ROCK AND ROLL CAGE MATCH

MUSIC'S GREATEST RIVALRIES, DECIDED

EDITED BY SEAN MANNING
FOREWORD BY ROB SHEFFIELD

THREE RIVERS PRESS
NEW YORK

Library of Congress Cataloging-in-Publication Data
Rock and roll cage match : music's greatest rivalries,
decided / edited by Sean Manning.—1st ed.
p.   cm.
1. Rock music—History and criticism. I. Manning, Sean.
ML3534.R6123 2008
781.66—dc22   2008003092

ISBN 978-0-307-39627-3
Printed in the United States of America
Design by Maria Elias

10 9 8 7 6 5 4 3 2 1
First Edition

Contents

Foreword

Rob Sheffield

Rock and roll is full of fateful choices. Beatles or Stones? Elvis or Ann-Margret? Sixties James Brown or seventies James Brown? Maggie May or Hot Legs? Peggy Sue or Mary Lou or Cherry Red or Midnight Blue? John Taylor or Simon Le Bon? Biggie or Rakim? Jimi Hendrix or Jimmy Page? Charlie Watts or Keith Moon? Doobie Brothers or Pointer Sisters? Tigra or Bunny? Born to run, or Revved up like a deuce? "Two Out of Three Ain't Bad" or "Total Eclipse of the Heart"? Did you ever have to make up your mind? That's what this book is all about.

When you're a music fan, you understand why these questions are life-and-death matters. Rock stars can chicken out of big decisions ("Love is a temple, love a higher law"—come on, Bono, which is it?), but we, the fans, must face them down. Like Zen monks pondering koans ("What is the sound of one hand clapping?"), we argue over questions that have no final answer, because in the asking, we discern the inner Buddha nature of the universe. (Fun fact: Four out of five Zen monks agree that Charlie Watts crushes Keith Moon, and the sound of one hand clapping beats any band with two drummers.)

The writers in this book have faced these questions with fortitude, rigor, and (I'm just guessing) a stack of Zimas behind the laptop. So who rocked harder, the Stones or the Velvets? Who won the epic rap battle between Jay-Z and Nas? Most valuable Beatle, John or Paul? Best eighties band, U2 or R.E.M.? More evil, Trent Reznor or Marilyn Manson? The answers are here. Parliament vs. Funkadelic? Guided by Voices vs. Pavement? Nirvana vs. Metallica? Who's your piano man, Elton or Billy? Who made you smear your mascara, Morrissey or Robert Smith? You're standing at the jukebox with a quarter in your hand, so what's it going to be: Simon & Garfunkel or Hall & Oates?

These writers have made the tough calls, and I am in awe, even when I think they're full of crap. Some readers will be outraged. Tears will be shed. Personally, I'm demanding a recount on Phil Collins's narrow victory over Sting. (I have reason to believe there were underreported write-in ballots from the Zenyattà Mondatta precinct.) But that's rock and roll—the music will never die, because pointless and ridiculous arguments like these help keep it alive. And if you're the kind of fan who jumps into the argument, then as David Bowie said—Ziggy Bowie, not Berlin Bowie—you're not alone. As for my personal quandary, here you go:

Okay, Berlin Bowie or Ziggy Bowie? Let's make this quick. Berlin Bowie: cooler hair. Ziggy Bowie: shinier boots. Berlin Bowie: Carlos Alomar and Ricky Gardiner on guitar. Ziggy Bowie: Mick Ronson on guitar. Berlin Bowie: Brian Eno. Ziggy Bowie: the Spiders from Mars. Berlin Bowie: "Sound and Vision." Ziggy Bowie: "Moonage Daydream." Berlin Bowie: the song about meeting your lover by the Berlin Wall and getting shot at by the guards but nothing can tear you apart because you're lovers and that is that. Ziggy Bowie: the song about your God-given ass. Berlin Bowie: "You're such a wonderful person, but you got problems." Ziggy Bowie: "Hey, that's far-out, so you heard him too?" Berlin Bowie: depraved sex night and day. Ziggy Bowie: depraved sex day and night.

I couldn't live without either Bowie, but for me, the choice is clear. Berlin Bowie. And that is that.

Introduction

Sean Manning

I know what you're thinking. *Metallica vs. Nirvana? Shouldn't it be Metallica vs. Megadeth and Nirvana vs. Pearl Jam?* Or maybe you're wondering what's up with Patsy Cline vs. Kitty Wells but no Johnny Cash vs. Merle Haggard, Jay-Z vs. Nas but no Tupac vs. Biggie. Or could be you think George was the best Beatle or Van Halen was better with that dude from Extreme than with either Sammy or Dave. That's the thing about musical rivalries: Somebody's always going to protest, if not the matchups then the outcomes.

Just ask Dan Kois, whose "R.E.M. vs. U2: Who Was the Best Rock Band of the '80s?" (appearing originally in the November 9, 2006, *Slate,* and here in an expanded version) could be described without exaggeration as the article that launched a thousand blog comments. Hordes of music and culture websites rushed to weigh in—and asked their readers to do the same. The response was overwhelming. *USA Today*'s Pop Candy blog received close to a hundred comments. (Compare that to its previous post's twenty.) *Rolling Stone*'s Rock & Roll Daily blog and entertainment blogger Stereogum both received well more than that number—or roughly ten times the typical number of comments per post. And yet that was only a third as many as the three-hundred-plus comments Rock & Roll Daily received on its related post two days later asking readers to select "the most compelling music-related rivalries." The suggestions ranged from the obvious (Blur vs. Oasis) to the arcane (Angels and Airwaves vs. +44) to the downright ridiculous (Thom Yorke vs. Clay Aiken), and the exchanges got plenty heated:

> **Frank:** Nirvana was better . . . the [last] few albums from pearl jam all sound the same, boring, not very creative and forced sounding . . .
>
> **Ace:** Pearl Jam's last few albums do not sound the same you moron . . . you are TONE-DEAF, & you MUST BE to think Nirvana was better . . .
>
> **Frank:** We could argue this point until the end of time and neither of us would budge, well you would a little because you're riding eddie's dick . . .
>
> **Ace:** Yeh nice work Frank . . . How old are you? 12 . . . I think you should go and do your chores now . . .
>
> **Frank:** Good one jack ass, and as for my chores, i don't want to wear your mother out so I gave her the day off . . .

But one thing—the *only* thing—everyone seemed to agree on was the worthiness and fun of such debates.

Why do we get so fired up about this shit? What—beyond mankind's innate fickleness, our ingrained tendency toward bifurcation (heaven/hell, yin/yang, tastes great/less filling)—makes us identify with one artist or band over another? Well, for Nashville native Laura Cantrell, having grown up just down the block from Kitty Wells, proximity plays a big part. Same, though in the complete opposite way, for Russ Meneve and Bruce Springsteen, whose singing, Meneve writes, "is almost always in praise of his New Jersey roots and in praise of how proud he is of the state. I'm from Jersey. *I prays* I never have to go back to that shithole." For both Gideon Yago and myself, attire, specifically jackets, has something do with it, while for Whitney Pastorek, it's a matter of phonetics: "My name is Whitney. I was born and raised in

Houston. Because of that early coincidence—or perhaps in spite of it and the twenty years of chortled jokes I've patiently endured since—there is no question as to whom I give my allegiance." But to varying degrees all of us, contributors and readers alike, are well served by Richard Hell's explanation: "A rock and roll show is about the audience agreeing to surrender to the band in such a way that the band gives back that which it's received from the crowd in the form of the crowd's pleasure in itself, in the form of the crowd's ideal of itself, of its own glory (as personified by the band's front man)." Or as Michaelangelo Matos puts it: "We respond to creators whose impulses match our own, or seem to—people we imagine we have some understanding of, or with, were we to meet them." Nowhere is this sentiment better exemplified than in Marc Spitz's essay, in which he contrasts the experience of interviewing, on separate occasions, the Cure's and the Smiths' respective front men, Robert Smith and Morrissey: "When the Robert Smith interview was done, I took the subway home. I'm sure I played lots of Cure albums on my stereo, but I didn't feel like I couldn't recover from it all rather quickly. When the Morrissey interview was done, and I'd walked him and his manager out, I went back to the bungalow we'd rented and stole the teacup that he was drinking from. Then I went back to my room and called everyone I'd ever met—and when you do that from a hotel phone you've clearly lost your shit."

However, this book strives to serve an even greater purpose than defining, to crib another line from Matos, "what guides a lot of how fandom works in general." Are you aware of the recent bit of revisionism alleging that both the American Revolution and the Civil War stemmed from disagreements over music? Sure, the founding fathers were tired of taxation without representation, but their real beef, the theorists contend, was George III digging Handel over Bach. And while the North and South were certainly at odds over slavery, turns out it was actually Jefferson Davis's insistence that "Camptown Races" was Stephen Foster's kickinest jam—not "Oh! Susanna," as was Lincoln's contention—that prompted the Confederate attack on Fort Sumter. Now once more the country stands divided. Iraq. Immigration. Gay marriage. Abortion. Stem-cell research. If we're ever to reconcile our differences, clearly we must heed history's counsel and first address those questions more fundamental to our national identity: Michael Jackson or Prince? Elton John or Billy Joel? Van Halen or Van Hagar?

(. . . or, fine, the Extreme dude—seriously, let it go already!)

R.E.M.

vs.

U2

Dan Kois

1. You can tell a lot about a guy by how he tells his own story. Does he make of it an ornate drama, one featuring pomp, pageantry, and a healthy dose of self-aggrandizing? Or does he tell it modestly, taking pride in his accomplishments but expressing more pleasure in the work he's done over his time in this world?

In the fall of 2006, two products appeared in the Borderses of America telling the stories of two bands that—though very different— in many ways represented the peak of intelligent rock music in the

(This essay is an expanded version of the article that originally appeared in the Nov. 9, 2006, issue of *Slate*.)

1980s: R.E.M.'s *And I Feel Fine,* a two-disc collection of songs from their early years, 1982 to 1987, featuring eleven short pages of liner notes in which the four founding members relate thoughtful, often very funny, mostly self-deprecating stories of the band's early years and how individual songs were born into the world; and, in weighty contrast to this slim text, *U2 by U2,* a forty-dollar coffee-table book that exhaustively recounts—in 352 pages of interviews, Anton Corbijn photographs, and splashy graphics—the band's birth, struggles, and modern-day success.

Now that U2 has become America's spokesband for human dignity, it's difficult to remember that R.E.M., the quiet Georgians with the elliptical lyrics, once competed with Bono and company for the title of world's best rock band. But the differences in those two retrospectives—one focusing on the music, the other on the myth—can help us remember that R.E.M., not U2, made the most important music of the 1980s.

2. **Throughout that decade** and the early 1990s, a fierce, bitter rivalry existed between R.E.M. and U2—not in real life, mind you, but in my head. By 1988 I was in high school and as obsessed as any high schooler with making sense of the world, usually by dividing it into false dichotomies. Jocks vs. nerds. Friends vs. phonies. Artists vs. sellouts. Liberals vs. fascists. In my mind—and, I've come to learn, in those of other floppy-haired music nerds of the era—you were either an R.E.M. person or a U2 person. (This assumed, of course, you had already made it through the brutal culling of People Who Cared About Music vs. People Who Were Morons and Just Listened to Rick Astley, or Extreme.)

To R.E.M. people, U2 represented the triumph of bombast over subtlety. To U2 people, R.E.M. represented preciousness and willful obscurity. To both, their own band represented the peak of musical relevance.

Who's more relevant now? Well, that's easy. This R.E.M. person has spent the last six years in agony watching his onetime heroes release several drab albums. Meanwhile, after a few years in the wilderness, U2 opened up their 2001 tour with Bono announcing they were "reapplying for the job" of "best band in the world." In doing so, U2 were famously proclaiming their intention to *matter* once again—and through a combination of hit singles, canny marketing, and Bono's admirable humanitarian advocacy, they've succeeded.

Though fans like me might fervently wish for R.E.M. to make a similar pronouncement, it's hard to imagine such a thing given the determination with which they pursued their off-center Southern muses for so many years. For all of their ambition—and you can't become as popular as R.E.M. once was without some measure of ambition—R.E.M.'s music in the 1980s *was* willfully obscure.

3. And I'm not just talking about the words. Much has been made of Michael Stipe's mumbly lyrics, but with a lot of early R.E.M. songs, the point wasn't that you couldn't make out the words—you *could* make out a lot of the words, but you didn't know what the hell they meant. As the liner notes in *And I Feel Fine* reveal, neither did the band. "I still have no idea what the song is about," Stipe writes about "Pilgrimage," and bassist Mike Mills says the same about "Gardening at Night" (while drummer Bill Berry claims—in jest?—that it's based on a euphemism for peeing along the side of the road during an all-night drive).

Berry goes further into the issue of the band's lyrics. "Very early on," he writes, "I made a point not to confront Michael with queries regarding lyrical origin or significance. Just as I wouldn't peer into his diary if it fell into my possession, I didn't feel I merited any more privy than the average listener." To that average listener, the lyrics could mean anything, and therefore they meant everything, weighted as they were with mystery, resonance, and passion. "It's not necessarily what we meant," writes Mills, "but whatever you think." A friend of mine once gave his sister, for her birthday in 1988, a complete collection of R.E.M. lyrics, painstakingly hand transcribed from repeated listens to the songs. Were they right? It hardly mattered.

Even R.E.M.'s "political" songs of the era, like "Fall on Me" or "Exhuming McCarthy," are tricky to parse. "Fall on Me" could maybe be about acid rain, or maybe environmental degradation in general, or maybe, uh, missile defense? Whereas U2's political songs of the 1980s are a little easier to work out: "Pride (In the Name of Love)" is about Martin Luther King, for example, and "Sunday Bloody Sunday" is about Sunday, Bloody Sunday. Stirring as those songs are, there's very little a listener can bring to them; they are Bono's take, not yours, unlike "Fall on Me," which, for me in 1987, was a deeply personal song about the crushing whatever of existence.

When U2's songs weren't on-the-nose political anthems, they were heroically uplifting but intentionally vague—filled with signifiers but signifying nothing. There's a huge difference between being vague and being elliptical. Vagueness feels fuzzy, as if Bono's broad strokes were meant to obscure the lack of anything real to say. Rightly or not, Michael Stipe's lyrics felt as if they hinted at hidden stories and meanings that only the most dedicated of listeners could ferret out. Drenched in Southern detail, allusive and elusive, R.E.M. songs sounded like fables or folk wisdom; U2's majestic uplift, in contrast, often felt like the outtakes of a melodically gifted youth-group minister. And each band's music so often mirrored its lyrics! When U2 Can't Find What They're Looking For, they back up their words with ringing chords and gospel inflections. When R.E.M. is Still a Ways Away, they turn their words into mournful country folk.

R. There's a charming modesty in R.E.M.'s liner-note stories of how they learned to create these songs. Guitarist Peter Buck writes that when the band signed with I.R.S. the president of the label suggested the band write some slow songs—an idea that had never actually occurred to them. Mills devotes paragraphs to explaining why it was fun to play bass within the framework of Buck's guitar. And in the notes on the collection's best unreleased track, a slowed-down version of

"Gardening at Night," the band explains how, struggling with the song in the studio, they tried playing it slowly—to see if, in Mills's words, "it might hold up well with a softer treatment." Unlike most previously unreleased demos, this version is a treasure: The intricacies of Mills and Buck's interplay at a slower pace, overlaid by Stipe's falsetto and supported by Berry's expressive drumming, reveal new beauty behind the familiar drive of the original.

If in the studio R.E.M. was tentative and exploratory, U2 was as straightforwardly ambitious as a band could be. "We're going to make the big music," says Bono in *U2 by U2* about the band's mind-set leading up to the recording of 1984's *The Unforgettable Fire.* "That's who we are. We're not Indie, we're not miserable, we're full of joy, and we are going to take over where Phil Spector left off. Big ideas, big themes, big sound." Then he adds, "We knew that the world was ready to receive the heirs of the Who. All we had to do was keep doing what we were doing and we would become the biggest band since Led Zeppelin, without a doubt." R.E.M., still convinced they weren't even the equal of their heroes in Athens, Georgia—new-wave predecessors Pylon—not by a long shot, never offer such bombast.

Live, the two bands were markedly different. In *U2 by U2* the Edge describes an outdoor concert in Dublin in 1985: "We really had done it. This wasn't a band that was doing OK, this was a band that was topping the charts and had broken America and the world. . . . There was an entire stadium jumping up and down in time to 'Pride.' " There are a lot of triumphant concert stories in *U2 by U2,* brimming with tales of Bono climbing the stage rigging and leaping into the audience, and it's illuminating to compare them to Peter Buck's story from *And I Feel Fine*'s liner notes about a 1983 show in Holland: "We played and we weren't very good. We were walking off on our way to the dressing room, and this little punk chick with a mohawk comes up to me, shakes her fist in my face and says, 'In a fart there is more music!' " Buck adds: "There hasn't been much more trenchant criticism than that in my entire career."

5

Contrast Bono's enthusiastic courting of—and connection to—an audience with Stipe hiding behind the drum kit when David Letterman came over to interview the band on *Late Night* in 1983. Even when Stipe engaged an audience live—as with the long, rambling stories he would tell about the origins of songs like "Life and How to Live It"—he was adding to the band's mystique, confirming fans' belief that there was always more to R.E.M.'s songs than words could possibly express. (In *And I Feel Fine*'s liner notes, Stipe alludes to the band's preciousness in his notes on the much-parsed faux-folk "Swan Swan H": "Let's just go ahead and call the song 'Swan Swan Hummingbird,'" he writes. "Now maybe Mike will finally forgive me my affectations when I was in my mid-Twenties." To which my sixteen-year-old self replies: *Now* you tell me.)

Even the bands' public personas at that time suggested—to me, at least—that one was modest and serious while the other was stereotypically given to excess. While R.E.M. championed obscure artists like Pylon, filmmaker Jem Cohen, and the Southern outsider artist Howard Finster, U2 embarked, with *Rattle & Hum,* on a dilettante's tour of the American South even as the band hung out with supermodels. ("Rock stars and supermodels," the Edge writes in *U2 by U2.* "It is a little bit of a cliché but we were happy to live with the cliché because the supermodels we got to know are great people and we still count them as very close friends.")

5. **"There's nothing like** being at Number One," Bono says in *U2 by U2.* "It's just better than Number Two." In the early 1990s both bands were Number One: U2 with *Achtung Baby* and "One," R.E.M. with *Out of Time* and "Losing My Religion." By the late 1990s, though, both bands were in career lulls. U2's dabbling in electronica with *Zooropa* and *Pop* had turned off many hard-core fans. R.E.M.'s Berry had amicably left the commercially floundering band after suffering an aneurysm onstage during a concert.

Without Berry, R.E.M. has recorded three quiet, unimpressive albums, the third of which I didn't even buy—an unthinkable omission to my younger self, who so idolized the band and fetishized its output that I memorized not only the real running order of 1986's *Lifes Rich Pageant* but the cheeky fake running order listed on the cassette's back cover. Meanwhile, U2 is on top of the rock heap again, a brand as much as a band, representing both sincerity and success. Just check out their Successories-ready aphorisms in *U2 by U2:* "I always thought the job was to be as great as you could be," says Bono. "If it is not absolutely the best it can be, why bother?" says bassist Adam Clayton. And that's just in the flap copy!

6. I should step back for a moment, though, and admit the truth: There never really was a rivalry, of course. Despite the dramatic differences between the bands, and despite all my righteous teenage anger, U2 and R.E.M. were, and remain, entirely friendly. In 1992 members of the two groups combined to perform a sweet version of "One" at MTV's Inaugural Ball. Bono testified at Peter Buck's 2002 trial on charges that he attacked a British Airways crew while on a flight to London. Bono even discusses meeting Stipe in *U2 by U2:* "this odd-looking bohemian with tiny little plaits in his hair," he calls him. "Michael Stipe's friendship means more to me than I can ever tell you," he says on page 162. Then, of course, he doesn't mention Stipe's name again in the book.

Do I sound bitter? I am! Whether the rivalry was real or not, it existed for me. And at the peak of my R.E.M. fandom I was infuriated on R.E.M.'s behalf every time the band was slighted in favor of U2. That's the thing about rock and roll rivalries, real or imagined: People get really passionate about their pronouncements.

In 2006 I wrote the *Slate* article from which this essay is adapted, the headline of which read, R.E.M. VS. U2: WHO WAS THE BEST ROCK BAND OF THE '80s? On *Slate*'s message boards, on music blogs, and in my inbox, hundreds of music fans angrily weighed in to explain why I was totally wrong—either because U2 was so obviously better than R.E.M., or because my entire article was built on a false comparison and the *real* best rock band of the 1980s was *obviously* the Smiths/the Replacements/ the Pixies/the Cure/the Police/New Order/Hüsker Dü/the Minutemen/ Van Halen/GN'F'n'R, MOTHERFUCKER!!!!

And here's why all those arguments are so vehement: because all those people are right. Far more than any other art form, music hits us not in our brains but in our hearts (or, on certain occasions, in our rumps), so any fan who argues that her band is better than my band is, for all intents and purposes, right.

You say that XTC meant everything to you in the 1980s, so they're clearly a better band than R.E.M.? You're right!

You shout that AC/DC fucking kicks R.E.M.'s ass? You're right!

You explain that maybe those bands were good in their time, but Weezer's recorded output inarguably dwarfs that of R.E.M. and U2 put together? Um, I guess by the bullshit rules I've established, I'm forced to admit that you're right, too.

But I'll forever remain convinced that R.E.M. is not only the band of the 1980s, but the band of my life, no matter how crappy their recent albums have been. And I'm not the only one; mixed in with the messages telling me that clearly the Georgia Satellites were the best rock band of the eighties were heartfelt e-mails and posts from fans who wrote that R.E.M. held the same place in their hearts that the band holds in mine.

And that's why in the end the rivalry between R.E.M. and U2 isn't about how U2 are a bunch of preening posers. At least, it's not *only* about that. It's about defending the band we love and struggling to express the reasons their music meant so much to us for so long.

The delicacy at the heart of R.E.M.'s 1980s albums fostered introspection and brotherhood among those of us who loved them in those years. Introspection because the mystery and melancholy of the songs pushed the listener inward to find resonance in every line. Brotherhood because we had to band together to defend our heroes against the un-feeling jerks who found R.E.M. precious and opaque.

I assumed, of course, that those jerks were U2 fans.

Phil Spector

vs.

Timbaland

Michaelangelo Matos

The producer as auteur in pop music wasn't Phil Spector's invention. To start with, there's Jerry Leiber and Mike Stoller, with whom Spector apprenticed; hell, you could claim the title for Ralph Peer, who conceived country music in one gesture by lugging a tape machine to Tennessee in 1927. But even given Leiber and Stoller's radio-influenced playlets with the Coasters and their introduction of Latin rhythms and strings into R&B, changing rock and roll entirely and pop forever, Spector was the first pop producer with an identifiable *sound*. Given the way things have been going for five decades since, this is no small thing. Spector changed the sound of the radio, influenced countless others in his path, and turned the studio into an instrument in itself. For good or bad, his massed multiple guitars and seas of reverb point the way to compression-heavy record engineering; more than anyone, he turned recordings of songs into events unto themselves. In this way Spector invented modern pop as much as anyone this side of James Brown. But he isn't the greatest record producer of all time. Timbaland is.

This is perhaps unfair to Spector, but only in the sense that comparing any other producer to Timbaland is unfair. Prior to Spector, producers were either songwriters with perfectionist streaks (like Leiber and Stoller), or engineers made good, or (usually) A&R folks. (Jerry Wexler is the ultimate example of the latter; his fifties Atlantic Records cohort Tom Dowd fits the middle category.) No one in their right mind would discount those folks' work. But Spector turned producing into more than getting the best possible performance from all involved—he made producing the pursuit of a singular, signature aural item that simultaneously fits in with everything else on the radio and leaps out from it.

There are producers with "sounds" you can spot on tiny speakers a room away: Mutt Lange, for example, who is probably the key exponent of Spector-style mass. It's tempting to add Rick Rubin here, too, but only in his hip-hop work does Rubin have an identifiable sonic style—hard, crunchy, rude, exuberant, masculine. But he's a good example of the split I'm trying to describe. Like most of his peers, in rock mode Rubin is more in the mold of the pre-Spector type—a glorified coach. Certainly there's no "Rick Rubin sound" on the Johnny Cash *American* albums; Rubin's job was to find material and coax believable performances.

Nothing about this is dismissible; frequently the difference between a championship team and a mediocre one is good coaching. (Also, Cash over "King of Rock" probably wouldn't work even as novelty.) But there are fundamental differences between being a sounding board and enacting one's methodology hands-on, between decision making and beat making, between working with (or over) what is given you and building something from the bottom up. That's what hip-hop producers share with Spector and other meddler types: They're often responsible for the track, if not the song, and frequently have a hand in the latter as well.

This is why comparisons to Timbaland are invariably unfair: He's been responsible for more distinctive *sounds,* for longer, than any other producer. Pitting him against Spector is almost a category error—not because Timbaland emphasizes rhythm and Spector melody, or because Timbaland's best work is frequently minimal while Spector's is anything but, or because Spector petered out after a half decade (at best) and Tim has stayed strong for more than twice as long (and counting). It's because the basic nature of their work is completely different.

If Timbaland feels inspired, he can knock out a track in a night with minimal help: program the right rhythms, sample the right babies, extra coffee for the engineer, boom. Spector had to do a lot more legwork. Walls of sound don't construct themselves, cathedral-like recording studios don't book themselves, lead sheets for session players don't notate themselves. (His dick didn't suck itself, either, but we'll stick to the music and not the man or his automatic weapons here.) Even if Spector didn't do all of this work himself (and he most certainly didn't), he had a lot more to oversee to make three minutes of his kind of magic than Tim does for five.

Even with that caveat, though, Tim wins this thing by a mile. The reason is ideas. Spector had one; Tim overflows with them. Spector was going strong from 1961 to 1966, from Ben E. King's "Spanish Harlem" to Ike & Tina Turner's "River Deep Mountain High." (As wonderful as the first two John Lennon solo albums are, no one thinks of them as Spector's work even though Spector produced them.) (Well, maybe *Imagine*'s "I Don't Want to Be a Soldier.")

But even then he wasn't half as creative as Timbaland has been for any similar stretch of time you'd want to isolate. Choose either 1996 to 2000 or 2001 to 2006 or any subdivision therein; glory abounds, much of it unalike. I love "Be My Baby" as much as every human being should, but I'll be damned if Spector's other records ever really diverged from what made that one great. He even tried to make the Beatles sound like Phil Spector—for Christ's sake, people, *the Beatles*. (Not that it would have done him a damn bit of good if it really had worked, since the Beatles became the greatest band of all time by sounding like everybody else anyway.) Rock is full of monotonous great artists, but there are few with as little dimension as Spector. Timbaland, on the other hand, discards old formulas and improvises new ones as a matter of habit.

None of which, I realize, may necessarily convince you I even know what I'm talking about. After all, the binaries I'm establishing are not only more or less false, they may well be irrelevant: Pop music has a lot of room for the single-minded. Maybe not as much as movies, which, despite their inherently collaborative nature, are the domain of megalo-maniacs so grandiose they make the likes of Spector (not to mention Timbaland) look like Boy Scouts. But there's a case to be made for the bloody-minded visionary, the person who does the same thing repeat-edly and with minor variation for more or less their entire career. Spec-tor is one of those people, maybe in pop music *the* person, if you want to be absolute about it, which would be only fair considering the terms of the discussion.

When I became interested in pop music—when my engagement shifted from keen acknowledgment to obsession—I wanted to hear and know as much as possible about it. That's been my MO as a writer, too; there's gold in them thar hills, if you have the time and interest to dig constantly, which as a full-time critic I get to do, and that gold is more or less as variegated as you care to discover. But that approach— everythingism, to put an ungainly tag on it—has its pitfalls. If your mandate is to know something about a large number of things, you're less likely to know everything about one thing. In itself this isn't so bad, but it sometimes leads me to wonder whether I'm not missing out on a fulfilling relationship with the entire discography of someone I love be-cause I'm too busy playing catch-up with things I only marginally care about, that I'll forget in three years, that I have to crank something out about on deadline instead of going out and getting a real job like everybody else.

The counterargument is that by trying new things I'll find new things to love, deeper pleasures lying in wait that I wouldn't have known about if I didn't give a shot to some buzz album or random e-mailed mp3 link. That's the obvious upside, and it goes beyond wanting to be first on my block (almost wrote "blog" there, and not entirely by accident) to talk about something great to the portion of the world I can reach. But if mania can blind, it can also illuminate. There are certain types of recorded music—the jump blues that preceded rock and roll, protojungle rave from the early nineties, early-seventies soul—I am naturally inclined toward, that I'll listen to no matter what. We all have our favorites; they're what make music (art, life) a pleasure. And we respond to creators whose impulses match our own, or seem to—people we imagine we have some understanding of, or with, were we to meet them.

I'm not planning to meet Timbaland anytime soon, and I can't imagine we'd have anything to discuss beyond my possibly interviewing him. (A journalist—even one who primarily writes criticism—never knows whom he'll end up interviewing.) The point is that through his work he comes across as someone who's eager to find the next thing. Actually, not *the* next thing—*his* next thing, the thing that makes him feel like he's making music again for the first time, just as I look for things that make me feel like I'm hearing music again for the first time. Again, this has nothing to do with personalities, though I figure it's okay to presume that the part-time bodybuilder would be a lot more congenial a dinner companion than the accused murderer. It has to do with overall creative thrust. I prefer Timbaland over Spector for symbolic reasons as much as musical ones, and while that might sound shallow, it's also what guides a lot of how fandom works in general.

It's also not to discount the one-man-one-vision-one-sound part of the deal. If I find Spector limited, it's partly because his singularity of approach allows for easy cherry-picking. The most rabid fans of *Back to*

Mono I know, or know of, veer toward the ideological; they seem to love the idea of the Phil Spector sound as much as the sound itself. I intend no harsh criticism by this. Everyone does it to some degree, like I do with early rave. It's an identifying marker, shorthand for other, related things. Spector's music is overly romantic, impractical, clings to youth as an ideal, and was made by an acknowledged control freak. Those things can probably be applied, to one degree or other, to his superfans as well, just as proudly displaying the banner of rave makes me, by proxy, immature, easily dazzled by cheap gimmicks, misguidedly utopian, and probably best not taken seriously.

What does being a Timbaland fan mean, though? *Does* it mean anything? It's debatable. A lot of people can instantly ID a Timbaland track but primarily know him from the radio and couldn't care less about his fitness regimen or what he tells journalists, just the way most people felt when Spector was ruling the airwaves. (Though it's a lot likelier those people had read, or at least heard of, Tom Wolfe's 1964 *New York* magazine profile of Spector, "The First Tycoon of Teen," than it is that Tim fans have read even the best pieces on him—I'd nominate Sasha Frere-Jones's 1999 interview in *The Wire* and Dave Tompkins's 2005 profile from *Scratch*.) But Timbaland fandom is, at this juncture at least, less concerned with identification—either with him as a figure or with the particular epoch in which he works—than Spector fandom. That's largely because we're still in the middle of the Timbaland Era, and as I write this it looks like we'll continue to be for the foreseeable future. But it also has to do with his curious facelessness.

The thing I told my friends when I was preparing to write this was that the one place where Spector had Timbaland beat was albums. Tim has made four solo CDs, none of them great, though 1997's *Welcome to Our World* (co-credited to rapper Magoo) is superb. *A Christmas Gift for You from Phil Spector* (1963), though, is a flat-out classic, probably the best holiday album in rock history. Nearly everyone I mentioned this to called foul: *Christmas Gift* isn't really a single-artist album, they pointed out, but a compilation featuring tracks by four singing groups, with

Spector alone credited for the closing track, "Silent Night." Besides, he'd only top-billed himself once compared to Tim's quartet, which probably counts for something.

Still, even if *Christmas Gift* features "Christmas (Baby Please Come Home)," which might be Spector's greatest hit (besides "Be My Baby," I mean, duh, nothing touches "Be My Baby"), you'd never call it a Darlene Love album. Even beyond the guests Tim calls in for his own projects, those never come across as forcefully *his* as *Christmas Gift* does for Spector. Maybe that's because for all his sonic eccentricity, in human terms Timbaland's greatest gift is his apparent flexibility. Even if he knocks out tracks by the gross more or less alone with the engineer (let's have a big hand for Jimmy Douglass, a studio veteran who's worked extensively with Tim since before his breakthrough), he's never projected the kind of loner-with-machinery vibe of many of his more auteurist hip-hop contemporaries, from DJ Premier to the late J Dilla. He's willing to adapt his style to that of someone else—it's hard to imagine another producer of his stature as willing to subsume his own ego to that of a collaborator like Björk, as Tim does on two tracks from 2007's *Volta*. He's boisterous: The way he gesticulates while auditioning the track that will become "Dirt Off Your Shoulder" for Jay-Z is the unquestioned highlight of the documentary *Fade to Black*. Timbaland exudes pleasure; there's little of Spector's dictatorial feeling in his work. If you're gonna pick a guy for one reason alone, that one is as good as any.

The Smiths

vs.

The Cure

Marc Spitz

It was in the very late summer of 2007 that I received a pair of e-mailed press releases, both of which I could not reflexively delete. I rarely write for monthly magazines or daily papers anymore as my time is spent cleaning fish tanks, scrubbing pots, walking dogs, and generally recovering from twenty years of heroic drinking. I also write an occasional book. I was, however, a monthly columnist for about a decade, and still get about twenty or so urgent dispatches each day as a result. (About fifteen more end up in my spam folder.) I didn't change my e-mail address after leaving *Spin* magazine in 2006. It can be a nuisance, what with all the no longer professionally useful or interesting clutter, but I preserve and maintain this hub for two reasons. For one, it's a private account, so I didn't have to forfeit it to the company, and the ISP is free. The other reason is far less simple: That same year I'd given my e-mail address (along with a copy of my second novel, *Too Much, Too Late*—the one I did not write about him) to Morrissey. Morrissey did not give me his in return. I'm still holding out the faint hope that one day he will read the book, although he never would admit to me that he'd read the first novel, *How Soon Is Never*—the one that I did write about him and yet did not give to him. (I do know that he once purchased a copy at Book Soup in West Hollywood, but I never confronted him about this.) After he finishes the book, he will think about it, and he will e-mail me and ask me out to tea to talk about it.

> "Is the title a play on the second New York Dolls album title, the one that might have been the last ever had I not brought them back together for that Meltdown festival I curated?"
>
> "Why, yes, Morrissey. It is. Although both, as I'm sure you well know, pay homage to theatrical grand dame Diana Barrymore's autobiography."

If it was hot, we'd consider a cold bubble tea. I know it's gonna happen someday.

This might seem like an aside but it's actually both a segue and a verdict on this Smiths-Cure badminton match that I've been asked to participate in.

Segue first: One of the above mentioned e-mails happened to be from Morrissey's publicist. It read, in part:

> Finally, in an effort to stop the speculation and kill off the rumor mongers who seem to use these things to take advantage of committed fans, we can tell you that one thing the future will not bring is a Smiths reunion tour. Per recent reports, Morrissey was approached during the course of the

summer by a consortium of promoters, in the wake of the
success of The Police, U2 and The Rolling Stones tours,
with a $75,000,000 offer to tour in 2008 and/or 2009. The
offer called for Morrissey to do a minimum of 50 shows all
over the world under The Smiths' name with the only pro-
viso being that Johnný Marr was also in the band. The offer
has been refused.

There will never be an essay that argues whether or not seventy-five
million dollars is a lot of fucking money. It's not Abba-reunion money
(the Swedish pop-godhead quartet reportedly once declined a billion-
dollar offer to reunite). It is, however, more Police-tour money than, say,
Squeeze- or Crowded House–headlined, reunion-tour-of-respectable-
capacity-theaters money. As with the Pixies, and on a much smaller
scale Gang of Four, time and an embrace from two or three younger
generations via compilation CDs and older brothers or sisters (although
amazingly not [legal] digital downloading, as at the time of this writing
and that offer, only *Hatful of Hollow* is available on iTunes) has transformed the Smiths, defunct since 1987, into a bigger draw than they
ever were while an active band, perhaps even a stadium act (certainly in
stronghold cities like Los Angeles where culturally it's frequently still
1987). Only, unlike Gang of Four and the Pixies, the Smiths will never,
ever, ever reunite. Ever. Never. Not even for Abba money. Not even for
Oprah money. Gates and Buffett money. Morrissey has publicly stated
that he would rather eat his own testicles than re-form. "And I'm a vegetarian," he added for (hardly needed) emphasis. They are dead. And,
although dying is surely no fun, there's almost nothing cooler than
being dead.

While writing *How Soon Is Never* in 2002, I drew from a time in my
life (roughly age fourteen through, well . . . thirty-three) when the
Smiths meant absolutely everything to me. I'm not going to waste the
time and space explaining why. Buy my book. And if you don't want to
buy my book, buy that *Hatful of Hollow* on iTunes, which is more than

enough to do the job. If you're reading through this book, it's a safe bet that you have heard at least two or three Smiths songs, or perhaps the theme song to *Charmed*. You probably, at the very least, know that they were Johnny Marr's first band before Modest Mouse (apologies to the The, the Pretenders, the Talking Heads, Bryan Ferry, Electronic, and the Healers . . . or perhaps just . . . Healers). I'll qualify a little in case you happen to be browsing in your local superstore and aren't sure you want to commit to buying this book for fear that it's full of off-putting, elitist, rock-boy and rock-girl snobbery: The Smiths were a four-piece formed in 1982 in Manchester, England. They released four albums and two compilations of singles, B-sides, and/or Peel sessions. One live record. Then they broke up. And when they did, it was worse than when my parents divorced. It was worse than getting my nose broken in a baseball game and in a fight. It was worse than getting arrested. Worse than getting dumped. Worse than being audited. Worse than when my grandparents died. It left me empty and distrustful and vulnerable to horrible things like heroin and cowboy boots and art-school girls. I was only seventeen and my life was over. When I discovered the Smiths, I felt at once superior and empathic toward my fellow humans (not to mention hopeful and yet full of gorgeous, swooning despair in my guts). I had wanted that feeling back ever since '87 and it was only after writing that book that I managed to exorcise (some) of that terrible loss. Now not only do I not want them to reunite, I think that not reuniting is the coolest thing they ever did. Everyone reunites. One day they are going to figure out how to clone dead rock stars and reunite them with their surviving bandmates. You know it's going to happen. But the Smiths will stay pure. They are—and Morrissey might roll his eyes at this (although he'd probably like hearing it as well)—the James Deans of modern rock: forever young, beautiful, true, incorruptible, and invulnerable to plaintive quasi-fiction, eight-figure dangling carrots, or anything else you might want to chuck at them.

That same week, as I said, I received another press release—this one from the Cure's publicist. And because its subject said "The" and

"Cure" I opened it. This memorandum announced the postponement of the band's arena tour, in support of its upcoming double album (that's *double* album), from fall to spring in order to better work the (many) new songs into the set:

> The schedule as it stands only gives us a couple of weeks to finish our new double album before we hit the road again, and we know this just isn't enough time to complete the project to our total satisfaction . . . believe us we have been looking forward to the tour more than anyone and know there will be a lot of disappointed people out there, but we honestly feel that in the bigger picture we are making the right decision.

The Cure, as you may or may not know (buy this book, already!), have threatened to break up 157 times since forming in Sussex, England, circa the great British punk year zero of '76. They never break up. Ever. The Cure break up like Sinatra and Ziggy Stardust retired. Like Jay-Z retires. Like Cher retires. Nobody will need to clone the members of the Cure, because they will be touring happily (or happily unhappy) forever and ever. They are vampires, see. You couldn't kill them with a stick unless it was a sharp one, thrust into the heart muscle by moonlight.

If the Smiths are its James Dean, the Cure are the Marlon Brando of modern rock. They predated the Smiths (as Brando predated Dean, who idolized him). They were far more successful commercially (although you can't hold it against Dean for making no hit movies after dying in a Porsche wreck in 1955 . . . at twenty-six). Unfortunately, like Brando and unlike Dean, the Cure have, some say, turned into a bloated self-parody (playing up the goth androgyny well past its aesthetic sell-by date). And finally, like Brando, the Cure, although still respected by younger bands like Interpol and the Rapture (who both performed on 2004's self-congratulatory Curiosa Festival), kept going creatively when perhaps it might have been better for the legend if they had, well . . . stopped.

If the Smiths had not broken up twenty-some-odd years ago, of course, there might have been a *Wild Mood Swings* to tarnish their immaculate discography, too. At least a "Mint Car" somewhere in the singles output. It's not an argument I'm going to belabor. It's the age-old what-if premise. What if the Beatles didn't break up? Would they have eventually started to suck? Would "Back Off Boogaloo" or "Crackerbox Palace" or "Mind Games" or "Wonderful Christmastime" have become Beatles songs instead of subpar solo material? The Rolling Stones have released about a dozen shitty records since the spring of 1970 (when their biggest rivals opted out of the race), but they also released two deathless eternal classics (three if you count *Some Girls*) before the seventies were through (and '81's *Tattoo You* is almost perfect). In other words: They're still the fucking Stones and they will kill your best with their best so buy the merch and suck on their new single because "Sympathy for the Devil" is coming next. Or at least "Shattered."

The Cure have created enough similarly timeless music that any number of reaching albums that strain for relevance, or nearly there pop forays that hope to burrow into our collective brains, can never, ever change that. They got there, and nobody stays there. Unless they die. That's the only testimonial required to underscore just how high a level the Cure operated on in their prime (roughly '79 to '89). They joined the Stones club. If they broke up after, say, "Just Like Heaven," in 1987, the same year that their own personal Beatles disbanded, they'd be sexier and probably more pure, and somebody would be offering them sub-Abba money to re-form for Coachella or something. And yes, cinematically, Robert Smith might remain more Jett Rink than Colonel Kurtz (or Dr. Moreau). But then we wouldn't have *Disintegration,* and without *Disintegration* many of my close friends would have to pick a new favorite album of all time.

This is a roundabout way of saying that I will always love the Cure despite their myth inferiority and diminished culture stock. In their own way they mean as much to me as the Smiths do. I lost my virginity while "Catch" was playing. And it wasn't by chance. I wanted to lose my virginity while "Catch" was playing. Or at least "Like Cockatoos." And so, when I figured the deal was about to go down (as I was not, for the first time . . . alone), I slid *Kiss Me, Kiss Me, Kiss Me* into the CD player and thought of England.

When putting the Cure and the Smiths head-to-head, the posterity factor remains dicey and the personal-significance factor amounts to an audiobook recital of William Styron's *Sophie's Choice* as read by *120 Minutes'* Dave Kendall. It may ultimately be best to let Morrissey and Robert Smith slug it out themselves, not least of all because, well, they have been for years anyway.

In the fall of 1989, the Cure were enjoying the greatest success of their career with the release of the *Disintegration* album: the pervasive "Love Song" single vying for top-forty airspace with Paula Abdul, a sold-out tour of America's football stadiums. In fact, it was probably the greatest success any alternative-rock act had ever enjoyed. Will ever enjoy. There was no bigger band than the Cure in '89. But right in the midst of their glory, Morrissey took care to publicly take them down a peg or two. In England (and in certain cities like Los Angeles, and here in New York, where it is still occasionally 1989 . . . in my one-bedroom apartment, anyway) everybody but *everybody* reads the *NME*. It's the music paper of record: a tabloid that commands the weight of the *Observer* or the *Guardian* on the rock scene. In a questionnaire-formatted interview (to promote the Mozzer's far less commercially successful "Interesting Drug" single) in the September 16 issue, he listed under "Absolutely Vile": "The Cure, a new dimension to the word 'crap.' " Under "Election Promises": "McDonald's bombed and Robert Smith popped (both actions require a similar voltage of explosives)."

Smith did not retaliate immediately, although there is a quote attributed to him along the lines of, "If Morrissey doesn't eat meat, then I'm going to eat meat because I hate Morrissey." This is probably apocryphal, and if not, it's clearly an attempt at the arch English sarcasm that Morrissey wielded so ferociously.

The Smiths' and the Cure's shared well water was poisoned by those who zoned their properties so close in the first place. That is to say, people like me. Journos. They are, in truth, nothing alike. There are so few classic-era modern-rock superstar acts with explosively charismatic lead singers (truthfully, would you give a flip or even a toss about a New Order–Depeche Mode beef . . . or an Echo & the Bunnymen–Siouxsie and the Banshees spell of high hair pulling . . . maybe an armed death match between those two brothers from Gene Loves Jezebel?) that I suppose they must be placed alongside each other, but the Smiths and the Cure could not be more different, and to compare their styles is to interlock opposing extremes.

Musically, the Cure are darker and play doomy chord structures (with an occasional classic pop offering like "Close to Me" or "Friday I'm in Love"). The Smiths draw predominantly from the classic English and American records they cherished (Swinging London, Motown) and despite prejudices remained musically jubilant barring only a few instances of rainy brooding. Smiths lyrics were direct ("I'd like to smash every tooth in your head"), the Cure's often abstract ("You want to know why I hate you? Well, I'll try and explain . . ."). The Smiths were a songwriting partnership: Morrissey-Marr. The Cure is a rotating lineup of temporary foils for Robert Smith. Morrissey was androgynous by suggestion. In truth he was an athletic northern boy who happened to love the New York Dolls, Ziggy Stardust, and Jobriath. Robert Smith wore lipstick and pancake. Smith allegedly took smack and acid with his lager. Morrissey, chocolate bars and crisps.

They hate each other partly because they have been deprived, by some anyway, of the individuality that any basic analysis of their personality, art, and style would clearly entitle them to. Even the Loser's Lounge, the semi-regular live musical tribute night that's been floating around New York City for a decade, combined the two bands once they finally got around to honoring them (whereas Paul Williams, who wrote "The Rainbow Connection" and "Evergreen," got his own night). But ultimately, and this is only my (expert) opinion, they hate each other because Robert Smith believes that the Smiths are perceived as more authentic and romantic. And because the Cure sell (many) more records and Morrissey does not think that they deserve to.

Robert Smith is actually much smarter than most rock stars I've met. (Rock stars are less intelligent than rock writers, but they have a lot more money.) Smith looks you in the eye when he speaks to you. He radiates intelligence and awareness and is quick to explain or defend a point in his long career (the licensing of the heretofore wonderfully obscure cult hit "I Dig You," which he'd recorded with his postman under the moniker Cult Hero, to monster.com, in my case) with steely logic and confidence of vision. Smith is a living (undead) legend: an icon, his hair ratted, his eyes raccoon-ringed. He brought modern rock up from the underground two years before Nirvana's *Nevermind*. He defeated Mecha-Streisand. But Morrissey, who is the same age, risks invalidating all of that with one well-timed thrust of his notorious rapier. He vexes Smith in a palpable, non-WrestleManiacal way. You'd think Robert Smith could just shrug it off, enjoy a pint and a football match, or purchase a brewery and a football team.

"[Morrissey] was constantly saying horrible things about the Cure," Smith complained to *Entertainment Weekly* in 2004, the year that I first interviewed him for *Spin*. "In the end, I kind of snapped and started retaliating. And it turned into some kind of petty feud. I've never liked anything he's done musically, but I don't have any kind of strong feelings of animosity towards him as a person because I've never met him."

The interview that I conducted with Robert Smith took place in a midtown-Manhattan hotel suite. I recall being felt out beforehand by his representatives. They were concerned about whether I intended to bring up the subject of Morrissey during our sit-down. The *EW* story had been picked up by several music sites and papers like the *New York Post*. I suppose my recently published book had made me Morrissey-identified, but I was no sympathizer. This was Robert Smith, and like I said . . . that was a huge, virginity-loss-memorializing deal. I didn't and wouldn't bring it up. I was much too nervous to even have an agenda. I'd had a cocktail before the interview in order to calm my nerves, and when that didn't work, I had three more. By the time I sat down in a private room with Smith, I was slurry. The first thing I did was tell him that I lost my virginity to his music. "So . . . thanks for that." I shrugged. He was polite and funny and engaging, and the interview ultimately went so well that when I asked to interview him again at a later date for a *Spin* anniversary issue, he readily accepted.

I was thrilled to interview Robert Smith. But—and here's the verdict that I mentioned in the first paragraph—I didn't give Robert Smith my e-mail address, and I don't have a fantasy that he will one day acquire it (via an army of obedient and overgrown spider-men) and ask me to go for tea . . . or meat. And I also didn't call my editor ten minutes before the interview to quit my job, as I did before meeting Morrissey (for the first time) the following year at the Beverly Hills Hotel in L.A. "I cannot do this," I said then, while hiding in the back patio of the hotel's Polo Lounge, dreading the Mozzer's imminent arrival. "It's like meeting my maker. It's like dying. You're killing me. This assignment is killing me and I quit. I'm leaving. I'm not coming back. I'm going to the ocean." The fact that this man was the voice of the Smiths made me want to drown myself. That the Robert Smith who chatted with me the previous year was the voice of "The Love Cats" (and "Push" and "A Strange Day" and "Bananafishbones") was just . . . merely . . . amazing.

Both interviews were jobs. They required a level of cool professionalism, ultimately, and I did pull myself together (more or less) for the respective hours in which I sat face-to-face with these titanic dudes. And I did my research (you know, in high school). But when the Robert Smith interview was done, I took the subway home. I'm sure I played lots of Cure albums on my stereo, but I didn't feel like I couldn't recover from it all rather quickly. When the Morrissey interview was done, and I'd walked him and his manager out, I went back to the bungalow we'd rented and stole the teacup that he was drinking from. Then I went back to my room and called everyone I'd ever met—and when you do that from a hotel phone you've clearly lost your shit. I smuggled the teacup back to New York in my suitcase and eventually gave it to my friend Sarah "Ultragrrrl" Lewitinn as a present. I'm not sure if she drinks tea out of it. I had a similar reaction after meeting Johnny Marr. Less of one after interviewing Mike Joyce and Andy Rourke, but even then, it was much more of a soul shaker than it might have been had I shared a beer or a smoke or a pair of phone ends with Porl Thompson.

I suspect that it all comes down to who is the greater power in the ongoing war of words for me. Who is the better writer. The better articulator of loves and hates and passions just like mine. As opposed to plastic passion. And in the end, it's the words set to music, not pissy words in newsprint, that win out. The Penis Mightier Than the Sword (as Morrissey said, or wrote and posted in a famous photo). And while I loved "A Forest" and "The Hanging Garden," it was "William, It Was Really Nothing" and "Sheila Take a Bow" and "The Headmaster Ritual" and other urgent, immediate, clear, and passionate words that provided a genuinely useful beacon out of those dark woods of early-eighties teendom and, on certain (only certain) days, adulthood. I know several people who feel this way about the Cure. I acknowledge there are people who feel this way about Fall Out Boy, too. Or Clay Aiken. Or real religion. Or cookies. And I don't mean this as an invalidation. Whatever gets you through the night . . . as John Lennon said in one of his better could-have-been-Paul-instead-of-Elton-harmonizing solo hits . . . it's all right.

Whitney Houston

vs.

Mariah Carey

Whitney Pastorek

My name is Whitney. I was born and raised in Houston. Because of that early coincidence—or perhaps in spite of it, and the twenty years of chortled jokes I've patiently endured since—there is no question as to whom I give my allegiance in this thunderdome of melismatic proportions. I'm Team Whitney, through and through.

Obviously there is more to be said; we'll get to my deeper, largely overwritten logic in a bit. First, though, a little business.

For anyone confused as to why Houston and Carey have been pitted head-to-head—you were hoping for a Houston-Dion battle, perhaps, or Carey–fruit bat?—I'd like to point out that, on paper at least, they are the most even matchup the music world has to offer, with the possible exception of Velvet Revolver vs. Audioslave. Don't believe me? Look no further than *American Idol,* within the context of which Houston and Carey are the lone artists considered no-no's for all but the most talented to tackle—and even Melinda Doolittle tanked her shot. Furthermore, *Idol* recently had the audacity to include a Beatles medley in its season finale, so for that show to call *anything* off-limits is really saying something.

I'd also like to make it clear that when I first started thinking about this assignment, I took it as a purely academic exercise, but quickly became frighteningly subjective about the whole thing. I now believe my brand of blatantly biased personal opinion is completely appropriate. After all, unlike sports—where the numbers rarely lie, unless you are discussing Barry Bonds—it is nearly impossible to use mathematical reasoning to evaluate music. There are no real stats for singing. Record sales have become irrelevant, since no one buys the damn things anymore; awards totals are somewhat less than credible so long as the National Academy of Recording Arts and Sciences continues to distribute Grammys to bands like Train. Frankly, dry recitations of figures are just too easily negated by simple things like, say, bringing up someone's horrible taste in choosing movie roles. Watch, I'll do it right now: Yes, Mariah has seventeen number one singles, and Whitney only eleven. But Whitney made *The Bodyguard,* which is basically a classic, and Mariah starred in *Glitter,* a colossal suckfest of crapitude that should disqualify her on the spot.

This seems a good place to assure readers that, although I regularly use her as something of a chew toy, I do inherently *like* Mariah Carey, as well as several of her songs—and I'm not just saying that because a bunch of her more vehement fans have my e-mail address. Likewise, I don't want anyone to think I'm going easy on Whitney just because at the moment she is God only knows where, having fallen from the public eye like tears of lost potential. We aim for critical analysis here, not charity, and anyway, I expect that if Ms. Houston wanted a comeback (and Clive Davis said it was okay), she could swipe the national spotlight from the crotches of our current starlets in a heartbeat. Case in point: I recently saw Lauryn Hill rock a sold-out crowd in San Diego despite bearing little resemblance, vocally or physically, to the once devastatingly beautiful Fugees singer and *Sister Act 2* star I knew her to be. And my God, Whitney Houston is like nine billion times more iconic than Lauryn Hill.

Next, I want to mention that, overall, this is barely my taste in music. I was raised by symphony musicians, and like a preacher's kid to grain alcohol, I often chose to rebel via rock and roll—the louder the better. During both of these women's heydays, I'd prefer history to remember that I was listening to Guns N' Roses and Nine Inch Nails, although I'm not too cool to admit I owned tapes of Whitney's first two albums, and like everyone else in America I wore out my *Bodyguard* soundtrack. There was also a *very* brief period in the mid-nineties during which the soundtrack to *The Preacher's Wife* could be found on my CD rack, but only because of "I Believe in You and Me," and I swear I sold the thing back as soon as humanly possible. Although prior to the writing of this essay I had never physically possessed any of Carey's work (boy, was *that* trip to Amoeba awkward), I find the crisp pop of "Always Be My Baby" completely infectious, and her performance of "Hero" on the post-9/11 *Tribute to Heroes* telethon gives me goose bumps. That one video where she flees a beachfront resort via Jet Ski? I could watch it again and again; I believe it may have inspired my later attachment to the television series *Alias*. And okay, fine, "Dreamlover" is kind of an awesome song, but tell anybody I said that and I'll call you a liar.

Finally, please be advised that I am aware of Houston and Carey's 1998 duet, "When You Believe," and agree that it would be a most logical springboard from which to launch this conversation. But since the song is basically unlistenable, and appears to have been recorded from separate bunkers at least a thirty-minute drive away from each other after both women had spent the previous night doing Jäger bombs at a very loud bar, it will remain absent from the discussion. I apologize, and hope you'll stay with me anyway, as we begin.

Whitney Houston was released in 1985, and the expectations were high; Houston is, after all, Aretha Franklin's goddaughter, and I think somehow related to Dionne Warwick. She didn't disappoint. From the opening number, "You Give Good Love," the choir girl's tone is clear, her structure simple and relatively unadorned; the song is what I'd call an emotional journey, as she forces us to take her heart, *take it,* before slipping back into murmured satisfaction at the end. At times her voice is ever so slightly off pitch—not so much as to be uncomfortable, mind you, but just enough to ensure that it's actually her, singing, straight into a microphone, no fancy machines involved. "Saving All My Love for You," "All at Once"—they overflow with the twenty-one-year-old Houston's precocious, earthy passion. And then, of course, there is the incomparable "Greatest Love of All," a song that doesn't have to compete on mortal levels thanks to the simple fact that it is, hands down, the finest set of lyrics to recite in a faux-melodramatic setting, ever. I *do* believe the children are our future. So do you. So does everyone. For providing the world that endless mine of comedic gold alone, Whitney Houston can fall asleep proud. She should also probably pat herself on the back for the racial barriers her debut brought crashing down, at least within the scope of the MTV generation: She was the lone female African-American voice amid my Caucasian collection of cassingles, and the cassingles of most of my friends. I doubt we realized the impact she had at the time. I also suspect we would have listened to a giraffe if it was singing "How Will I Know."

One could argue that the trail blazed by Houston led to the immediate popular success of 1990's *Mariah Carey*—although we'll give Mariah some credit, too. Her opener, "Vision of Love," features a vocal that's as strong and clear as her predecessor's; in fact, at just twenty years of age, Mariah was growling her way into words she now might prefer to fluff like a teensy baby chick. "Love Takes Time" soars with shocking assurance, "Someday" is the most pleasant fuck-you-loser song of all time, and on the dramatic torch single "I Don't Wanna Cry," I find myself marveling at how she dips down low at the end to scoop up the last of her tears and deposit them in a sweet, sweet pile at our feet. Overall, this collection of songs manages to be much better than I'd ever bothered to notice.

But let's return to that very first track and listen through once more, shall we? For somewhere around the 2:50 mark . . . it happens. There is . . . a noise. What is it? It is certainly . . . high. And it doesn't appear to be emanating from Carey, who is all the while delivering a gutsy riff on the lyric back down in the sonic range of humans. No, that noise is something strange, foreign, hovering above our heads like a UFO—it spins, blinds us ever so slightly, then zips out of sight, leaving us to wonder if it was really ever there at all.

Yeah. It was.

That Noise, as I will begin capitalizing it now just for fun, remains the enduring hallmark of Carey's work, and if you like it, you like her. If you don't—well, let's just say the only way I'd take a Mariah Carey CD to my desert island is if I thought it might help me better communicate with friendly dolphins in order to hitch a ride home. I just can't deal. For me, That Noise has never managed to be anything more than a novelty, a spectacularly lucrative party trick, and since I know Carey has written a vast number of her own songs—the one category in which she's got Houston soundly beat—I suspect she is largely to blame for its persistence. But just because God gave you a seventy-four-octave range doesn't mean you have to use it, and discretion is almost certainly the better part of singing valor. Also not helping? The way That Noise tends to be accompanied by its friends, Too Much High End in the Mix and Generic Nineties R&B Dingy-Dingy Sound. I hate those guys. But they're largely cosmetic and could be forgiven were I more certain of one crucial thing: Could Carey's career have reached such stratospheric heights if her voice did not?

Whitney's got something that deserves capitalizing too, but it's so far away from That Noise on the awesome spectrum I almost feel bad mentioning it in the same relative breath. I am talking, naturally, about The Catharsis: the glorious boom of a key change that arrives three quarters of the way through "I Will Always Love You," anchoring what is, with apologies to the White Stripes, the best Dolly Parton cover in history. The Catharsis is in effect elsewhere throughout Houston's career—you can find it as far back as "How Will I Know"—but the modulation she pulls off in "I Will Always Love You" is perfection embodied. I fail to find a way to break this down scientifically, or even articulately; all I can hope is that you have experienced a great key change at some point in your life and you know the rush, the transcendent ping that goes off in your brain and brings emotions you barely knew you had rushing to the surface and spilling out all over the place for no good reason whatsoever. A good key change can save your life. Whitney Houston has given us countless great ones.

So. That Noise vs. The Catharsis. To me there is no doubt which prevails. But what the musical component of this contest comes down to, ultimately, unavoidably, is that Whitney Houston is the soundtrack to my childhood, and Mariah Carey is the flittering blip that emerges from my somewhat terrified perspective on the downfall of MTV and resultant screamfest of the *Total Request Live* years. I may have *liked* much of what she did, but I never *identified* with it. It never buckled my knees, never moved me to tears, never caused me to clutch my pillow and dream silly dreams. By the time 1990 rolled around, I was already a crabby high schooler, and as the Carey era progressed—and my personal life did not, by any stretch of the imagination—I found I had little use for her lovey-dovey squealings, or for much of pop radio in general. To this day Mariah continues to be little more than a pleasant diversion, someone whose songs I won't necessarily skip if they pop up in my iTunes but that I won't necessarily skip other things to get to, either. Whitney Houston, on the other hand, practically raised me.

Beyond the music, of course, there are all kinds of surface-level battles to be fought involving wardrobe, onstage sweat levels, dramatic weight loss/gain, and whether or not the singer in question has ever restricted herself solely to a diet of pink foods. Several of these cosmetic categories are deeply one-sided—Whitney kills when it comes to album titles, for example, mainly thanks to the fact that she never named anything *Charmbracelet*—but there remains one key toss-up that will lead us into the second, briefer section of this essay, and it's a doozy:

Is it better to marry (and then divorce) Tommy Mottola, a music mogul twice your age who's offering you a career, or to marry (and then divorce) Bobby Brown, an attractive but waning pop star notorious for his brushes with the law?

I know. It's tough, right? And here's the thing: There is no answer. It's a trick question. Both options are equally doomed, and like the worst *Choose Your Own Adventure* book ever conceived, both will lead you to a public breakdown of massive proportions.

Mariah's journey to the brink was pretty straightforward: The girl married her svengali, thus inexorably blurring the line between personal life and career. (One can only imagine those dinner-table conversations. Mariah: "Chicken or fish tonight, dear?" Tommy: "Who cares? Your fucking album still doesn't have a single!") After three short years, Carey had the sense to free herself from his fatherly clutches, but the damage had been done. Her divorce led to a change in labels, the label switch led to a reported eighty-million-dollar contract with Virgin, and that ginormous sum of money most likely led to crushing amounts of self-doubt, as no sane person could ever imagine their singing ability is worth the same amount of money they pay baseball players. So the pressure mounted, and Mariah soon fell prey to "exhaustion," that most unavoidable of celebrity afflictions. During the summer of 2001 she randomly showed up at *TRL* with an ice cream cart and took off some clothes, said some nutty shit on her website, and checked herself into a hospital. And *then* they released *Glitter.* By 2002, Virgin had offered her the princely sum of twenty-eight million dollars just to go the hell away.

But like the butterflies she loves, Carey's chrysalis of pain would soon yield new life. Since 2003 Mariah has been on a steady upswing, and 2005's *The Emancipation of Mimi* got her back on the Grammy horse. Even though the kinds of people who pay close attention to these things say her voice is a shadow of its former self, I dunno. "We Belong Together" seems like a decent-enough song. But frankly, I mostly don't care.

And why don't I care? Because I believe that if you're going to have a breakdown, you should do us the favor of not coming back from it so damn fast, if at all. Don't just dangle your crazies in front of Carson Daly, then claw your way to sanity—go out like a *champ,* and if at all possible, take others with you.

Go out, in other words, like Whitney Houston.

It's easy: Become famous at an early age. Experience mind-boggling levels of international success. Face some lesbian rumors. Marry a presumably sympathetic former child star then accuse him of smacking you around. Act in a movie, then record a song for the soundtrack that every single person on earth loves so much that you are forced to sing it over and over and over and over again to the exclusion of almost anything else for nearly a decade. Act in a couple more movies to try and get the world to move on. Record some pretty great stuff that is different from, but not worse than, where you started your career. Sign a one-hundred-million-dollar contract. Sweat. Sing that one song a couple thousand more times. Deal with public speculation over status of marriage and fidelity of husband. Cancel a couple gigs. Get caught with pot while boarding a plane. Resurface on TV in order to swear that you would never do crack, because crack is wack. Disappear off the face of the earth. Lose a significant amount of weight. Resurface on TV again, this time to star in a reality series documenting your husband's release from jail and subsequent failure to deal with humanity on any rational level. Coin a variety of phrases including the eternally useful "Oh, hell to the no" and its less handy but no less spectacular cousins "That's very Italian" and "I am not doing this with him to-*daaaaaay.*" Perform an impromptu gift-shop ditty called "Do You Like These Sunglasses (They Work for Me)," which turns out better than anything you've released in five years. Come off as crazier than your husband. Finally divorce him. Et cetera.

Please tell me you see how completely and utterly brilliant Whitney Houston's downfall has been. I'm not trying to be callous or insensitive to victims of domestic violence or substance abuse here, and I recognize that she is most likely a very unhealthy person who needs a great deal of psychological assistance just to shop for clothes. Hell, I used to wander the streets of New York City like a ghost, moaning to anyone who would listen that the collapse of Whitney Houston was the collapse of everything good in the world. It's just that once I scabbed over the heartbreak of watching the frilly, flirty, upstanding adopted namesake of my childhood morph into the Gollumesque creature of *Being Bobby Brown,* I started to see the whole situation not as tragedy but as testament to her unparalleled abilities as a public figure.

First of all, Whitney lasted until about the age of forty before completely and irretrievably losing her shit. That's nearly twice as long as Britney Spears managed to hold it together—and yet the benchmark of crazy that Houston has set is something the Lost Mouseketeer can only dream of. Britney shaved her head and stole some stuff from a photo shoot? Whatevs. Whitney Houston, a multigazillionaire, had to auction off her *underwear* at a *warehouse* in *Jersey,* for crying out loud. She is, in a word, amazing.

And that, at long last, is why Whitney Houston is the greatest diva of all: because whether she's singing or fucking up, the woman just does it better. Chicks like Mariah or Britney or Lindsay Lohan or, God, I dunno, Fergie and her stupid crystal meth—they may try, but they can never match the carnage of her train wreck, and they *certainly* cannot hold a candle to Houston as an artist. Whitney may come out with a new album someday; she may not. She may die a horrific, Layne Staleyesque death; she may not. It doesn't matter. In both chapters of her extraordinary life, she has been absolutely dominant, and now the rest is gravy. On every conceivable level she reigns supreme. Always has, always will.

Lots of love, kid. Get well soon.

The Rolling Stones

vs.

The Velvet Underground

Richard Hell

My first thought was that it'd be fun to crush the Beatles with Guided by Voices. But that would take too much research. Those bands were prolific. Then I thought of the Velvet Underground and the Rolling Stones. I'd been surprised the first time I saw the title of the Velvets bootleg I have called *The Psychopath's Rolling Stones*. And the Velvets only released four albums during their entire existence, so that'd reduce the homework. Furthermore, I only own one Beatles album and never play it, while I often play many of the large number of Velvets and Stones recordings I have.

(A little aside here, regarding the phrases "crush the beatles with guided by voices" and "the velvet underground and the rolling stones."

I don't know if I can duplicate the experience for you by describing it, but those phrases, when I read them where I'd typed them on the computer screen, unexpectedly took place in my brain separated from their rock and roll band applications, and it was a mental kick, like true poetry, maybe as high an instance of it as rock and roll can achieve. Never mind.)

The first order of business has to be getting our opponents into the same weight class, since the Stones have made so many more records than the Velvets. To do that, I'll restrict the albums considered to each band's output during the years that the Velvets existed, 1966 to 1970. (Their first public appearance was actually in December 1965.) This works out neatly, since not only is Lou Reed (born March 2, 1942) practically the same age as Jagger and Richards (July 26 and December 18, 1943), but the Stones album—their fifth—that came out in mid-1966, *Aftermath,* was their first of entirely original songs. All the Velvets' records contained strictly original material, and they recorded their first album in the same period as *Aftermath,* May 1966 (though it was released, as *The Velvet Underground & Nico,* only in early '67).

One was an international-megahit-making group of superstars, considered by many the greatest rock and roll band in the world; the other an abject commercial failure widely reviled, excoriated, and dismissed. The Stones' records were crystal clear and crisp, no matter how driving and aggressive, while most of the Velvets' were a scratchy, fuzzy clatter of muffled screeching noises, beats, drones, and snarls. A retrospective distinction of the Velvets, though—one in a class with being regarded for a time as "the greatest rock and roll band in the world"—is that they became the first completely hitless rock and roll band to end up in everyone's short-list pantheon of all-time-best groups.

The obvious things the two groups have in common are (1) instincts and skills for the construction and arrangement of catchy rock and roll songs and (2) full scary sexy worlds of attitude and style, style auras like silvery sick-thought balloons or dim naked-limb-filled miasmas that each group emanated and in which everything they were and did took place. This phenomenon of whole extreme environments associated with specific musicians is at the center of rock and roll. People love bands and their music for the alternate worlds they betoken as much as for anything else about the music. The music-business promoters know it, too. Stones manager Andrew Loog Oldham's liners on their very first album (1964) included the slogan "The Rolling Stones are more than just a group, they are a way of life," while a radio ad for the Velvets' third album (1969) intoned, ". . . here are expressions of a new dimension in honesty, purity, and feeling . . . not a probe, not an exploration, not an experience, but a whole complete reality: the Velvet Underground."

As for the music's roots, the Stones came out of a mix of blues and early R&B, Chuck Berry, Bo Diddley, and rockabilly, while the Velvets deemphasized the blues, Bo, and Berry in favor of the subsequent rock and roll development of largely urban, Brill Building–pop songwriting and doo-wop (Brian Wilson was big to Lou Reed too), along with the early-sixties raga/modal drone John Cale had been playing with La Monte Young and Reed's partiality to free jazz (which had already been affected by Indian·music in the fifties). In terms of song ideal, probably the meeting point of the Stones and Velvets is Phil Spector. Both bands adored the idea he formulated of the stunning pop gem, the resplendent, massive, white-lit wall of glittering sound.

Rock and roll is wallpaper, like tendrily patterns, on a wall of sound, and the wall surrounds a way of life, various ones for every great rock and roll maker, and in each of those worlds the song is like a cup, and in that cup is the lead singer's voice. Elvis's or James Brown's or Dylan's or Mick Jagger's or Lou Reed's. Sneers and swagger are almost always ingredients. Part of the Beatles' problem was that they were deficient in sneers. There are great oeuvres that are pretty wholesome—Beatles hero Buddy Holly for instance—but it's a handicap. Teenybopper music is a weak strain of rock and roll. (Holly strutted and threatened more than it might appear at first glance. Consider the lyrics to "That'll Be the Day.")

Rock and roll is aggressive self-assertion. Full-fledged front men have to be difficult, egotistical people, and, if they write the songs too, then the songs are likely to have plenty of that meanness and egotism as well. Part of the job description of the front person is to be godlike for teenagers. A rock and roll show is about the audience agreeing to surrender to the band in such a way that the band gives back that which it's received from the crowd in the form of the crowd's pleasure in itself, in the form of the crowd's ideal of itself, of its own glory (as personified by the band's front man). And teenagers need to swagger and be sarcastic and furious because they have so little power (or self-assurance either) otherwise and elsewhere, and because sex chemicals are pouring through them. The music, strictly aurally, physically, in sound waves and rhythms, embodies and unleashes power too, and emotion, but it's the human thing, the focal point presented by the front person, that's the essence of the band, and it's dirty and mean. The lead singer is a dick. The lead singer is a cunt. When a person needs to have that power—a godlike power enabling him to confer a feeling of immortality to his audience—to perform well, needs to have that absolute self-assurance that is required to satisfy audiences ravenous for the thrill of its reflection in themselves ("I'll be your mirror"), that driven self-certainty will make him a creep. (It's really not easy on the performers either, as seen not just by their level of sheer crankiness but by their fatality rate.)

Maybe I'm just talking about my own tastes, because after all there are also Bruce Springsteen and Joey Ramone and Joe Strummer, all of whom are pretty flatly nice people. But I don't find them interesting as performers. I can't get into proletariat rock, cartoon rock, jam rock, or college-kid-irony rock. I believe in the idea of no-hero rock and roll, but prefer the music of monstrously self-involved front men. I don't have to like them or admire them. Still, I'm grateful for them, and believe they deserve all the pampering they need.

My original notes for this article had the heading "The Beautiful Music of Nasty Little Shits." It just gets complicated, one's feelings toward people who make works that have made one's life better, and the difficulty of separating the talent from the character, or trying to figure out the relationship between the talent and the character. In rock and roll, the expression is so direct and personal seeming. (What's more personal and expressive than a voice?) A soulful thing about Keith Richards (more on that later) is his tolerance for the nastiness of front men. He has said about Jagger, "It's a hard gig, out front there.... You gotta be able to actually believe you're semi-divine when you're out there. Then come offstage and know that you ain't. That's the problem, that eventually the reaction times get slower and you still think you're semi-divine in the limo and semi-divine at the hotel...."[1] I mean, Richards let Chuck Berry hit him in the face. (About which he said, "He can hit me in the eye again anytime.... See, Chuck fascinates me—he's an absolute asshole but I've had lots of experience working with them. And to me it's kind of a lovable trait. It's not a big deal that a guy is an asshole. It doesn't mean that you don't bother with him. To me, it's more intriguing than a guy who's fairly well balanced and has all the answers...."[2])

Back to how the bands compare. First: Despite Reed's many loving references to the term, it seems correct to call the Stones a "rock and roll" band, but not the Velvets. The Velvets *are* a rock and roll band, but one for a new age in which words have to be put in quotation marks. The Sex Pistols liked to claim to have destroyed rock and roll, but it was the Velvets who did. By comparison the Pistols were classic rock. The VU are the original white low-fi band, but that's not the important thing. Maybe you could say they're art rock, but that's unfairly precious sounding. What they were was metarock. Not a subset of rock but a superior set, an arch to the point of overarching set. They're the first rock and roll band to play rock and roll that's about rock and roll. They're reconsidering it. They're a step removed.

The Velvets are linear, surface, compared to the Stones, whose best

1. Keith Richards, quoted in Stanley Booth, *Keith: Standing in the Shadows* (New York: St. Martin's Press, 1995), 157–158.
2. Ibid., 176–177.

records have real depths. "Surface" isn't bad, though. Spector's mono-phonic wall of sound was surface, like a tidal wave. As Andy Warhol, the Velvets' first manager-promoter and Reed's mentor, said in 1967, "If you want to know all about Andy Warhol, just look at the surface of my paintings and films and me, and there I am. There's nothing behind it."[3] The Velvets are like that: without differentiation. (I remember how it blew my mind when it first really hit me that each moment of a record-ing is only one sound—one single sound of a given pitch, timbre, and loudness, no matter how many noises of what type went into producing it.) There had never been anything like that free-jazz, Eastern, paradox-ically frenzied drone that the Velvets in Cale's period (the first two al-bums) brought to rock and roll. Cale's amplified viola on "Heroin" and Reed's guitar solo on "I Heard Her Call My Name" are more interesting and important and innovative than anything the Stones did musically. There hadn't been the confrontational intensity of the Velvets' sound ei-ther—this is their main contribution to "punk" style. The band reveled in offending people with decibel levels and aural chaos. (Warhol en-couraged this too, recommending, "Always leave them wanting less."[4])

Speaking of "punk," you can find the basis of so many bands' and stars' whole sounds and styles in specific Velvets songs: The Modern Lovers came out of "Sweet Jane" and "Sister Ray" ("Roadrunner" by an-other name); my nomination for song most revealing of Tom Verlaine's debt to Lou Reed would be "Temptation Inside Your Heart" (recorded in 1968 though not officially released until *VU* in 1985)—Television's style is an anal version of the way that song sounds; half of Bob Quine's guitar style can be heard in "Some Kinda Love"; Sonic Youth is prefigured in the long monotonous stuttering rhythmic droney sitar-sounding distorted

3. Andy Warhol, quoted in Gretchen Berg, "Nothing to Lose: An Interview with Andy Warhol" in *Andy Warhol: Film Factory,* ed. Michael O'Pray (London: British Film Institute, 1989), 56.

4. Andy Warhol, quoted in Victor Bockris, *Transformer* (New York: Simon & Schuster, 1994), 120.

shrieking and feedback break on "European Son"; Patti Smith's singing style sounds were enabled by the Doug Yule of "Oh! Sweet Nuthin'," and her lyric-writing approach would appear to have taken seriously such Reed efforts as "I'm Beginning to See the Light":

> *I wore my teeth in my hands*
> *So I could mess the hair of the night*
> *Baby I'm beginning to see the light*
> *Now now now now now now now*
> *Baby I'm beginning to see the light*
> *It's coming closer*
> *Hey now baby I'm beginning to see the light*
> *I met myself in a dream*
> *And I just wanna tell you everything was all right*
> *Hey now baby I'm beginning to see the light*
> *Here comes two of you*
> *Which one will you choose*
> *One is black and one is blue*
> *Don't know just what to do*
> *Well I'm beginning to see the light*

The whole original alternative-rock college-kid slew of bands like Pavement derived their disjunctive, non-sequitur lyrical mode from songs like "Pale Blue Eyes":

> *Skip a life completely, stuff it in a cup*
> *She said, Money is like us in time*
> *It lies but can't stand up*
> *Down for you is up*
> *Linger on, your pale blue eyes*

Reed's lyrics probably do come the closest to poetry of any in rock and roll. Dylan is his only competition. Dylan rules, but I'd venture that the lyrics on *The Velvet Underground* are the best as a suite, as an album set, of any in rock and roll history:

> *Candy says, "I've come to hate my body*
> *and all that it requires in this world"*
> *Candy says, "I'd like to know completely*
> *what others so discreetly talk about"*
>
> —"Candy Says"

> *Put jelly on your shoulder*
> *Lie down on the carpet*
> *Between thought and expression*
> *Let us now kiss the culprit*
>
> —"Some Kinda Love"

> *Linger on, your pale blue eyes*
>
> —"Pale Blue Eyes"

> *Jesus, help me find my proper place*
> *Help me in my weakness*
> *cuz I'm falling out of grace*
>
> —"Jesus"

> *I'm beginning to see the light*
>
> —"Beginning to See the Light"

> *I've been set free, and I've been bound*
> *Let me tell you people what I found*
> *I saw my head laughing, rolling on the ground*
> *And now I'm set free*
> *I'm set free*
> *To find a new illusion*
>
> —"I'm Set Free"

The Rolling Stones vs. The Velvet Underground

That's the story of my life
That's the difference between wrong and right
But Billy said both those words are dead
That's the story of my life
————The entire lyrics to "That's the Story of My Life"

Consistent with the general ironic, meta viewpoint of Reed's Velvets musicmaking, though, he sings all his lyrics flippantly, sarcastically (with the rare exceptions of a breathless, monotonous, Nico-like "Sunday Morning" or two). He mocks everything. The music supplies a sturdy foundation with its incontrovertible drive, but it too is unsentimental—rough—to the point of near parody (though it got notably more mellow toward the end, post-Cale, especially on *Loaded*). There are pretty harmonies, but they're rec-room style too. It all has no frills and makes no concessions to pop polish. And if a song is to be sung with any innocence or sincerity, it has to be sung by someone other than Reed (Maureen Tucker on "After Hours" and "I'm Sticking with You"; Doug Yule on "Who Loves the Sun," "A New Age," and "Oh! Sweet Nuthin' ").

There is a weird, oblique contact point between Jagger's and Reed's otherwise fairly dissimilar singing styles. Jagger is a mimic of the blues-roots and backwoods American singing from the small-label "race" and rockabilly records that his band grew out of. But if you listen cold to Reed's singing on "White Light/White Heat," you realize he sounds as if he were in blackface, like a parody of a vaudeville minstrel (which is already a mockery), not just down to the broad Southern *a* sound in words like "mind" and "blind" (*mahnd* and *blahnd*), but in black idioms too: "Ooo have mercy / White light have it goodness knows," "I surely do love to watch that stuff," "Hey there foxy mama," "Goin' upside yo head," "Goodness knows, work it!" The music sounds crazed and rabid but, unlike the way Jagger sings in a threatening style on the more aggressive Stones songs, Reed, true to his form, just gets all the more goofy and mocking over this insanely violent speed-freak rave. The mysterious thing is how even though Reed's singing style is one that screams with its every burlesque inflection that none of it matters, the world is fake ("I'm set free to find a new illusion"), it's the Stones who by comparison come off sounding artificial.

Gee, I didn't really intend to go this direction. During the period under consideration, the Rolling Stones released *Aftermath, Between the Buttons, Their Satanic Majesties Request, Beggars Banquet,* and *Let It Bleed,* along with such singles as "Nineteenth Nervous Breakdown," "Paint It, Black," "Mother's Little Helper," "Have You Seen Your Mother, Baby, Standing in the Shadows?," "Who's Driving My Plane," "Let's Spend the Night Together," "Ruby Tuesday," and "Jumpin' Jack Flash." Good God. Those are some snappy recordings.

The main thing that the Stones have that the Velvets don't is Keith Richards, meaning: soul. Lou Reed has a lot going for himself, but soul isn't part of it. You have to grant that he explicitly rejected it ("no blues licks" is said to have been a rule for the Velvets), but still, soul is usually a desirable quality. What is soul? It's humane empathy that in music gets expressed as loose swing (no matter how harsh and biting the chords might be, or pumping the beat); it's the sound of musicians respecting one another and submerging their egos to create conjunctive syncopated rhythms that make the listener's body sympathize and want to play off them by moving around to them. (You could object that artists such as James Brown and Ike Turner were obsessively controlling egomaniacs who dictated some of the deepest, most sexily greasy soul music of all time, but that's another essay. Maybe titled "They Contained Multitudes, Each of Whom Loved Each Other and Played Separate Rhythm Parts.") Richards is a hero of that kind of musical generosity. Lou Reed is not generous.

Neither, though, do the Velvets have a Jagger or a Charlie Watts. What Jagger brings is the apotheosis of that front-man function. Not only can he do a lot more with his voice than Reed, but he's the leaping monkey who serves that "appointed god to make us perfect" role for his audience in a way Reed couldn't begin to try. As for Charlie, maybe he even exceeds Keith's contribution in the battle with the Velvets. The snap, bam, and sliding virility of the way his drum kit makes Stones recordings riveting puts them in another class altogether from the VU in the percussion department. Maureen's drumming is perfect in its one-dimensional way, but Charlie makes every other drummer in rock and roll sound handicapped.

The most striking difference between the Stones and the Velvets, though, is the Stones' committed commerciality. Sometimes this works in their favor and sometimes it doesn't. *Aftermath* seems the most relentless and fun catalog of misogyny (or honesty about how boys wish they could act toward girls, but that only star-level charisma enables) ever to thrill teenagers, with "Stupid Girl," "Lady Jane," "Under My Thumb," and "High and Dry," until *Between the Buttons* comes along and ramps the level up further with "Yesterday's Papers":

> *Who wants yesterday's papers*
> *Who wants yesterday's girl*

"Back Street Girl":

> *Please don't you call me at home*
> *Please don't come knocking at night*
> *Please never ring on the phone*
> *Your manners are never quite right . . .*
> *Don't want you part of my world*
> *Just you be my back street girl*

"Cool, Calm & Collected," "Please Go Home," and "Miss Amanda Jones." All these tracks drive and syncopate and are thrilling and they're also all like novelty songs, pop concoctions with lots of harmonies and echo and reverb and hand claps and—thanks to Brian Jones's versatility—exotic instruments like recorder, sitar, slide guitar, bells, and marimbas. The world they talk about is one of fashion and money and drugs, which is the world the group, Jagger especially, inhabited, even if the girls of that world are viciously mocked by the street-kid rock and roll stars. But the star is a fastidious snob too (viz. "Back Street Girl"). I don't mean to be playing superior to this stuff. I liked it then and I like it now. Contrasted with the Velvets it does seem fey, but you could interpret its pop aspirations as respect for an audience as much as some deficiency of integrity. Or at least as honest ambition. Every rock and roll band wants to be popular and rich and pursued by sex objects. These songs are timelessly exciting and charged with pleasure.

It's hard to excuse *Satanic Majesties Request,* though. At best you could take it as endearing in a certain way: the Stones showing their true colors as determined to keep up with all trends, no matter how lame and inappropriate the results. It's only rock and roll. But unfortunately that record's not really rock and roll, and it's pretty inexcusably horrible. They did give it a good title. Changing the classic wording of a British royal invitation, "Her Brittanic Majesty requests," to "Satanic" was more outrageous than the ten-years-subsequent "God save the queen / She ain't no human being."

Following this faux-*Pepper* travesty, the group tried to redeem itself by coming down to earth, raising a glass "to the hardworking people," and taking political stands on their generation's big current events. But *Beggars Banquet* is as overwrought, in different ways, as the previous album was. It may not trick itself out in psychedelic effects, but it's boringly grandiose and bombastic, like old-fashioned bad acting: It's intended for stadiums. The songs aren't true or personal but are roles played (most likely imitating a Beatles mode again). The superficial appearance of political radicalism is betrayed by the lyrics too. The violent "Street Fighting Man," which sounds like a topically timely call to arms, is actually the meek opposite, a variation on the Beatles' recently released "Revolution" ("But when you talk about destruction / Don't you know that you can count me out"):

The Rolling Stones vs. The Velvet Underground

What can a poor boy do except to sing for a rock and roll
  band
Cuz in sleepy London town there's just no place for a street
  fighting man

Jagger takes on exaggerated hillbilly accents for a few hokey jokey songs ("Dear Doctor," "Prodigal Son"). The album is all poses and compromise.

Then comes *Let It Bleed*. You have to sit up for this one. You have to push everything out of the way. It's a strong contender for best rock and roll record ever made. Brian is gone. Keith played all the guitars on two of the set's most powerful cuts, "Gimme Shelter" and "Let It Bleed." These songs give you chills. Velvets songs don't give you chills. Not only do the tracks, with their monster guitar parts and whipping licks and fills and gospely and choral backup singing, reach you emotionally, but the music is physical in a way the Velvets never are. It's music that commands your body. You don't feel manipulated, as on *Beggars Banquet,* but uplifted. The lyrics and feelings are personal and plain and true to life. Even the down-home-mask adopting—"Love in Vain" and "Country Honk" ("Honky Tonk Women")—sounds genuine not just as tribute but as emotional identification, and, in the case of "Honk," as actual experience. The lyrics are the Stones' best ever. Their themes come out of the intense sixties drug pain fashion money and sex underworld the group had helped create, but they don't reflexively, defensively deride the debutantes so much, and they're more detailed and juicy than ever before while also being funny.

I got nasty habits, I take tea at three
Yes, and the meat I eat for dinner must be hung up for a week
My best friend he shoots water rats and feeds them to his
  geese
Doncha think there's a place for you in between the sheets
                                        —"Live with Me"

I'm a flea-bit peanut monkey, all my friends are junkies
That's not really true
I'm a cold Italian pizza I could use a lemon squeezer
How'd you do
                                        —"Monkey Man"

Jagger even seems to match Richards's soulfulness with his lyrics to songs such as "Gimme Shelter"—which has got to be one of the top three rock and roll tracks of all time, and which doesn't say much more than

War, children, it's just a shot away, it's just a shot away
It's just a shot away, it's just a shot away
Love, sister, it's just a kiss away, it's just a kiss away
It's just a kiss away, it's just a kiss away

and "You Can't Always Get What You Want"

You can't always get what you want
But if you try sometime you just might find
You get what you need

The record is scary and compassionate. You love being tossed around on it. It does that thing of taking you out of yourself into a whole ocean.

Oh, and to bring up the Stones' fruitful influence on subsequent bands: Their presence so permeated rock and roll culture for so long that it's almost impossible to isolate their mark—it's everywhere, especially in the countless great garage-punk groups of the mid and late sixties, as found on the *Nuggets* compilation albums, who played fuzz-box guitar and yelled and taunted and couldn't get much satisfaction because their sex drives were relentless but all the girls were too stuck-up and stupid. There are two specific great and important groups I can think of who owed a whole lot to the Rolling Stones: the New York Dolls, who of course were almost like a robust drag-queen hallucination

50

of the Stones (to find the roots of the Dolls' style, Johansen's singing especially, check "Doncha Bother Me" from *Aftermath*); and the Stooges of *Raw Power,* showcasing James Williamson's K. Richards–besotted guitar and songwriting.

I remember being surprised to notice that when Keith gets asked about first knowing and working with Mick, he always mentions how Mick came from a higher social class. Jagger's father was a physical-education instructor for schoolkids, whereas Keith's worked in a factory. This seems like a fine distinction to me, but those minutely calibrated social classifications are still how people think in England. The Stones were the classic rock and roll story of white underclass kids who surprised themselves by becoming rich and famous playing the even more underclass music (usually African-American) they loved, like Elvis before and Eminem later. The shock of success was further exaggerated by the extreme British class consciousness, combined with the amperage of youth trends in the sixties when the baby boom created the greatest number of teenagers the world had ever seen. So the Stones were these street kids thrust into the middle of a world of commercial hitmaking and upper-class attentions. They kept their self-respect by defying social conventions and emphasizing their rebellious, impolite attitudes, but at the same time, as proud young players in the world of pop music—and contemporaries of the Beatles—they accepted the standard of sales figures being the measure of their achievement. (Notice for instance how whenever Keith is asked in interviews about his friend Gram Parsons, he always remarks on how impressed he is by people's interest in Parsons even though he never made a hit record. Richards can't think of public respect for his rock and roll peers except in categories of record sales.)

The Velvets were a world away from that classic-hit rock and roll scenario. The Velvets were Americans (except for Welshman John Cale) and middle-class—citizens of a place where, though economic class levels certainly exist, social class levels are a lot more permeable than in Britain. And the Velvets were intellectuals. Lou Reed's first mentor (or at least his fantasy mentor) was the brilliant (speed-freak) American poet Delmore Schwartz, with whom he studied at Syracuse University. Musically, Reed was as excited by rarefied avant-garde noise jazz and faceless white professional songwriting (like Goffin and King, Barry and Greenwich) as he was by roots rock and roll. Cale was a serious modern classical musician who studied composition at the college level for years and was influenced by avant-garde classical musician La Monte Young, with whom he studied and played, and John Cage. Sterling Morrison started out majoring in physics at university, and, after the Velvets, returned to school and ended up being a college professor of literature.

The Velvets were a rock and roll band, but they took all of recent music, from Bo Diddley through Phil Spector through John Cage, Ornette Coleman, and La Monte Young, as their province. They were high artists, bent on making the most stimulating and aesthetically interesting music—built on the foundations of their broadly various musical preoccupations—that they could. Their world was as outlaw and depraved and scornful of conventional social values as the Stones' (this is built into rock and roll too, because it's the teenage view of what's desirable) but was a great deal more intellectually oriented, a new thing in rock and roll. It might sound strange that the intellectual approach has cruder results, the way the Velvets' music is so much messier sounding than the Stones', but it's not. It's comparable to the way, say, Duchamp's *Fountain,* a signed urinal, made Picasso look like a commercial artist. The Velvets made the choice of being strictly faithful to their own advanced ideas of what was most interesting to do in rock and roll without conceding anything to less sophisticated conventional tastes that would have packaged their ideas in pop-music sheen. They wrote beautiful ballads and visceral, driving rock and roll, but only paid attention to their personal ideas about what were the important features of that music to present.

My expectation of which band would come out on top here has changed a few times in the course of this writing. In a way, rock and roll that's not hit music is failed rock and roll. Rock and roll is pop teenage music. If masses of kids don't respond to it, then by definition it isn't good. Also, a lot of what we love about rock and roll is that wallpaper quality, where a given song is pasted everywhere on the (youth) culture for a few months so that it comes to represent that time and place forever, as well as provide alternate or idealized identities to its fans by the world of feelings and values embodied in it. The Rolling Stones have this to a degree that obliterates the Velvets.

Of course, you don't have to choose. You can like it all. When you are a kid, your identity is your favorite band. But you realize, when you know more, that you can like them all. Or not. It is interesting how preferences and interests fluctuate. So the winner has to be provisional. I was kind of looking forward to beating up the Velvets with the Stones. Lou Reed was obnoxious enough in the Velvets, but he really became insufferable in his subsequent career (which is devoid of Velvets-caliber records too). I would have liked to try to bring him down a peg. But it began to look like it wasn't going to turn out that way. Then I came to *Let It Bleed* and I started reconsidering again. That record is uniquely magnificent. But here at the moment of truth, the Velvets can't be denied. They take the crown. Lou Reed is queen for a day.

Jay-Z

vs.

Nas

Tom Breihan

Rap rivalries are different from pop rivalries. Pop musicians tend to respond to adversaries by stepping up their sounds or visuals, by keeping close tabs on each other's advancements, maybe by letting a guarded reference or two slip in an interview. Even when they make explicit references to each other in their songs, those references hardly ever amount to thrown gauntlets. In "Sweet Home Alabama," Ronnie Van Zant didn't threaten to kill Neil Young. He didn't question Neil Young's sexuality or brag about fucking Neil Young's wife. He just said a Southern man don't need Neil Young around and that Neil Young should remember that.

But rap is different. It has direct competition in its DNA. Before a single rap record was ever released, graffiti writers and dancers and rappers gained stature in part by trashing each other: scrawling over each other's pieces, mockingly mimicking each other's moves, piling scorn on each other's names. Kool Moe Dee to Busy Bee, 1982: "Hold on, Busy Bee, I don't mean to be bold / But put that paw-diddy-paw bullshit on hold." LL Cool J to Kool Moe Dee, 1988: "How you like me now? I'm getting busier / I'm double-platinum, watching you get dizzier." Canibus to LL Cool J, 1997: "Now watch me rip the tat from your arm / Kick you in your groin, stick you for your Vanguard Award / In front of your mom, your first, second, and third born / Make your wife get on the horn, call Minister Farrakhan."

In rap there's a prevailing illusion that it's like sports, that one rapper can objectively be considered better than another, that every rapper threatens the supremacy of every other rapper, that art is like sports. That's why rap crews hardly ever stay together and why rap alliances splinter in the blink of an eye. Young men raised in poverty and degradation, by necessity conditioned from birth not to trust anyone, find themselves successful and powerful because of the stuff that they say and the way that they say it. But that success and power, even after years of work, comes so suddenly that it feels tentative and illusory, like it could disappear any day. And so everyone else who succeeded in the same way becomes an immediate threat, a problem to be dealt with. In New York, four years after Biggie died, two of these young men both claimed to be the city's greatest rapper. Worse, they both had legitimate reasons for declaring their supremacy. Things were always going to explode.

Here's the first thing to remember about the feud between Jay-Z and Nas: Their symmetries far outnumber their differences. They're both New York rappers born within a few years of each other.

They both came to prominence during New York rap's mid-nineties halcyon period, releasing sweeping but dense and uncompromising debut albums, then gradually changing their styles to reach larger and larger audiences. They've collaborated with many of the same rappers and producers. They both like to quote gangster movies and talk about their diamonds. When both of them recall their crime experiences, real or imaginary, they're as likely to lapse into regretful dejection and soul-searching introspection as they are to sneer and declare dominance. And, perhaps most important, they both continually pay tribute to Christopher Wallace, Biggie Smalls, their fallen contemporary.

Before Biggie died on March 9, 1997, he was the best rapper in New York and the best rapper in the world. After he died, he left a sudden vacuum at the top of the pile, and both Jay and Nas rushed to claim his absent throne. The phrase "King of New York" came up over and over again during their feud, and it gradually came to take on a totemic significance, almost as if it were a real title and not just an imagined primacy. To both of these guys, the very idea that New York could support two dominant superstar rappers was unthinkable. This town wasn't big enough for the two of them.

There was other stuff, too, of course. Jay's early single "Dead Presidents II" sampled a line from Nas's "The World Is Yours." Jay wanted Nas to appear on the record and in the video. Nas refused. Predictably, there was a woman involved: Carmen Bryan, who had a baby by Nas, slept with Jay, and a few years later wrote a trashy tell-all book about her experiences with both. But it's a lot more interesting to consider the feud's gestation through rap's intricate web of coded slights and violent threats perceptible only to a few.

Years before the two went ahead and started naming names, they hid their insults against each other as quick little lyrical asides, burying them under mountains of implication. Think about Jay's line from 1997's "Where I'm From," from the album *In My Lifetime, Vol. 1:* "I'm from where niggas pull your card and argue all day about / Who's the best MC: Biggie, Jay-Z, or Nas." On one hand, Jay was paying tribute to Nas and Biggie, still warm in his grave. On the other, he was brashly declaring himself the equal of the other two. *Reasonable Doubt,* Jay's first album, had been released just a year earlier, and Nas was a relative veteran. On the same album, Jay had a single called "The City Is Mine," which he framed as a letter to Biggie: "A world with amnesia won't forget your name / You held it down long enough, let me take those reins." Nas's answer didn't come until 1999, with the first verse of his "We Will Survive," similarly addressed to Biggie: "It used to be fun, making records to see your response / But now competition is none, now that you're gone / And these niggas is wrong, taking your name in vain / And they claim to be New York's king? It ain't about that."

This sort of thing happens all the time: rappers subtly hinting at rivalries in lyrics, refusing to name their adversaries, leaving us to piece together mysterious behind-the-scenes stories with whatever ghostly and incomplete information we might have. More often than not, these issues evaporate before they come to light. Sometimes, though, the insults keep coming and building up steam until they turn into something bigger. That's what happened here, though Jay himself was absent during most of the early hostilities.

After Nas released a single called "Nas Is Like," Jay-Z's young and rangy protégé Memphis Bleek recorded the vastly inferior but conceptually identical track "Memphis Bleek Is. . . ." Nas, not amused, fired a warning shot, flipping a line from Bleek's track "What You Think of That" on his own single "Nastradamus": "You wanna ball till you fall, I could help you with that / You want beef? I could let a slug melt in your hat." Then Bleek, nearly a year later, on "My Mind Right": "Only a few fit in / Play your position / So who you supposed to be? Play your position."

None of this is quite on the level of Tupac telling Biggie he fucked Biggie's wife. Instead it was an intricate and half-secret series of jabs and counters. Two potential opponents feeling each other out, secretly massing forces along their borders. As Bleek and Nas traded insults, they certainly knew when they were being addressed, but most of the rest of us were in the dark and not really paying much attention anyway. Until the summer of 2001.

Things exploded, or anyway started exploding, at Hot 97's annual Summer Jam concert in 2001. In New York, Summer Jam is a big deal. Rappers bring out special guests and try to one-up each other with theatrical, headline-grabbing stunts. That year, Jay-Z brought out special surprise guest Michael Jackson, pretty much the be-all and end-all of special surprise guests. He also premiered "Takeover," a song that scathingly attacked the Queensbridge rap duo Mobb Deep, sometime allies of Nas. "When I was pushing weight / Back in '88 / You was a ballerina / I got the pictures, I seen ya," Jay sneered as a childhood photo of Mobb Deep rapper Prodigy in dance-class tights flashed on the enormous screens at Giants Stadium. The verse was devastating enough that it nearly ended Mobb Deep's career; the group never managed to scrape together an adequate response. And it ended thusly: "You guys don't want it with Hov / Ask Nas: He don't want it with Hov, no!"

That was it; the floodgates were open. Nas, in a long radio-station freestyle, responded: "Is he H to the izzo, M to the izzo / For shizzle, yo phony, the rapping version of Sisqó." Then Jay raised the stakes further. On September 11, 2001, he released *The Blueprint,* which included an expanded version of "Takeover" that even more explicitly addressed Nas.

"Takeover" remains the greatest dis track in rap history. Kanye West, a relative newcomer at the time, turns a looped sample of the Doors' "Five to One" into a gargantuan march, Josey Scott of the also-ran rap-metal band Saliva wails in the background, and Jay utterly nails the haughty, regal disdain he'd spent years perfecting. First, Nas is a once-great rapper who has sharply deteriorated: "Went from Nasty Nas to Esco's trash / Had a spark when you started, but now you're just garbage." Then he's a writerly rapper who pretends to have real-world criminal experience: "Nigga, you ain't live it, you witnessed it from your folks' pad / You scribbled in your notepad and created your life." He's a bad businessman who doesn't play to his strengths: "Yeah, I sampled your voice, you was using it wrong / You made it a hot line; I made it a hot song ["Dead Presidents II"]." And he caps it off by alluding to their shared past with Carmen Bryan: "You know who did you know what to you know who / Just keep that between me and you."

One of Jay's greatest gifts as a rapper was always his unflappable confidence; even on his first album he sounded like rap was an idle hobby, an impression that rumors about his big-money drug-dealing past only reinforced. And so "Takeover" is more frustrated sigh than splenetic rant; Jay addresses Nas the way a bored principal might talk to an underachieving shop-class burnout.

In the months after September 11, rap listeners were hungry for any news that didn't revolve around the destruction of the World Trade Center, and thus "Takeover" immediately took on a totemic significance; we feverishly debated whether Nas or Mobb Deep would come back with a response, whether that response could possibly equal the first song's impact. And then it happened: Nas came back hard.

"Ether" hit the airwaves a couple of weeks after "Takeover," but it sounded like Nas wrote it in one feverish, sleepless night. In contrast to Jay's exquisite arrogance, Nas is all scrappy underdog bluster, swinging wildly at anything resembling a target. Rather than meticulously pointing out Jay's weaknesses, Nas careens haphazardly from one point to the next, never bothering to tie them all together. He slurs homophobically against Jay, accuses him of being envious and duplicitous, claims he stole his album's title from KRS-One, lambasts him for comparing himself to Biggie, obliquely threatens his life, and coins the deathless phrase "dick-suckin' lips"—and that's just the first verse. In subsequent verses, Nas calls Jay a misogynist and a money-grubbing philistine, makes fun of his whiskers, feigns confusion that Jay would name his record label after someone who died of AIDS, and unfavorably compares Jay to both Eminem and protégé Beanie Sigel. And he does it all with palpable bile, ignoring quaint concepts like song structure, and letting it all come out as a near-unbroken rant: "You a fan, a phony, a fake, a pussy, a Stan." In isolation, none of the shots Nas takes would add up to much. But taken in blurry, unfocused sequence, all that anger adds up to something monolithic and overwhelming. In virtually every way, "Takeover" is a better song than "Ether": its delivery more assured and controlled, its beat fuller and more fiery, its concepts less scattered and more logical. But Nas's wild-eyed fury felt like a force of nature. And it soon became part of a mythical story: the down-on-his-luck veteran facing impossible odds and coming back to deliver an unprecedented knockout blow.

By normal rap-battle standards, Nas won, gaining public sympathy and recharging his career in the process. Jay eventually responded with "Super Ugly," a radio freestyle that scored most of its points by explicitly discussing Jay's relationship with Carmen Bryan: "I came in your Bentley backseat / Skeeted in your Jeep / Left condoms in your baby seat." After the righteous rage of "Ether," though, the allegations, no matter how true, felt petty and unnecessary. Suddenly Jay no longer looked like unimpeachable rap royalty; he just looked like an asshole bully with no sense of decorum. A few days later, on Hot 97, Jay apologized for the song, sounding chastened and claiming that his mother had been appalled.

That apology was basically an admission of defeat, and it mostly signaled the end of the feud. From that point on, when the two would discuss the beef in their lyrics, they generally sounded mellow and ruminative, not angry or animated. On the next year's "Blueprint 2," Jay couldn't resist taking a few bitter shots at Nas's lyrical inconsistencies: "Y'all buy the shit, caught up in the hype / Cause the nigga wear a kufi, it don't mean that he bright / Cause you don't understand him, it don't mean that he nice / It just mean you don't understand all the bullshit that he write / Is it 'Oochie Wally Wally' or is it 'One Mic' / Is it 'Black Girl Lost' or shorty owe you for ice?" On the same song, though, Jay came as close to resigned conciliation as the world's most arrogant rapper ever could: "I will not lose, for even in defeat / There's a valuable lesson learned, so it evens up for me / When the grass is cut, the snakes will show / I gotta thank the little homey Nas for that, though." Nas's final word on the subject was equally withdrawn and contemplative: "Last Real Nigga Alive," a fascinating step-by-step reminiscence on how the Jay beef and a few other under-the-radar rap squabbles had come to their various boiling points. The book was closed, and Nas and Jay both seemed comfortable admitting that Nas had won the battle.

But here's the thing: Nas didn't win. Jay won—won before it even started. If we're measuring these things by which competitor had a greater and more lasting impact on mass culture in general and rap culture in particular, Jay wins in a walk; Nas isn't even in the running. If we're considering who made better music, Jay wins. If we're wondering who's a better rapper or a better rap star, Jay wins. If we consider who made the more convincing dis song, Jay wins. The wild, pyrotechnic, mouth-foaming fury that Nas displayed on "Ether" was so fierce and so unprecedented that it fooled all of us at first. When someone clearly wanted the victory that badly, it was hard not to award it to him, and Nas sounded invested in the feud in a way that Jay wasn't. But Nas and Jay were contemporaries for five years before their feud really erupted, and they remained contemporaries for years after it died down. During that time Jay had a seismic impact on rap in general, while Nas just sort of chugged along, alternating between moments of stunning brilliance and long periods of inert boredom. Jay was built for the future, and Nas was built for the past.

On "Takeover," when Jay accused Nas of scribbling in his notepad and creating his life, he may as well have been paying a compliment. Nas was always the prototypical observational rapper, more comfortable and convincing when he was staring out his windows and watching stories unfold than when he actually imagined himself at the center of those stories. His delivery was a flat, affectless monotone—an omniscient-narrator tone. Part of the reason "Ether" hit so hard, in fact, was Nas's decision to abandon that tone for a derisive sneer; it was a shock hearing him displaying an actual emotion that wasn't wistful nostalgia, Nas's stock in trade since before he'd even hit drinking age. *Illmatic,* his wunderkind debut album, had been suffused with a melancholy yearning for childhood and for previous eras in rap. Stylistically he was a direct descendent of Rakim; his densely allusive mutter an even more introspective take on Rakim's own. And when Nas allowed himself to practice those hermetic, distanced musings without outside interference, the effect could be stunning. *Illmatic* remains one of the most moving and complete rap albums in history, and even Jay had to let a little bit of awe creep into his voice when he said the album's title on "Takeover."

But rap changed, and Nas never really succeeded in changing with it. Biggie, who released his own classic debut, *Ready to Die,* around the same time as *Illmatic,* heralded the maturation of rap's flashy, dangerous, larger-than-life ghetto-superhero archetype. Nas tried to force himself to fulfill that archetype and always looked faintly ridiculous: trying on a pink suit in the *Casino*-parody video for "Street Dreams," posing in front of a slow-motion explosion in the bombastic "Hate Me Now" video, alternately claiming the King of New York title and admitting that the title meant nothing. By the time Jay got around to making "Takeover," Nas had spent years thrashing around trying to figure out his own identity, and he'd go back to that futile quest as soon as the feud settled itself.

"Name a rapper that I ain't influenced," says Nas on "Ether," but that's not really much of a challenge. In the years since *Illmatic,* his style of passive, descriptive, densely allusive rap has gradually fallen out of favor. By contrast, it's hard to imagine what rap would look like today without Jay's influence. Jay built on Biggie's big-money drug-dealer persona: suits and cigars, ostentatious boasts of wealth, specific stories about criminal life, unimpeachable confidence. Both Jay and Biggie had a way of digging up all the crippling internal conflicts that come with profiting from other people's misery while still somehow managing to glamorize that profit. Biggie's lyrics were much more concrete and intricate, but Jay turned out to be more of a musician than Biggie—and Nas—ever was. His innovations were all in the use of his voice. Jay never strained his thick, husky monotone, not even when he was making death threats.

Instead he submerged that voice deep within his tracks, spacing his words out to give each of them maximum meaning. He could say more with an extended pause than most rappers could with an entire verse. When every other New York rapper was hitting up producers like Swizz Beatz for tinny synth-horn fanfares, Jay was commissioning tracks from innovative Southern beatmakers like Timbaland, learning how to fit that voice into different cadences and finding himself a wider appeal in the process. (He also used those Swizz Beatz fanfares and managed to sound better over them than anyone else.) By the time his problems with Nas started, he'd drifted back to a languid wide-screen version of classic sample-based New York rap, nurturing amazing young in-house producers Just Blaze and Kanye West. And throughout his career (at least up until his would-be retirement in 2003), he kept up an amazing workload, releasing an album a year for six years and making a ton of guest appearances in the process. Before the feud he was already a titanic figure, but he needed that chastening to make him great. When Nas so publicly scolded him, he took on a certain depth and reflexivity he'd never quite found before. In a way, he won by losing.

Of course, the point is entirely moot now. In 2005 Nas stepped onstage with Jay-Z at one of Jay's big post-retirement shows. I was in the crowd at New Jersey's Continental Airlines Arena that night, and while it was an electric moment, it wasn't quite a surprise; rumors had been circulating on the Internet all week. A few months later, Jay signed Nas to Def Jam Recordings, where he'd become president. The two of them showed up at the 2006 MTV Video Music Awards on a double date. They're friends now. And in a way, neither of them much matters. Rap has moved south, and the genre's biggest hits, as I'm writing this, are simplistic and hooky dance songs, not sweeping and cinematic Horatio Alger stories. Jay and Nas are still working, but they're men out of time. The difference between them: Jay had a hand in shaping this world. Nas is just trapped here.

Band Aid
vs.
USA for Africa

Dan LeRoy

Considered from one perspective, no one involved with this book had an easier argument to make. Compare the beginning of Saint Bob Geldof's crusade for Africa with the Los Angeles didactifest "We Are the World." Isn't that the definition of a rhetorical slam dunk?

Yet there is a complication: How do you criticize an undertaking that earned hundreds of millions of dollars for charity? Whatever the flaws of "We Are the World," doesn't that fact trump all other concerns?

To be sure, there are plenty of aesthetic reasons to argue that Band Aid's "Do They Know It's Christmas?" is a superior record to its American counterpart. The song Bono once described as "a hymn" has a peculiar timelessness, made more improbable considering it was created during one of the most highly stylized periods in music history. The graceful arrangement—the stark opening giving way to what is largely an ensemble-sung number, punctuated by "clanging chimes of doom"—helps obscure its eighties origins. And the lyrics' dignified appeal to holiday charity stands in stark contrast to the song it inspired. If "We Are the World" is a hymn, it is a hymn to the celebrity activist.

But in this argument, the simplest point is also the strongest. Namely, the primary reason "Do They Know It's Christmas?" is the better single is that it happened first. Which begs the question: What if it hadn't?

Singer Harry Belafonte famously remarked—after "Do They Know It's Christmas?" became a huge hit on both sides of the Atlantic—that he was "ashamed and embarrassed at seeing a bunch of white English kids doing what black Americans ought to have been doing." Geography was probably a factor: Britain is closer to Africa than America is, perhaps making it more likely the British would take the issue of Ethiopia seriously—as the BBC's Michael Buerk, who prepared the now famous report on the famine, certainly did.

Also, Britain (and the British music industry) is far smaller than America (and the American music industry), which is no small point when it comes to organizing such an endeavor as an all-star charity record. In addition, Geldof had some connections: his then-wife, Paula Yates, was copresenter of the TV program *The Tube*—although only in the tiny, hypercompressed world of U.K. pop could Yates have made a significant difference.

Regardless: Had one of the stars to whom Belafonte was presumably speaking—a Lionel Richie or a Michael Jackson, at the peak of their almost unimaginable commercial success—originated the idea of feeding the world, then the effort would undoubtedly have moved units and raised funds. Had Quincy Jones first seen the BBC documentary and been moved to organize a charity endeavor, he would have drawn the same sort of star-packed studio.

Yet obscured by the story of Band Aid and all it begat is this important fact: The man responsible for this single was no longer a famous and successful pop star. In fact, Bob Geldof was, in the autumn of 1984, a self-described "old has-been," a man whose band, the Boomtown Rats, was on the verge of disintegration and whose own prospects after the breakup were none too rosy. Somehow, this washed-up singer managed to convince nearly every important figure in U.K. music circles to join him—with almost no notice, and no promise of reward—in recording "Do They Know It's Christmas?"

If an American singer in comparable career circumstances had tried what Geldof attempted, it would simply never have worked. The improbable victory of the old has-been is perhaps the greatest miracle of the many necessary to bring "Do They Know It's Christmas?"—and, in its considerable wake, "We Are the World"—to life.

But back to those aesthetic differences, which would be apparent even if you knew nothing of the history behind "We Are the World," in particular. On the night when Lionel Richie famously posted a sign that read CHECK YOUR EGO AT THE DOOR, there was still enough rampant self-esteem in the room at A&M Studios—and among absent friends, like the famously MIA Prince—to stymie any project without direct appeal to all the celebrated me's, myselves, and I's.

As momentous as organizer Ken Kragen's feat was, ego suffuses every groove of "We Are the World." From the it's-all-about-us title to the unfortunate line, "We're saving our own lives"—which, translated, is analogous to the "If I give this bum some money, maybe he won't rob me later" sentiment beloved by so many on the left—the lyrics are nearly a parody of socially conscious pop. It came as little surprise, twenty years after the fact, to learn that the words for the song had been drafted by Richie and Jackson at the last minute.

Band Aid vs. USA for Africa

Not surprisingly, the composers and producer Jones felt the music for "We Are the World" had to match the scale of the stars it attracted. The ensuing vastness seems as much an affront as the fish stuffed with caviar that made Bob Geldof recoil when he traveled to Los Angeles to observe the "We Are the World" recording session. But while the massive drums and sickly sweet synths may be as cloying as the lyrics, to criticize "We Are the World"—with its top-dollar production, Olympian guest list, and "I care; therefore, I scream" vocalizing—for its size alone is to miss the larger issue. By the time United Support of Artists for Africa formed, in early 1985, famine relief had become an *event,* with all the self-consciousness and Big Gestures that inevitably entails.

There are other, more subtle, ways to mark the difference in character of these two songs. One of the best examples comes via Sting, a participant in the Band Aid session. His involvement recalls Sherlock Holmes's famous quote about the incident of the dog in the nighttime. Like the silent canine, it is what Sting didn't do that was curious.

Here was the owner not only of a healthy ego but of one of the world's most singular voices. The Police were dormant in the fall of 1984, yes, and Sting was still several months removed from his official solo career. Yet if anyone had the clout to approach Bob Geldof and request his own space, it was Sting. Geldof had saved the first lines of the song for David Bowie; when it became apparent Bowie could not attend, Geldof turned the lines over to Paul Young. And Sting didn't have a case for claiming those lines for himself? He did, but evidently chose not to make it, instead providing a beautiful counterpoint to the vocals of Simon Le Bon and Bono.

Understatement can be overrated, especially when it comes to songs about issues. For every hopelessly simplistic "Give Peace a Chance," there are ten imagined obscure profundities that could be about war, peace, or the contents of a now-empty bong. Achieving the elusive middle ground of "Do They Know It's Christmas?" and delivering a coherent message with grace is a rarity. It is a grace born, at least in part, of unformed expectations—the unformed expectations that are the blessing of the pioneer.

George Michael and Boy George would hang on awhile longer. A few others, such as Duran Duran and Paul Weller, would evolve, survive, and ultimately thrive. Bono and Sting were already operating on a different plane than their peers, and would go on to transcend pop itself. Still, if one is charting the close of what has come to be considered the "age of the haircut" in popular music—the end of the second British invasion, the last moment before the asteroid hit and wiped out the colorful dinosaurs of new pop—then Band Aid seems the most fitting moment. Which is all the more ironic, given the contrast between the style-over-substance philosophy commonly attributed to this era, and the reality of what this generation of musicians actually accomplished with "Do They Know It's Christmas?"

The asteroid in question landed, in fact, at nearly the same moment the musicians of Band Aid were gathering at Sarm West Studios in November 1984. It was a new single from a Liverpool group called Dead or Alive, but it would end up being much more than that. The song was a piece of audio kryptonite that would sterilize British pop for years to come.

It didn't seem that way at first, when "You Spin Me Round (Like a Record)" began its slow climb to the chart summit. There was something beguiling, in those days, when MIDI and sequencing were still in their infancy, about the crispness and perfection of the song, the way its interlocking parts fit seamlessly together. It was a precision that had only been matched, perhaps, by Kraftwerk, and it was a precision that had attracted Dead or Alive's flamboyant lead singer, Pete Burns, in search of the hard, metallic disco sound of his dreams.

"You Spin Me Round," with its dense layers of chattering syncopation, was a star-making moment. What no one realized then was that the star it was making would not, in the long run, be Burns. Instead, the single was the first step toward unprecedented domination of the British charts by a production team with a lawyerly name that suggested its ruthless efficiency. Mike Stock, Matt Aitken, and Pete Waterman—eventually known as simply SAW—would go on to score more than two hundred hits and a baker's dozen U.K. number ones with variations on the programmed, processed sound of Dead or Alive's breakthrough.

The trio would defend their music as a modern variation of Motown's assembly line, and the comparison was not unreasonable. But the digital blandness of their Eurobeat spread far beyond the bounteous crop of SAW singles. It infiltrated almost every nook and cranny of British pop for years—as well as a fair percentage of the American market—making cold studio exactitude dominant and singers an interchangeable variable. Stock, Aitken, and Waterman concluded their partnership long ago, but their aesthetic has lingered; tracing it to today's pop-idol-ized wasteland can certainly make one nostalgic for the more organic new wave SAW replaced.

So it's somewhat ironic to recall that it was Stock, Aitken, and Waterman, then at the pinnacle of their success, who first revived Band Aid, back in 1989, at Geldof's request. It was an awkward moment, in retrospect; the new version occurred too early to benefit from the usual pop nostalgia, and lacked the direct participation of Geldof and his cowriter, Midge Ure. Both of those factors would later make the 2004 rerecording of "Do They Know It's Christmas?" defensible historically, if not musically.

Instead, Stock, Aitken, and Waterman remade the song with a supporting cast that featured several of their own creations, and an arrangement that skirted every bit of the original's urgency, which was sequenced neatly out of the lockstep groove. But the truly regrettable part of Band Aid II was its promotional video, which interspersed scenes of continuing African starvation with well-coiffed pop stars giggling and mugging and even doing the Running Man. (In fairness, there had been a bit of this horseplay in the original Band Aid promo, but at least it hadn't been contrasted directly with images of the famine.)

Still, it must be reiterated that famine relief was, after "Do They Know It's Christmas?" an *event,* first and foremost. The self-consciousness of stardom would become increasingly unavoidable, even in such grotesque shapes as revealed in the Band Aid II video. As it recedes into pop history, the overall sense of gravitas and selflessness that marked November 25, 1984, makes it seem more and more like a moment that cannot—that could not—have been repeated, in any other time or place.

The next time you hear "Do They Know It's Christmas?" with Paul Young whispering and Bono bellowing and that familiar dozen-note chorus, and the next time you hear "We Are the World," all-warm Brother Ray and shrill Cyndi Lauper and the sound of backslaps echoing alongside the gargantuan snare hits, remember that the world would be a lesser place without either song. Goodwill is goodwill, and famine relief rightfully recognizes none of the finer points of music criticism.

But remember as well that without the first tune, the second wouldn't have occurred. If good works, as Mother Teresa once observed, are links in a chain of love, then that chain in modern pop music—a chain that continues, in some form, in every charity event attempted by musicians since, from "We Are the World" to Live Aid to Live 8—began in London one November Sunday almost a quarter century ago. So thank God for Bob Geldof and the BBC and the peculiarities of geography and the British music industry. Without all of them, working in divine and improbable tandem, this would be a hungrier, more cynical world indeed.

Guided by Voices

vs.

Pavement

Elizabeth Goodman

In 2004, when I was freelancing for a handful of rock magazines and writing essays about the tricuspid heart valve for PBS, I interviewed Stephen Malkmus. Matador had just announced it would be releasing a deluxe edition of Pavement's second album, *Crooked Rain, Crooked Rain,* and I was assigned a short piece on the reissue. During a listening session held at the perfectly ramshackle Matador offices (lots of overgrown houseplants, lots of golden New York City light), I remember hearing the rambling low-fi gem "Same Way of Saying." In this track Malkmus casually strums his guitar while delivering elusive streams of lyrics that walk the band's trademark tightrope between sincerity and parody. Midway through, somebody in the recording studio shouts, "Let's smoke some butts, Steve," and "Let's smoke some butts, come on!" immediately becomes the song's new refrain. The track then devolves into a messy, seemingly improvised stream-of-consciousness antipoem about having or not having babies ("Now I'm getting older / Maybe I'd like to fuck a woman and make one / But I don't know if I should because I don't have a real steady job / Because I don't have a real special . . .").

When I spoke with Malkmus the following day I wanted to get him talking about this specific song as an example of Pavement's casual throwaway genius. It was to be a serious discussion in which he revealed the indefinable secret to productively fucking around. We never got there. Instead I managed to give Malkmus the impression, via a nervous question about the Peel session tracks on the album, that I didn't know who John Peel was. After enduring his justifiably amused and vaguely derisive explanation of the DJ's international reputation as one of the most influential people in rock history, I folded and spent the rest of the interview letting Malkmus evade all Is-Pavement-reuniting questions by discussing his and the other band members' obsession with fantasy football. "Stephen Malkmus thinks I don't know who John Peel is," I thought as he explained how teams are picked. "Stephen Malkmus thinks I don't know who John Peel is," I thought after I hung up the phone. "Stephen Malkmus thinks I don't know who John Peel is," I thought after I turned in the piece the next day. "Stephen Malkmus thinks I don't know who John Peel is," I thought years later when I finally got a job with health benefits. "Stephen Malkmus thinks I don't know who John Peel is," I presume I'll be thinking on my wedding day/ deathbed.

I would never have gotten flustered in front of Bob Pollard. And even if I had, I would have recovered much more quickly. And even if I hadn't, I certainly wouldn't be haunted by it four years later. I really cared what Malkmus thought of me. I still do. And that's because he's cooler than me. He's cooler than you, too.

Pavement is not a better band than Guided by Voices because the members play their instruments better, or write better songs, or are more electrifying onstage. After all, neither GbV nor Pavement were about displaying their technical music-playing prowess; Bob Pollard is one of the greatest pop songwriters of his generation, and Guided by Voices were more reliably awesome live than Pavement. Pavement is the better band because they embodied that elusive indefinable quality that separates the great from the merely good. It's not a rational, academically explicable thing and it's not supposed to be. Some bands are better than others for mysterious, almost spiritual reasons that can't be deduced via careful thought, or diligent track-by-track comparisons, or fucking calculus. This is rock and roll, not math class.

Bob Pollard is like your cousin's drinking buddy who plays in a local rock band you go see on the weekends, except that rock band is one of your generation's best and the drinking buddy is a preternaturally observant, incomparably prolific rock poet. Armed with an infallible sense of melody and one of the many battered notebooks in which he translates the inspired drunken ramblings of those around him into dark but uplifting lyrics, Pollard calls into being pristine pop songs, then takes them downtown and beats the shit out of them with a four-track in a gritty basement studio. Pollard has probably written as many (if not more) perfect songs than Stephen Malkmus, but they're harder to find because there's so much more half-finished material to sift through in the search. For Guided by Voices fans, that process is part of the fun. There are several consistent Guided by Voices albums but the perfect one doesn't exist, so as a fan you make your own. If you happen to be one of the handful of people (most of whom actually played in the band) who knew Guided by Voices existed back in the early eighties, you could have twenty-five years of self-made mix tapes, each containing a different favorite arrangement of the band's tunes.

My personal favorite Guided by Voices album is the TDK cassette titled *I Am a Lost Soul, I Shoot Myself With Rock & Roll* that rests in a shoe box in my parents' closet in New Mexico. It was made for me by the same almost-boyfriend from college who loaned me his copy of

Pavement's *Watery, Domestic,* which I still have. (We had a falling-out before he got around to repossessing it, and I'd be lying if I said that I didn't avoid my last college reunion in part because I worried he might be there, track me down, and ask for it back.) Side A contains early GbV gems like "Game of Pricks" and "Pendulum" and "I Am a Scientist." Side B is all later brilliance like "I Am a Tree," "Bulldog Skin," and my (current) favorite Guided by Voices tune ever, "Glad Girls." I still harbor a dangerous sense of nostalgia for this guy just because he weeded through the pounds of good GbV tunes and fished out the great ones for me.

Pavement appeared to have a laissez-faire looseness in common with Guided by Voices, but for a band that seemed so willfully uninterested in having its shit together, Pavement produced five remarkably cohesive, visionary, and filler-free albums. Before Pavement even got around to putting out their wickedly irreverent debut, *Slanted and Enchanted,* they released three casually flawless EPs: 1989's *Slay Tracks,* 1990's *Demolition Plot J-7,* and 1991's *Perfect Sound Forever,* all of which were recorded by Stephen Malkmus and Spiral Stairs (aka Scott Kannberg) at Louder Than You Think, the home studio of Gary Young, a bonkers ex-hippie who lived in their hometown of Stockton, California. The deceptively elegant low-fi pop songs contained on these EPs herald what would become a canon of remarkably consistent, well-constructed records that showcase the band's evolution from shambolic preppy rabble-rousers to wry experimental pop stars.

Slanted and Enchanted is widely considered one of the greatest indie-rock records of the nineties, and mid-decade critics were already writing about it as one of the most influential records in recent rock history. Writing about *S&E* in 1995, *Mojo's* Barney Hoskyns called it a "cryptically-packaged debut which instantly had the hallmark of Certifiable Classic all over it." *Crooked Rain, Crooked Rain* is a gorgeous collection of precisely nonchalant classic-rock tunes that makes listeners feel, for forty-two minutes, like they are privileged, witty, naturally tan, khaki-wearing golden children who might later that day star in a Wes

Anderson movie or endow a boarding school. This much is generally agreed upon. But each of the remaining three Pavement albums—1995's *Wowee Zowee,* 1997's *Brighten the Corners,* and 1999's *Terror Twilight*—are underappreciated, or at least misunderstood.

Wowee Zowee initially seemed like a disappointment. In the post-Nirvana nineties it was briefly believed that indie-rock visionaries like Malkmus could directly connect with alternative-culture-obsessed kids and their chain wallets. *Crooked Rain,* with its comparatively accessible sound and almost-hit "Cut Your Hair," suggested that the boys from Stockton could one day be chart-topping, arena-filling moneymakers. Then they released *Wowee Zowee,* an eighteen-track album filled with understated, deliberately obscure weirdness. By this point in their career they were past the initial giddy thrill of getting to make a record (which they displayed on *Slanted and Enchanted*), past the need to show off how aggressively perfect their albums could be (which they showcased on *Crooked Rain*), and had finally settled into their most versatile, wittiest sonic and lyrical style.

In 1995 Guided by Voices were also experiencing a creative high. In fact, when their perfectly unfinished operetta of indie-rock awesomeness, *Alien Lanes,* came out in March of that year, two weeks before *Wowee Zowee,* it felt like Guided by Voices had just released the best Pavement album ever. *Alien Lanes* was Guided by Voices' first album for Matador, but it serves as a center point in the Guided by Voices holy triumvirate that includes 1994's *Bee Thousand* and 1996's *Under the Bushes, Under the Stars. Bee Thousand* not only heralded the official arrival of these unparalleled low-fi pop merchants but also perfectly encapsulated that fusion of messiness and melody that made indie rock thrilling. By the time they released *Alien Lanes* the following year, everybody knew this band understood how to make basement rock shimmer with surprise catchiness, but no one expected them to release an album so comparatively cohesive. This record—with its chaotic stream-of-consciousness sampling of every major rock genre, from British-invasion pop to garage rock to psychedelic to punk—seemed to be the accessible but still indisputably indie-pop album *Wowee Zowee* wasn't.

Pavement were always ahead of their own image, and by the time fans and critics came around to *Wowee Zowee*'s brilliant meandering weirdness, Pavement were already onto their next incarnation via their slickest, most produced album yet, *Brighten the Corners*. Pavement's fourth album was criticized when it came out for being too polished, but it's a mistake to think that Pavement's best stuff is their sloppiest. On the surface *Brighten the Corners* seems willfully accessible, but it's every bit as deranged ("Stereo"), sarcastic ("Shady Lane/J Vs. S"), and pastiche ("Blue Hawaiian") as the records that preceded it.

Guided by Voices had always been and will always be Bob Pollard and whomever was playing with him when he decided one of the 369,000 tunes he'd written was a GbV tune. However, in March of 1996, when Guided by Voices released *Under the Bushes, Under the Stars,* their last album with the so-called traditional lineup featuring, among others, guitarist Tobin Sprout, there was a sense that the original incarnation of the band was coming to an end. The album features comparatively sophisticated production and was actually recorded in a real live studio, but *Under the Bushes* is still plenty bizarre, with slews of minute-ish-long songs deconstructing one after another like drug-fueled almost revelations. Guided by Voices would go on to release other strong records throughout the rest of the nineties and through the band's official retirement in 2004, but for Pavement, *Terror Twilight* and the end of the nineties were it.

Terror Twilight is Pavement's least consistent album, but even in its unsettledness it's oddly perfect, considering it's Pavement's last and it sonically documents their loss of focus. *Terror Twilight* reveals an unraveling sense of purpose and emerging restlessness, but it's still a relatively high-concept and coherent record featuring great songs including the obvious ("Spit on a Stranger," ". . . and Carrot Rope") and the less obvious ("You Are the Light"). *Terror Twilight* made it pretty clear Pavement were done being Pavement, but it did so without compromising the band.

Guided by Voices vs. Pavement

The ideal GbV best-of might rival a comparable Pavement collection, but Pavement did more in less time, all while pretending to do nothing. This kind of secretly organized, productive casualness is ultimately the game-winning difference between Pavement and Guided by Voices. Of course, there is also the style factor. When Stephen Malkmus sang the line "I've got style / Miles and miles / So much style that it's wasted" on *Watery, Domestic*'s "Frontwards," he wasn't being ironic. Pavement weren't stylish in an obnoxious bandannas-and-leather-sporting way. Their style perfectly reflected their ethos: It was seemingly effortless, precise but nonchalant, both pastiche and sincere, and totally original. Until Kanye West started sporting pastel Polo shirts, the world had not seen another musician successfully rock garden-party wear. But this was Pavement's specialty, the depraved but Waspy look of boarding-school drug dealers, and to this day there remains a small but significant subset of the rock-worshipping female population that fetishizes pink oxford shirts and Top-Siders all because of Stephen Malkmus.

However, Bob Pollard wins major style points for his incontestably magnetic stage presence; he is definitely more of an obvious front man than Malkmus. Pollard borrowed the signature move of every great rock front person and repurposed it as his own. The result was this totally inspired, theatrical onstage aura that, via Townshendlike windmills, karate kicks, Daltrey-inspired mike swings, and Jaggeresque struts, triggered a cathartic celebration of everything good and pure and right about rock and roll. During a great Guided by Voices show it felt like you were rocking out through Pollard, like he was a medium through which the rock energy flowed out of the amps and into you.

Bob Pollard understood that it was his job to perform but that part of doing that job meant including the audience in the performance. He was an unparalleled front man. Stephen Malkmus didn't even like front men. "When I watch bands, I watch drummers," Malkmus said in a 1997 interview with *Ray Gun*. "I really think singers are kind of boring to watch." Malkmus liked the idea that the audience might look at

Pavement and see a bunch of normalish dudes doing something that seemed tenable. "I like this music thing that we do. It's sort of inefficient, it's like blood and guts. And people can see him [points to Bob Nastanovich] or anyone in the band and say, 'What's he doing up there? I could do that.' "

Pavement intentionally communicated an aura of whateverness, so much so that it seemed possible that any dude with decent hair and a pair of Dockers could be part of the band (bassist Mark Ibold started out as Pavement's biggest fan). The larger effect of this recalls that moment in high school when someone more popular invites you to sit at their lunch table or offers you a piece of gum. The line separating you and your inherent regularness from their effortless greatness seems temporarily nonexistent. Of course, not anyone could be in Pavement, but the band succeeded in making it feel that way. Pavement were a bunch of rock stars who came across like everymen; Guided by Voices were everymen who transformed into rock stars.

Why isn't Stephen Malkmus more of a mess? He's a generation-defining artist with an expansive, complex body of work and a nearly twenty-year-long career in rock and roll. Yet he lives in a nice house with a yard in Portland, Oregon, raising a new baby and hanging out with his wife. Being an artistic visionary doesn't theoretically have to coincide with being fucked-up, but it usually does. The narrative of alcoholic poet/pill-popping painter/heroin-abusing rock star is so cliché that there's flocks of desperate kids snorting shit cocaine in bathrooms in the Lower East Side at this very moment in the hope that the ritual alone might trigger inspiration. But Stephen Malkmus manages to be one of the most visionary rockers of his generation *and* an alarmingly normal guy.

I once interviewed Jim Greer, former touring member of Guided by Voices, *Spin* editor, and author of *Guided by Voices: A Brief History: Twenty-one Years of Hunting Accidents in the Forests of Rock and Roll.* We were discussing Matador in the nineties and Pavement came up. Greer remembered being down in Australia during festival season and observing the band's incongruous normalcy. "They would call me when they were having a Scrabble tournament," Greer recalls. "They'd call the room and I'm like, 'I'm going to the bar,' you know? The most they would do is get stoned or something, but not even that much. Scott and Bob also played tennis and they were always trying to get me to play because I used to play tennis pretty well. They were always very preppy and totally normal; Pavement was the most normal group of people in the world."

I admire Pavement's unconscious wholesomeness only slightly more than I admire GbV's unpretentious debauchery. Pavement were normal people who might, after writing an absurdly witty piece of serrated low-fi pop, hit the courts. Guided by Voices were normal people who liked to drink and play rock and roll, not because they felt obligated to but because they would have anyway. Some people play Scrabble, some people drink beer.

Phil Collins
vs.
Sting

Sean Manning

Phil Collins and Sting were both born in 1951, in
England, in towns home to breweries. Both were leaders of seminal
eighties bands—singers as well as instrumentalists. They performed together at Live Aid. They appeared—separately—in film and television
versions of rock operas by the Who. They made other equally forget-
table forays into acting. Each put out three critically acclaimed pop albums, followed by more conservative, adult-contemporary fare. Then,
of course, there are the Disney soundtracks, to say nothing of the countless Grammys won, millions of records sold, and millions more dollars
made. But the reasons I've long equated the two—as opposed to, say,
Sting and Bono, what with the pretentious pseudonyms, the self-serving

political activism, the short-lived mullets and their uncanny ability to somehow, someway make them work—are far more personal and date back twenty-odd years to the Christmas of '85.

I was six years old. My cousin Rex was ten. Nine years and ten months, to be exact, which, smarting with the inferiority of a younger sibling, I always was. I say sibling because, as Rex and I were so close in age, both only children, and lived only twenty miles apart and spent the night at each other's house practically every weekend, we were more like brothers than cousins. Accordingly, from our other, older cousins and aunts and uncles and grandmother, so as not to make either of us feel slighted, we'd always get the same gifts at Christmas. Until the Police jacket, that is.

It was the satin kind pitchers wear in the dugout between innings. Royal blue with snap buttons and white trim around the collar, cuffs, and waist. Big across the back, in their trademark block letters, mingling red, yellow, orange, and purple thread, my grandma, an expert seamstress, had stitched the band's name.

Any other kid would've been relieved not to get something his grandmother made him—especially when getting Contra for his brand-new Nintendo instead. But ours wasn't one of those grandmothers always foisting on us some ill-fitting, heinously colored, animal-patterned monstrosity. She was too skilled and too proud to waste her time and talent on something we'd just spill food on or tear up on the playground. For her to have made Rex that jacket was a huge deal. It was her way of acknowledging he was getting older, more responsible, however much his jumping up and down, playing air bass, and shouting, "De do do do, de da da da," a full fifteen minutes after opening the gift suggested otherwise.

It was this conferral of status I was jealous of, not the jacket itself. Actually, I thought the jacket was kind of wussy—granted, in its craftsmanship, indistinguishable from Rex's vast collection of buttons, patches, posters, and other officially licensed band memorabilia, but wussy nonetheless. All those girly colors. That this was the same palette found on the *Zenyattà Mondatta* album cover made little difference; I thought *Zenyattà Mondatta* was wussy, too—"wussy" being what from ages six till eight (when "lame" came into vogue) I called things I didn't understand. And despite repeated, concentrated listening during my weekends at Rex's, while we played Flight Simulator on his Commodore 64 and gorged ourselves on Andy Capp's Hot Fries, goddammit if I still didn't understand the Police. *Zenyattà Mondatta* and *Reggatta de Blanc* and *Outlandos d'Amour* . . . why always such weird, hard-to-pronounce album names? Weirder and more befuddling still was the music itself. I mean, those lyrics! Honestly, who ever heard of someone complaining about their bed being too big? And this poor Roxanne character—what was so wrong about her walking the streets for money, anyway? The fifth and sixth graders at my elementary school had done that for a cancer charity and raised almost five hundred dollars for research.

That off-kilter drumming, tinny guitar, straining voice—it was all so unlike the catchy, conventional, and, in Rex's estimation, "cheese city" pop I preferred, be it *Thriller,* the only tape I owned outright, or Billy Joel's *An Innocent Man,* my favorite of my father's extensive adult-contempo catalog. At least it *was* my favorite. Then came the drive home from Rex's house that Christmas evening.

It was snowing, I remember. Highway traffic was slow going. Slunk low in the backseat, I felt ten times lower. My parents could tell. One of my favorite pastimes was opening my father's tapes (opening anything, really), and, hoping to console or at any rate distract me— since with my nubby, little-kid fingers it took me forever to get that pesky plastic off—he handed back the tape he'd received that afternoon in our extended-family gift exchange. I'd then been too overcome with disappointment over the jacket to notice who it was, and, resentful over the prospect of enduring the likes of Loggins or Lewis, thereby further widening the chasm between Rex and me, I didn't care now. In my preoccupation, I unconsciously felt along the sheathing, found a loose seam, peeled the packaging in one go, and passed it back to my dad, no doubt surprised by my newfound dexterity. He ejected *The Very Best of Burl*

Ives Christmas we'd enjoyed on the ride there and slipped this new one in. There was that standard couple seconds of fuzz, and then . . .

Some two decades later and slightly, just slightly, more knowledgeable about music, I can parse what I heard: the Roland, the Moog, the Phenix brass. But back then all I knew was that, notwithstanding how rotten I felt or my determination to dislike whatever was about to come out of those acoustically unflattering factory-system speakers, when it did, just as when Rex would make faces at me Sunday mornings in church, it dared me not to smile and quickly, thoroughly succeeded in shattering my resolve.

> *There's this girl that's been on my mind*
> *All the time, Sussudio*

I recognized the voice instantly. My dad owned *Face Value* and *Hello, I Must Be Going!* as well as Genesis's most recent, eponymously titled release. Aside from the snappy "You Can't Hurry Love," however, I didn't care for Phil Collins. He was too dark for my taste, too despairing. So far as I knew, so far as my father's cassette collection had led me to believe, love was simple, storybook—the stuff of Joe Cocker and Jennifer Warnes's "Up Where We Belong." Of course, as Billy stressed in "Tell Her About It," good communication was essential. And even then love didn't always last. Yet I preferred to attribute any such failure more to the crummy timing and squandered opportunities of Bruce Springsteen's "Bobby Jean" than to the suspicion and resentment fueling "In the Air Tonight," "I Don't Care Anymore," "Do You Know, Do You Care?," "That's All," "It Don't Matter to Me," even, though less pronouncedly, "Against All—" Wait a second. What the hell did he just say?

I asked my dad to pass back the liner notes. Sussudio indeed! By God, here was a lyric as confounding, as absurd, as downright wussy as anything by the Police! And speaking of the Police, look here! It says Sting sings backup on the song "Long, Long Way to Go." Well, if Phil

Collins met with Sting's approval, he'd certainly pass muster with Rex. And if not, all the better. I could just picture it: Rex comes over, eager to try out the thirty-lives cheat code, I pop the tape into my dad's hi-fi, and as soon as Rex starts in with that "cheese city" garbage, I say, "Oh yeah? I'd like to hear you say that to your good buddy Gordon Sumner." Then I shove his nose in the liner notes and watch him turn as red with embarrassment as Collins's face on the album cover.

So redeemed, I folded up the liner notes and was about to hand them back to my dad when something else about the cover struck me. That something, naturally, was the album's title. To many, this disclaimer would prove as random and ridiculous as "Sussudio." And it was—the result of Collins's having once been barred admittance to Chicago's Pump Room for failure to meet the restaurant's dress code. But to me, on of all nights this one, the title was beyond explicable; it was a sign. Maybe Rex doesn't even like the Police, it counseled. You ever consider that? Maybe he just says he does cause it's cool. Same reason he's got all that Police stuff, and same reason he gives you such crap about the music you like. Cause he's jealous you don't care about being cool. You don't care what other people think. You like what you like and that's that and you certainly don't need an embossed article of clothing to prove it.

Damn straight, no jacket required! I thought to myself.

Time would prove Rex's devotion to the Police to be utterly genuine. Make that his devotion to Sting. While forgoing Andy Summers's *XYZ* and Stewart Copeland's Animal Logic endeavors, he was quick to snap up the Spanish version of *Nothing Like the Sun,* the hard-to-find (especially in the Camelot Musics of northeastern Ohio) Gil Evans sessions, and, yes, even the *Demolition Man* soundtrack. All of this I found even more insufferable than the Police, whom in the intervening years I'd actually grown to appreciate, an appreciation that has thenceforth blossomed into love. I can't say the same about Sting's solo oeuvre. I like it as little now as I did then. "The Dream of the Blue Turtles," "Shadows in the Rain," "Love is the Seventh Wave," "Island of Souls," "The Wild, Wild Sea. . . ." All right, already. Water. A metaphor for all things.

We get it. And his reliance on those infernal Marsalis brothers! Fifty years of innovation from Miles, Monk, and Mingus for this imaginatively and emotionally bankrupt jazz lite? But the worst, and I mean the absolute worst, remains his "Little Wing" cover, though I suppose you could consider it a feat of some sort—managing to castrate a Hendrix tune.

Not that I'd graduated to bop or Jimi just yet. As with my ability to unfurl the rich tapestry that is "Sussudio," it's only recently that I've been able to decipher my disdain for Sting. No, back then I simply didn't like the guy because my father did.

Once Rex entered junior high, our weekends became more and more infrequent till eventually we only saw each other at holidays and the occasional family reunion. Yet when it came to championing Sting, my father was quick to pick up the mantle. I suppose I should've been surprised—that my father even knew who Sting was. After all, one of the first times I came home from a weekend at Rex's complaining about his listening to the Police, my father's response—precipitated by Rex's having had his share of run-ins with local law enforcement over such adolescent infractions as skateboarding on city property—was, "It's about time." But I wasn't. In breadth, my father's cassette collection was a distant second to his library of spirituality and self-help books. Joseph Campbell, Wayne Dyer, M. Scott Peck, and Hugh Prather were all favorites, and it wasn't uncommon after dinner, while my mother washed dishes and I encamped before the TV, to find him sitting in his recliner rereading *The Prophet* for the umpteenth time. So naturally he'd be taken in by that con man Sting, with his phony name and self-styled, spuriously metaphysical, New Age troubadour schlock.

Man, that came out way harsher than I intended. Guess it's the pain of imagining a time when my mother and father were still together. Riding in the same car. Living under the same roof. They divorced when I was thirteen. It wasn't like my friends' parents who got divorced. Dad schtupping the secretary. Mom suing the philandering son of a bitch for every penny. Each bad-mouthing the other within earshot of the kids during their court-appointed weekends. No, my mother and father were faithful to the last, and always, always agreed on what was best for me. They just couldn't make it work after twenty-one years of concerted effort. It wasn't anybody's fault—oh, how many times my parents reiterated this. I, in turn, told them they didn't have to, that it was okay, that I understood. Yeah, I tried to be real mature about the whole thing. But really I was devastated. And angry. Not least because Rex had been proven right after all. The music of my father, the music I loved and so unapologetically defended, with its underpinning knight-in-shining-armor, hand-in-hand-through-sunflower-filled-fields, love-conquers-all ethos, wasn't just cheese city. It was fucking bullshit.

All of it except Phil Collins. Suddenly, finally, I understood the despair, the bitterness, the indignation. Of course, so did my parents— much more so. The split was amicable, yes, but there was still the inevitable disappointment, hurt feelings, things unsaid and better left unsaid. Had they just copped to it, had they just been straight with me rather than putting on their respective good faces, then maybe . . . maybe what? It would've been easier? To know my parents cried into their pillows like I did? Hardly. No, my parents did right by shielding me from their pain—if that's in fact how it went. For all I know, they *were* straight with me. Aside from watching from my bedroom window my dad load up his car and drive away, and then, not knowing what to do but needing to do something, dribbling a basketball around the block for a good two hours straight, there's not a whole hell of a lot from that time I haven't repressed. So alleged an Upper West Side psychologist I went to see a couple times. Which is why I stopped seeing him, because of his allegation, and because his office took me for-fucking-ever to get to from Brooklyn. But maybe Dr. Kirshbaum was on to something after all. Maybe my parents did share, only I didn't want to, couldn't stand to hear it. Whatever the case, Phil Collins spoke to me in the honest way I wished my father would . . . or wouldn't.

Not that *I* was honest with *him*. I never told my father I was angry— not for years. I was too embarrassed to find I wasn't so mature after all, too ashamed at feeling anything but love and gratitude toward the man responsible for my existence. I, too, put on a good face. But my resentment was not to be bridled, and, bizarre as it seems, manifested itself in my hatred for Sting.

The year of the divorce—1993—was also the year of *Ten Summoner's Tales,* and I swear it seemed like every time my dad picked me up from freshman basketball practice or took me to dinner at Subway, goddamn "Fields of Gold" was playing in the car. That Christmas I bought him Collins's *Both Sides.* Rather, I bought it for myself and made sure it was kept in the glovebox at all times—there to spare me from Sting's latest ode to H_2O ("Heavy Cloud No Rain"), yet safely out of sight. Once puberty hit, I was no longer indifferent to others' opinions, as to survive high school, a different jacket, that of the varsity letterman, most certainly *was* required. Nowadays, with rappers sampling and nu-metal acts covering the hits, and the man himself voicing a character in *Grand Theft Auto,* it might not be social suicide to openly dig Phil Collins. But back then, with "Another Day in Paradise" having been released within the seniors' high school tenure, were anyone to expose my secret predilection, I'd have been sunk.

I was struggling to stay afloat as it was. I was too weak with my left to stand a chance at making varsity and had awful, Accutane-warranting acne. Which was one more reason I likened Sting and Phil, and vehemently favored the latter. Sting was almost Apollonian in beauty. Collins, on the other hand: Was he ever not bald? No matter. So what if he looked like Napoleon—alopecia wasn't the only thing the two had in common. In the superficial, appearance-obsessed recording industry, Collins proved just as unlikely a victor as the French commander. By sheer will and no shortage of talent, he'd become a bona fide megastar, i.e., he could bang whomever he wanted, however he wanted, whenever he wanted. But that was just it. He didn't want to, not if his songs were to be trusted. Unlike his tantra-obsessed counterpart, he wanted a monogamous, meaningful relationship. Same here. Sure, I had lunchtime reveries and nocturnal emissions about practically all of my female classmates and not a few of their mothers, but, in spite of my parents' divorce—*because* of my parents' divorce—I'd have shunned their collective desire to love and be loved by just one.

It took more than ten years and plenty of false starts for that to happen. Now that it has, now with Vanessa in my life, I'm not as cynical when it comes to love. Neither, I see now, is Phil Collins. Not entirely, anyway. For every "Doesn't Anybody Stay Together Anymore," there's "A Groovy Kind of Love." For every "Leaving Me Is Easy," a "Two Hearts." True, Collins can be, ahem, all wet at times: "The Roof Is Leaking," "I Wish It Would Rain Down," "River So Wide" . . . but on the whole his favorite subject is himself. His successes and failures. His hopes and fears. His joy and pain. This, above all and particularly in my attempted development as a writer, is why I continue to prize him over Sting—this penchant for the confessional. Tell your story, be as forthcoming as you can stomach . . . then a little bit more, and maybe somebody can derive a bit of solace from it. Maybe even yourself.

Hall & Oates

vs.

Simon & Garfunkel

Michael Showalter

Let me say this: "Bridge over Troubled Water" by Simon & Garfunkel is one of the top-ten best songs ever written. Let me also say: "Adult Education" by Hall & Oates . . . isn't. Based on this comparison, there is no contest. But I'm grading on a curve here; they cancel each other out. Moreover, Paul Simon didn't even write "Bridge over Troubled Water." God wrote it. "Adult Education" was all Hall.

So what are we dealing with here? Duos. Simon & Garfunkel, sixties folk-rock choirboy darlings, vs. Hall & Oates, eighties white R&B-pop crooners. Now, obviously, if it were a fistfight, Hall & Oates would win in a landslide. Paul Simon is a hobbit and Garfunkel never takes his hands out of his pockets (so he would have to fight with his feet, but you can't hurt anyone by kicking them when you're wearing Wallabees). In fairness, Garfunkel could fight with his Afro, but Oates could defend against Garfunkel's Afro with his Afro, and counterpunch with his mustache. Garfunkel would have no defense against Oates's mustache.

Meanwhile, Daryl Hall is like ten feet tall, kind of a spaz, and could take them both on by himself if he needed to. Like, let's say Oates was busy trimming his mustache—Hall could just twirl around with his arms out and knock them both out of their turtleneck sweaters. Simon & Garfunkel could even bring Edie Brickell & New Bohemians for backup, and Hall would still kick ass. He wears pointy boots. Score one for Hall & Oates. In a fistfight, Hall & Oates would demolish Simon & Garfunkel.

I know what you're thinking. You're thinking, "This is a joke, right? You're just saying Hall & Oates are better than Simon & Garfunkel to be ironic, right? It's like saying you love Ashlee Simpson or Bright Eyes just because it's cool to say you love something that sucks. Right?" Simon & Garfunkel have a compilation set that has fifty discs in it. Hall & Oates have a greatest hits CD with, like, ten songs on it, and only five of them are good. But it's true: I genuinely love Hall & Oates, and I genuinely think Simon & Garfunkel are one of the most overrated bands of all time.

I mean, can we even call Simon & Garfunkel a "band"? To me they are more of a "team" or a "pair" or perhaps a "klatch." They are a glee club minus the glee. Garfunkel doesn't even play any instruments! He sings harmonies and wears vests. Big deal. I've seen him shake that egg thing or the occasional tambourine, but honestly, anyone can do that. Truthfully, anyone with opposable thumbs can shake the egg thing. Even a slow loris, you ask? Yes! Even a slow loris. Conversely, Hall & Oates both play instruments. They are definitely a band. Enough said. Score two for Hall & Oates. Hall & Oates are a band. Simon & Garfunkel are a klatch.

Now look, there are many similarities between them: Primary among them is the combination of a seminormal-looking one and a buffoon. So in this situation we're dealing with the lesser of two evils. And here's the skinny: Oates knows he's a buffoon and has accepted it. I respect that. Oates has embraced his buffoonery and not apologized for it. And why should he?! There's no shame in the utterly buffoonish. Especially if it's self-acknowledged. But Garfunkel doesn't know he's a buffoon. I find that unacceptable. To the contrary, he has the audacity to think he's the opposite of a buffoon. Garfunkel thinks he's the shit. Garfunkel has a gigantic pole up his butt and I find that offensive. The only thing Oates has up his butt is his G-string, and I can respect that. But Garfunkel has a pole up his butt and a flag on the end of the pole that says, I'M ART GARFUNKEL AND I THINK I'M REALLY SMART AND COOL. That's not okay in my world. In conclusion: A buffoon with a high opinion of himself is worse than a buffoon who knows he's a buffoon. Garfunkel's lack of humility is off-putting to the extreme, and to boot, he's a pussy hound, which means that every time I look at his frizzy bouffant I have to think of his pubic hair, and I don't want that image running around inside my head. I don't want to have to imagine that Garfunkel's pubic hair resembles his bouffant, or that he grooms his pubes, or that his pubes also wear a vest. Score three for Hall & Oates.

Hey, Paul Simon! You're not off the hook, bub! Unless you're Ry Cooder, experimentation with third-world "rhythms" is the absolute mark of having lost the thread. *Graceland* was an unforgivable career move. It's rock and roll imperialism and it makes me physically ill. No, you know what? It's just easy. It's obvious. Like, just because it's African, I'm an asshole if I don't say I love it. Like, I'm a big heartless turd if I don't like something with African beats on it. Fuck that. I don't recall Daryl Hall's "inspired by tribal rhythms" solo album, do you? Of course not. Why? There isn't one. His solo album was more white R&B. Thank God! To me, "inspired by tribal rhythms" is a euphemism for "really rich and out of ideas." Score another one for Hall & Oates. They stayed true.

Stranded on a desert island with just one song to choose from, which would you rather have: "Scarborough Fair" or "Private Eyes"? Be honest!

It's only you and me here. Have you ever made out with "Scarborough Fair" humming in the backdrop? Of course not. Have you ever had an orgasm with "Scarborough Fair" humming in the backdrop? Doubtful. It's physically impossible to have an orgasm with that song humming in the backdrop. It'll kill an orgasm. I've had thousands of orgasms with "Private Eyes" humming in the backdrop. Literally thousands of orgasms. Like this one time, I was in seventh grade and my friend Joel's older sister had a make-out party and we were in the basement and the lights were off and everyone paired off and sucked face while "Private Eyes" was playing and I had an orgasm. Premature, yes. I mean, just the friction of rubbing my boner up against a girl's corduroys was enough to create a climax.

Let's try another one: "Feelin' Groovy" or "Kiss on My List"? Again, scan for number of orgasms and tally. I can remember going to second base for the first time with "Kiss on My List" crackling in the backdrop and having multiple orgasms. The only thing I know about "Feelin' Groovy" is that it's bullshit. "Hello lamppost"?! Is that an actual lyric?

"Hazy Shade of Winter," you say? The Bangles' cover of it was better! What does it say about you when the Bangles do better versions of your songs than you do? Susanna Hoffs is way hotter than Art Garfunkel. I would much rather go to second base on Susanna Hoffs than I would on Art Garfunkel.

"Homeward Bound," you say? "Maneater," I say. "I Am a Rock," you say? "Say It Isn't So," I say. "America," you say? "You Make My Dreams," I say. We're playing ping-pong here, and my forehand has way more topspin than yours. You keep hitting me these lobs and I keep smashing the ball back to you and you can't even hit it.

And don't even get me started on "Sara Smile." That song is perfect! It's like a summer day just as it's getting dark, just as the temperature is dropping down to where it's comfortable and cool, but it's a little sad, too. Like the perfection of the day makes you sad. And I'm on the football field and I'm cuddling with a girl and we're under the bleachers and we're smoking 100s and we're drinking warm beer that I stole from my parents and we're sharing my Walkman and "Sara Smile" is playing and we're majorly Frenching and I'm having multiple orgasms. "Punky's Dilemma" doesn't make me feel nostalgic like that. It makes me think about *Punky Brewster.*

"What about *The Graduate,* Michael? What about 'The Sound of Silence'? What about 'Mrs. Robinson'?" My answer is this: Screw "The Sound of Silence." It's an okay song, but do you ever actually listen to it? Have you ever put it on a mix tape? Of course not. The mix-tape litmus test is crucial. Have you ever put "Rich Girl" on a mix tape? I have. It's one of those songs. I can dance to it, I can French to it, I can blast it in my car and sing along to it. I can put it on a mix tape, and I do put it on a mix tape—as much as is humanly possible. With "The Sound of Silence" I just know that it's important. Big deal. Lots of things are important. For example: It's important to go to the dentist every six months but that doesn't mean it's better than Hall & Oates. See my point? And that other one, "Mrs. Robinson." "Where have you gone, Joe DiMaggio?" I'll tell you where you've gone. You've gone into the bargain rack at Coconuts. That's where you've gone. *The Graduate* was cool once, but so were trucker hats. Hall & Oates were never cool. That's the beauty in it.

I will always remember Simon & Garfunkel as those dudes in black turtlenecks, pouting for the camera, trying so hard to look "deep"; I will always remember Hall & Oates as the soundtrack of my youth. I will always remember Simon & Garfunkel for how good they thought they were; I will always remember Hall & Oates for how good I thought they were.

Blur

vs.

Oasis

Jim DeRogatis

It was the most pathetic, petty, school playground fight of all time.

—Damon Albarn, The Press Association Limited,
November 26, 1997

The American music scene of the nineties didn't lack for well-publicized musical feuds, but few of them seemed very amusing to those of us living through them, and that's even truer from the vantage point of a decade and a half later. Ultimately the conflict between Tupac Shakur and Biggie Smalls proved tragic for hip-hop and for two African-American artists who met violent ends well before their time, while the rivalries of the alternative-rock world—Kurt Cobain's sniping at Eddie Vedder; Pavement dissing the Smashing Pumpkins; Steve Albini vs. Urge Overkill; Courtney Love vs. the world—paled then as now for their comparative triviality.

For the era's most entertaining, no-holds-barred, blood 'n' guts cage match—an epic contest of both sheer, unbridled viciousness and utter, inane silliness—we must look across the ocean toward the motherland, to what its ever-punning music press gleefully dubbed "The Battle of Britpop." Yes, we must talk about Blur and Oasis.

The Blur-Oasis rivalry is often compared to that between the Beatles and the Rolling Stones, but in fact those '60s giants had a gentlemen's agreement not to release singles at the same time. Blur and Oasis, however, appear to loathe each other with a genuine and deep passion.

—Simon Reynolds, *New York Times,*
October 22, 1995

It began simply enough, as these Hatfield-McCoy enmities often do, and it seems likely, now that the dust has settled, that those of us in the peculiar substrata of the media firmament who write about music for a living were largely responsible for starting it.

By early 1995, the British press had tired of printing dispatches from its correspondents in Seattle charting the fallout from the alternative explosion triggered by the 1991 release of Nirvana's *Nevermind,* so critics and reporters began waving the Union Jack in their tirelessly hyperbolic way to signal a new, homegrown movement best synopsized by expatriate rock critic Simon Reynolds for the American readers of *The New York Times.* Noting that young British guitar bands were broaching the top-ten singles charts in the U.K. for the first time in more than a decade, brushing aside those upstart colonial grunge merchants and rappers, Reynolds wrote that "this so-called Britpop movement, which includes Blur, Oasis, Elastica, Pulp and Supergrass, harks back to the days when Britannia ruled the airwaves: the '60s (the Beatles, the Kinks, the Who) and the New Wave late '70s (Buzzcocks, Wire, the Jam).

"Britpop's parochial reference points, while appealing to large sections of British youth, may make it hard to export to America," Reynolds added. For many xenophobic residents of the faded empire, the music's veddy Britishness was a big part of its appeal: Here were choruses to be chanted at soccer and rugby matches, tunes to be cheered between pints at the corner pub. Nationalism alone wasn't enough to command readers' attentions, however; Fleet Street also needed a gripping narrative to capture imaginations and sell papers. That tale emerged on August 14, 1995, when "Country House," the first single from the fourth studio album by Blur, was released at the same time as "Roll with It," the second single from the second album by Oasis, setting up a thoroughly contrived competition for the toppermost of the poppermost.

THE RACE FOR NO.1: BLUR VS. OASIS
BLUR EDGE AHEAD IN RACE WITH OASIS
DISCORD IN DISC WORLD: THE RIVALRY
BETWEEN BLUR AND OASIS

This sampling of headlines from the second week of August 1995, drawn from newspapers as esteemed as the *Financial Times* and *The Independent* of London, pretty much tells the story. The question that lingers is: How much did Blur and Oasis really care at first? "More than competition with Oasis, it's competition with ourselves," Blur singer Damon Albarn told *Melody Maker* at the start of that week. "We've never had a Number One single. We want one." Oasis, which has always primarily meant songwriter and bandleader Noel Gallagher, responded via an unnamed spokesman, "Blur feel threatened by Oasis's musical success"—thus firing the first, relatively benign shot across the soon-to-be blood enemy's bow.

Inevitably, any examination of the Blur-Oasis dispute touches on the deep rifts caused by the English class system. But as a lifelong resident of a country where such distinctions allegedly do not exist, I've never been able to parse those murky waters, and it's revealing enough for our purposes to simply note the contrasts in the way the key members of each band grew up, which inevitably resulted in very different and often opposing goals, worldviews, and musical ambitions.

Albarn and his main conspirator, guitarist-vocalist Graham Coxon, met while attending the Stanway Comprehensive School in Aldan, Essex, where Coxon's father was a visiting music teacher, and the two reconnected a few years later at Goldsmiths College in London, which proudly boasts of being "the U.K.'s leading creative university." Albarn had enrolled in search of direction after dropping out of the East 15 Acting School, which had convinced him he wasn't much of a thespian, and it was only natural that he turned toward music: He was raised in what he's described as a "liberal, hippie household," and his father had managed psychedelic rock legends the Soft Machine. (Albarn once told me he recalled sitting backstage as a tyke, finger painting while Robert Wyatt and his bandmates performed.) Born in West Germany, where his father was playing in the RAF Band, Coxon had also been drawn toward music and could master any instrument he picked up, though he was working toward a fine-arts degree at Goldsmiths.

For their part, Noel and his vocalist brother Liam were raised by Irish parents in Burnage, a suburb of industrial Manchester, in a home eventually torn apart by their father's alcoholism. Regular truants, they committed the usual teenage crimes of breaking into cars and nicking bicycles, and at age thirteen Noel was sentenced to six months probation for robbing a corner shop. During that time he learned to play guitar and began to view music as his only hope for escaping the workaday drudgery that seemed to be his destiny, especially after he first toured the United States while serving as the guitar roadie for the second-tier "Madchester" dance band Inspiral Carpets.

In short, for Albarn and Coxon, pop music was part art project and part lark, one of several they could and would pursue, while for the Gallaghers it was a matter of life or a living blue-collar death. Alice Rawsthorn of the *Financial Times* summed up this dichotomy best when she wrote, "If Blur had not made it in the music business, they would have had their art school qualifications to fall back on. Oasis would probably have faced the same fate as Noel and Liam's elder brother, Paul, who recently lost his job laying pipes for the gas board."

> **That whole business was fuelled by very specific things between me and the two Gallagher brothers . . . There was a time early on in their career when we were very beneficial to them and they just never reciprocated. That was why we put the single "Country House" out the same week as theirs, because there had been quite a few occasions—silly little things like going to the party when they had their first No 1, just to say, "Well done lads," and being really made to feel like shits when you would have thought they'd have gone, "Cheers, let's have a drink."**

—Damon Albarn, *Independent,* February 2, 1997

Blur was much further along in its career than Oasis when the Battle of Britpop began. Albarn, Coxon, bassist Alex James, and drummer Dave Rowntree first started making music together in 1989 in a band called Seymour, named after the J. D. Salinger novella *Seymour: An Introduction* and indicative of their literary pretensions. On the strength of a demo that included "She's So High," which became their first hit, climbing to number forty-eight on the U.K. singles charts in October

1990, they signed to the independent Food Records, renamed themselves Blur, and released their debut album, *Leisure,* in the summer of 1991. It was a promising though hardly original bow, mixing equal parts then-ubiquitous Madchester dance groove and the swirling, psychedelic guitars of so-called shoegazer bands such as Ride, My Bloody Valentine, and Slowdive. But Blur was just warming up.

With the much more ambitious *Modern Life Is Rubbish* in 1993 and the even more remarkable *Parklife,* which made it to number one on the U.K. album charts in April 1994, Albarn emerged as lyrical heir to some of the best British songwriters, offering witty sociological portraits of distinctly English characters in the tradition of Ray Davies, Paul Weller, and Lennon and McCartney, while Coxon expanded Blur's musical palette to include horns, strings, synthesizers, and an increasingly impressive array of odd guitar sounds. Throughout they drew on a long and diverse list of British rock heroes ranging from Syd Barrett's Pink Floyd to Wire and XTC; T.Rex and David Bowie to art-rock god Brian Eno; and the soulful Walker Brothers to mod/psychedelic heroes the Creation.

At the other side of the ring, Oasis introduced itself to the world with a series of catchy, instantly familiar mod/glam/Beatlesesque singles ("Supersonic," "Shakermaker," "Live Forever") preceding the release of its debut album, *Definitely Maybe,* on Creation Records in August 1994. The mythology has it that Noel returned from his time on the road with Inspiral Carpets to find that his brother Liam had started a band, initially called the Rain, with drummer Tony McCarroll, rhythm guitarist Paul "Bonehead" Arthurs, and bassist Paul "Guigsy" McGuigan. Allegedly unimpressed, Noel nonetheless told this gang he'd take them out of Manchester and make them "bigger than the Beatles" so long as they let him write all the songs. They fell in line behind "the Chief"—though Liam would forever chafe at the tug of his brother's reins—and it wasn't long before Noel began to make good on his promise.

Oasis's winning streak continued when its second album, *(What's the Story) Morning Glory?,* and its first single, "Some Might Say," both debuted at number one in the U.K. in April 1995. The group hoped to keep the momentum going with its next single, "Roll with It," in August, but when Blur refused to change the release date for the first taste from its forthcoming album and/or playfully decided to have a go at derailing the Oasis gravy train, the battle lines were drawn.

> *He's got morning glory, life's a different story*
> *Everything's going Jackanory, in touch with his own*
>   *mortality*
> *He's reading Balzac, knocking back Prozac*
> *It's a helping hand that makes you feel wonderfully bland*
> *Oh it's the century's remedy*
> *For the faint at heart, a new start*
>   —Blur, "Country House"

> *You gotta roll with it*
> *You gotta take your time*
> *You gotta say what you say*
> *Don't let anybody get in your way*
> *'Cause it's all too much to take*
>   —Oasis, "Roll with It"

If neither single would ultimately be chosen by the musicians or their fans as the one to define the group for posterity—indeed, Coxon would say that he "grew to loathe" Blur's entry in the race—"Country House" and "Roll with It" are both as indicative of each bands' strengths and weaknesses as anything either ever recorded.

After a rolling, pseudosurf guitar intro, "Country House" settles into an old-time oom-pah groove punctuated by a sassy, intentionally campy brass section. In the great British music-hall tradition, it builds to a rousing sing-along finale, interrupted only by a flowery psychedelic breakdown two thirds of the way through. With its nods to literature great (French novelist and playwright Honoré de Balzac) and minor (*Jackanory* is a long-running BBC television show designed to encourage children to read), it's most interesting for its lyrics, which sarcastically portray a bourgeois gentleman wrestling with an existential crisis as he "lives in a house, a very big house in the country."

In contrast with "Country House" but in keeping with much of the Oasis discography, "Roll with It" doesn't really say much of anything—the basic message: "Take life as it comes, but don't fuck with me!"—though it says it in a typically catchy and swaggering way. The droning melody of the verses alternates with the more anthemic and bombastic choruses over a midtempo arena-rock beat accentuated by the band's trademark tambourine and decorated by Noel's massive, echo-drenched guitar, all of it resonant in an undeniable but indistinctive way of the Beatles circa *Revolver.*

At heart, Noel and Damon were both devoted to updating the innovations of Abbey Road in 1967 for a new, postmodern world. Though Gallagher wasn't immune to copping specific licks by the Beatles and others, as critics and occasional lawsuits attest, he focused more specifically on certain sounds and tempos from *Revolver* without ever acknowledging its intellectual content, spiritual aspirations, or artistic goals of opening oneself to myriad new sounds. "I don't know anything about psychedelic, really," Liam Gallagher told me in 2000. "Being psychedelic is what?—Being a fucking hippie? Being a loose free cannon?—and you can't be that. You've got to be on your fucking toes these days. The world's a harder place, and the kids won't take that!"

On the other hand, Albarn and his mates believed the open-minded psychedelic philosophy was as relevant at the dawn of a new century as it had ever been in the sixties, and they took a much broader and more original approach to throwing bits of the past into their transformative musical Cuisinart. "It's a case of stealing as much as possible, but not borrowing," is how Albarn put it when we talked after the release of

Parklife. "At the tail end of the century, there's a wonderful opportunity, because there's so much in grasp that's still in touch with what's happening now."

As stories about the competition filled the press, and the U.K. waited to see which band would be number one, Oasis evoked some famous Cockney beer-advert crooners when dismissing Blur as "Chas & Dave chimney-sweep music," while Blur called its opponents "Oasis Quo," nodding to the pedestrian early-seventies boogie band Status Quo. It was all still fairly good-natured ribbing. Then, on the evening of August 20, the British press breathlessly reported that Blur had "pipped" Oasis, relegating the Mancunians to second place. Albarn thanked the fans while graciously refraining from gloating, but the victory was short-lived.

In the weeks that followed, Oasis's sophomore album, arguably its finest moment, far outsold *The Great Escape,* an overall languid follow-up to the masterful *Parklife. (What's the Story) Morning Glory?* eventually became one of the best-selling albums in U.K. history as well as a quadruple-platinum success in the United States, which had always resisted Blur's charms, and the cliché would hold that Oasis lost the battle but won the war. Yet the Brothers Gallagher were hardly ready to call a cease-fire.

The bass player and the singer—I hope the pair of them catch AIDS and die, because I fucking hate them two.

—Noel Gallagher, *Observer,* February 19, 1996

Though Noel would later claim that this most infamous volley was prompted by a badgering journalist, and quickly issued an apology for his mean-spirited and politically incorrect jab, a week later, with no apparent irony, he was back slamming Blur for being "just so fucking two-faced." And so it went—on . . . and on . . . and on—spilling into the 1996

BRIT Awards (when Oasis won Best British Band and performed a version of "Parklife" that changed the lyrics to "shite life"); drawing in Albarn's then girlfriend, Elastica front woman Justine Frischmann (Noel: "I've got nothing against him—I just think his bird is ugly"; Frischmann: "[Damon] orchestrated the whole thing with Oasis, and he is far brighter than the Gallagher brothers. They just didn't stand a chance when it came to any form of intellectual sparring"); intensifying the class conflict (Albarn: "It was pretty obvious that in the context of being working-class heroes, Oasis were far closer than us to what the tabloids perceived as being authentic"); and continuing beyond Coxon's 2002 departure from Blur (Noel: "I'm sure Graham Coxon's tolerance has just snapped, because if your singer's saying stuff like he was . . . un-believable") and Albarn's success with the hip-hop side project, Gorillaz (Noel: "He's nothing, and it's fitting that he ended up as a cartoon: He always was a cartoon").

Even in the face of a very real war in Iraq in 2002, the Gallaghers couldn't seem to find perspective, scoffing at Albarn's vociferous and apparently heartfelt antiwar activism. "I don't understand all these pop stars saying, 'We should have a democratic debate about the war.' My opinion means nothing," Noel told the *New Musical Express,* while Liam added, "Nobody's gonna listen to knob'ead out of Blur—no one even listens to Bono." ("If I didn't have such an appalling history with Noel Gallagher, I'd say what I think about what he said, but it just perpetuates something which just negates from what we're actually trying to do," Albarn responded, evincing more disgust than usual at the never-ending back-and-forth.)

Today representatives of both sides are apt to groan or roll their eyes when asked about the opposition, though pressing just a little harder is still likely to produce a scathing insult. Regardless of the role of the press in starting the imbroglio, it has continued well past the point where the media can be blamed for perpetuating it, and in the end, all of it is a mere footnote to and distraction from the music.

Blur recovered from the disappointment of *The Great Escape* with a strong self-titled release in 1997 and the intensely personal *13* in 1999, both signaling a move away from Britpop in favor of inspiration from the American rock and hip-hop undergrounds. The group followed with the less satisfying, post-Coxon electronica of *Think Tank* in 2003, while on his own Albarn enjoyed phenomenal success with two albums by Gorillaz, fronted the modern supergroup the Good, the Bad & the Queen, and dabbled in world-beat side projects such as *Mali Music* (2002) and *Monkey: Journey to the West* (2007), an operatic adaptation of an ancient Chinese legend. At this writing, Blur is exploring the possibility of recording a new album with Coxon, and if the reunion takes, the only thing fans can predict is that the music will be unpredictable.

The same cannot be said of Oasis. Having found a winning formula with *(What's the Story) Morning Glory?,* the group continued mining the same ground with increasingly less revelatory results on *Be Here Now* (1997), *Standing on the Shoulder of Giants* (2000), *Heathen Chemistry* (2002), and *Don't Believe the Truth* (2005), and is currently recording its seventh studio album for release in 2008. The band never succeeded in fulfilling Noel's goal of becoming bigger than the Beatles, but it continues to be a multiplatinum force in the U.K. and the United States even as an increasing number of critics on these shores view it as the British version of ersatz rockers and retrofrauds such as Lenny Kravitz and the Black Crowes. Since I fall into that camp and unapologetically favor the merits of anything from Blur's discography over most of what Oasis has given us, for my money the last shot in the Battle of Britpop goes to Albarn.

"All credit to Oasis—the way they've managed to keep themselves together. They're threatening to be the Rolling Stones," Blur's leader told the World Entertainment News Network in June 2006. And he didn't mean that as a compliment.

Bernard Herrmann

vs.

Ennio Morricone

Dennis Lim

The composer Igor Stravinsky once described film music in terms of its "wallpaper function." It should have the same relationship to the drama, he said, that "somebody's piano playing in my living room has to the book I am reading."

Stravinsky, whose own *The Rite of Spring* took only three decades to evolve from riot-inciting shock of the new to soundtrack fodder for Disney's *Fantasia,* grossly understated the role of music in enriching or even transforming a narrative. But he had a point about the fundamentally subservient nature of film music. A film score exists not for its own sake but to fulfill the film's dramatic and expressive needs.

The concept of *Gesamtkunstwerk,* the "total artwork," which Wagner used in connection with opera, applies even more to film—the art that most voraciously encompasses the other arts. The medium's hybrid nature led to the rule of thumb, persistent in the early days of cinema and still not entirely banished, that film music—much like the "invisible" craft of film editing—should not be noticed. Since music often acts on the subconscious, the logic goes, film scores should operate subliminally and not distract from the main event. But the reductiveness of this notion is immediately apparent when you consider the film-scoring greats of the twentieth century, from Miklós Rózsa to Nino Rota to Toru Takemitsu and, most of all, the two film composers with the highest pop-culture profiles, Bernard Herrmann and Ennio Morricone.

Herrmann revolutionized the field of film music, redefining the relationship between sound and image; Morricone breathed new life into it, fusing symphonic traditions with pop eclecticism. Neither was predisposed to creating anything quite so meek or modest as wallpaper. The slashing violins that accompany the shower murder in *Psycho,* one of nine movies Herrmann scored for Alfred Hitchcock, constitute perhaps the most instantly recognizable music cue in film history—the critic and musicologist Jack Sullivan calls it "cinema's primal scream," the ultimate sonic signifier of terror. Morricone's twanging coyote-howl theme for *The Good, the Bad and the Ugly,* one of his six collaborations with spaghetti-western maestro Sergio Leone, is probably a close second. Can you still call it background music if it dominates the foreground?

Born in New York in 1911, Herrmann began his career as a composer at CBS Radio, where he worked on thousands of dramas. It was another radio prodigy, Orson Welles, who brought him to Hollywood. Welles's first film, *Citizen Kane,* was also Herrmann's. The composer won his first and only Oscar for his second score, the spooky, modernist folk suite for William Dieterle's *The Devil and Daniel Webster.* But like Welles, Herrmann could be irascible, and he quickly found himself in a prickly, mutually wary relationship with the Hollywood establishment that lasted his entire career—his fellow composer David Raksin memorably described him as "a virtuoso of unspecific anger."

Bernard Herrmann vs. Ennio Morricone

If Herrmann, again like Welles, positioned himself as the upstart outsider, it was with good reason. When he arrived in Hollywood the film-music tradition, despite being only a few years old, already seemed musty, descended as it was from the romantic orchestral style of the previous century. Not coincidentally, the major Hollywood composers of the time—Max Steiner, Dimitri Tiomkin, Erich Korngold—were European émigrés. ("Why need movie music be symphonic?" composer and part-time film scorer Aaron Copland lamented in 1941. "And why oh why, the nineteenth century?")

Music has been part of the film experience since the silent era, when screenings were accompanied by live pianists, organists, or even orchestras. Silent-film music was ubiquitous but it also tended to be generic. Scores were often literally interchangeable (Italian composer Giuseppe Becce published the *Kinobibliothek* in 1919, an accompanist's handbook that matched arrangements to a variety of on-screen scenarios), and they dipped freely into the classical canon (Joseph Carl Breil's score for D. W. Griffith's *The Birth of a Nation* was essentially a greatest-hits mix, drawing from Wagner, Grieg, Beethoven, and others).

The introduction of sound in the late 1920s is often discussed simply in terms of dialogue—hence the term *talkies*—but it also meant that specially commissioned music could be precisely spliced into a film. Now the score was not just blanketing the movie; it was hardwired into its DNA. This only increased the tendency toward musical overemphasis in the Hollywood films of the thirties and forties. A major culprit was the leitmotif, another Wagnerian concept, a recurring musical figure assigned to a particular character or action. Deployed with sophistication, this metonymic system can tease out themes and subtexts in the story. Clumsily used, it becomes crass, redundant shorthand. (A related form of literal-mindedness is the usually derided technique known as "Mickey Mousing," common in cartoons, in which the music mimics the on-screen action.)

Herrmann's great innovation was in freeing film music from its illustrative role. He once explained that the score supplements the work that the actors and technicians have done, or that they have been unable to do. (Implicit in this remark—as concise and complete a definition of the role of film music as you'll find—is the basic idea that the music need not state the obvious.) His dramatic sense honed by his experience with radio serials, Herrmann replaced the conventional use of the symphonic leitmotif with his own rhythmic patterns and instrumental palette. Instead of lush, winding melodies that were meant to echo the action but often just bogged it down, he favored brief, anxiously repeated figures—smaller, more supple musical units that better matched the fractured language of movies. Instead of a full orchestra, he emphasized select groupings of instruments (the low woodwinds at the start of *Citizen Kane,* brass and percussion for *Jason and the Argonauts,* and, most famously, strings for *Psycho*—a "black-and-white sound," he said, to match the black-and-white cinematography). In short, he provided what Copland had called for in his tirade against film music: "more differentiation, more feeling for the exact quality of each picture."

Despite a relatively low productivity rate, Herrmann's was an altogether remarkable career. He began with Welles and ended with Martin Scorsese. (Herrmann died in his sleep in December 1975, a few hours after the final recording session for *Taxi Driver.*) In between these towering bookends, he worked on nearly fifty films—a number that would surely have been higher if not for his temperament and his ambivalence about his profession. Herrmann was passionate enough about film scoring to be dismissive of most of its practitioners, but his lifelong aspiration was to conduct and compose for the concert hall. After his relationship with Hitchcock fell apart—the director bowed to Universal's demands and replaced Herrmann's dissonant music for 1966's *Torn Curtain* with a contemporary-pop score—he withdrew from Hollywood (he was already living in London by then) and worked mostly with European directors, including François Truffaut. It took a younger generation of fans—Scorsese and Brian De Palma, whom he worked with on the Hitchcock retreads *Sisters* and *Obsession*—to lure him back.

Herrmann's credits ranged from exemplary film noir (Nicholas Ray's *On Dangerous Ground*) to classic cold-war science fiction (Robert

Wise's *The Day the Earth Stood Still*). But he was defined above all by his alliance with Hitchcock, which earned him a reputation as a master of dread and suspense. ("[Henry] Mancini gets all the cheerful ones," he once said. "That's how it is.") There is one device in particular that Herrmann returned to time and again to conjure the sound of suspense. Musicologists have noted his fondness for the seventh chord, which contains dissonant intervals and, in musical terms, is said to seek resolution. Its repeated use, with that harmonic closure withheld or continually delayed, creates a mounting unease and a sense of infinite suspension.

In the case of *Psycho* (1960), by now a textbook study in the use of suspense music, Herrmann may have salvaged the film. Hitchcock supposedly had such little confidence in his rough cut that he considered editing it down for his television show. It was only after he heard Herrmann's relentless score, which easily equaled the film's starkness and sadism, that he changed his mind. This appears to have been an instance of the composer's willfulness paying off: Not only did Hitchcock have doubts about the film, he initially also told Herrmann not to write any music for the Bates Motel scenes, including the shower sequence.

Vertigo (1958), often called Hitchcock's crowning achievement, is Herrmann's as well. His self-consciously Wagnerian opus would appear to be one of his more traditional compositions, a full-orchestra throwback to the symphonic grandeur of golden-age Hollywood. But the music is anything but stodgy. The film is a gloriously perverse portrait of romantic pathology, in which an acrophobic detective becomes obsessed with a woman (or, more to the point, haunted by her image), and Herrmann's rhapsodic music both magnifies and plumbs the depths of the protagonist's irrational passion. From the woozy, spiraling arpeggios that accompany Saul Bass's hypnotic opening credits, the score diagnoses the hero's condition and transmits it to the viewer.

There have been plenty of great director-composer relationships over the years—James Whale and Franz Waxman, Federico Fellini and Nino Rota, David Cronenberg and Howard Shore—but only one other alliance has come close to matching the impact and influence of Hitchcock-

Herrmann: the swaggering duo of Sergio Leone and Ennio Morricone. Born in Rome and trained as a trumpeter, Morricone is one of the most prolific composers of all time—he has written nearly five hundred scores for film and TV, and at eighty is still actively composing.

A Fistful of Dollars (1964), a low-budget remake of Akira Kurosawa's samurai classic *Yojimbo,* put Leone and Morricone (and the film's star, Clint Eastwood) on the international map. The crazy-quilt score—a gleeful collision of trumpet, harmonica, electric guitar, Jew's harp, and ocarina, topped with whistles and choral chants—instantly established the Morricone sound, which was both cosmopolitan and deeply eccentric, a kind of alternate-universe world music. If Herrmann modernized the lush, symphonic approach to film scoring, Morricone matter-of-factly dismantled it. He went further than Herrmann in mixing up the instrumental palette. (The human voice is one of his favorites.) And while he can pull off symphonic sweep as well and as meticulously as anyone—he orchestrates all his own scores, as did Herrmann—he has never hesitated to crib from the pop idioms of the day, from garage rock and jazz to lounge and psychedelia.

Morricone's dizzying eclecticism is evident in individual scores and across his massive body of work. He was fortunate enough to have started his career during a period of extraordinary fertility in Italian movies. Besides Leone (his primary-school classmate), he collaborated with Bernardo Bertolucci (*Before the Revolution*), Gillo Pontecorvo (*The Battle of Algiers*), Elio Petri (*Investigation of a Citizen Above Suspicion*), and even bad-boy provocateur Pier Paolo Pasolini (the notorious *Salò*). He enjoyed mainstream success in America, earning Oscar nominations for collaborations with Terrence Malick (*Days of Heaven*), Roland Joffe (*The Mission*), De Palma (*The Untouchables*), and Barry Levinson (*Bugsy*). (He never won but was finally awarded an honorary Oscar in 2007.) He worked in every imaginable genre and had no fear of ostensibly disreputable ones. In fact, his excursions into the cult ghetto of so-called *giallo* horror (for Mario Bava and Dario Argento) were opportunities to indulge his mondo avant-garde side. (The 2005 compilation *Crime and Dissonance* is an excellent primer of his more outré work.)

Bernard Herrmann vs. Ennio Morricone

Because of this sheer variety, his admirers are not just legion but also all over the map. Yo-Yo Ma and John Zorn have recorded tribute albums. Celine Dion honored him at the Oscars. Metallica has introduced every live show since 1983 with "The Ecstasy of Gold," from *The Good, the Bad and the Ugly.*

The question of Herrmann vs. Morricone is a tricky one because it's not a level playing field. Morricone gets points for diversity, but that's no surprise given the volume of his output. Herrmann has a higher ratio of hits to misses, which is to be expected since he produced so much less. Time has distorted some of their achievements. Morricone's attentiveness to pop fashions has given his less enduring work the flavor of kitsch time capsules. To call Herrmann the more influential of the two is another way of saying that he—and *Psycho,* specifically—spawned the cattle-prod approach to horror and thriller scores. Attempts to evaluate a film score also unavoidably run into the peculiarities and contradictions of the form. To what degree should the music stand on its own? Need it survive the transposition to home listening or the concert hall? Can we judge a film score without the film?

With his treasure chest of hipster-friendly sonic innovations, Morricone is the more interesting composer, the one whose film scores tend to work almost as well divorced from their original contexts (and sometimes even better, since he scored his share of stinkers and obscurities). But Herrmann was the superior film composer. The movies he scored are unthinkable without his music. More than anyone, he wrote music that could shape the course of a narrative and set its emotional temperature. Just as the contours of its hero's madness are traced by the circular melodies of *Vertigo,* the menace and romance of Travis Bickle's grand delusions are inscribed in the luxuriant, sleazy swagger of *Taxi Driver*'s orchestral jazz score, its anachronistic swing reinforcing the antihero's alienation from the scum and grime of seventies New York. At their best, Herrmann's scores do for movies what some have deemed the sole province of literature: They speak the language of inner life.

Led Zeppelin

vs.

Black Sabbath

Robert Lanham

Author's note: *All discussion of Black Sabbath refers to their pre—Ronnie James Dio era, otherwise known as "the era when they didn't suck."*

WHO'S PARANOID OF A BRON-Y-AUR STOMP?

It's 1975. You're alone and walking home from school with your *Jaws* lunchbox and a backpack filled with textbooks. You decide to make a pit stop at the A&P to pick up some Sixlets with the quarters you swiped from your mom's change purse. As you enter the grocery store's vacant back lot, you see some older kids, teenagers, smoking behind the store's Dumpster. They spot you and suddenly you're approached by one of the "heads"—1975's idiom of choice for a hooligan—who makes it clear he intends to smash your fifth-grade face in, just for kicks. Escape is unlikely.

QUESTION: Given the following choices, which specific breed of head would you *least like* to receive your impending beating from?

A. A Black Sabbath fan wearing a *Sabbath Bloody Sabbath* T-shirt.

B. A Led Zeppelin fan wearing a *Houses of the Holy* T-shirt.

The answer is, of course, A.

Sure, an aggressive Led Zeppelin fan in a *Houses of the Holy* T-shirt smoking by the Dumpster behind the supermarket circa 1975 is definitely bad news. He's guaranteed to give you a solid, standard-issue beating, if only to charm his acid-washed-jeans-wearing girlfriend into giving him some backseat-of-the-Camaro nookie. He's likely to get all "Bron-Y-Aur Stomp" on your ass. Your beloved *Jaws* lunchbox is fucked.

But the prospect of taking a beating from a Sabbath fan is a much more frightening scenario altogether. Don't let his gaunt frame or his acne-clogged pores fool you. We're talking about a maladjusted, stoned, subversive social outcast who's probably been suspended for calling in a bomb threat. He's not just smoking behind that Dumpster, he's huffing Drano back there. There could be a decapitated crow back there, too. There could be knives. Sure, the Zeppelin fan would in all likelihood give you a worse beating than his pasty, Ozzy-worshipping counterpart, but if you're tangling with a Sabbath fan, there's the off chance you're going to get killed.

THE BATTLE OF EVERMORE

When it comes to metal, there's always an inherent rivalry between bands. Who rocks the hardest? Who's got the loudest riffs? Whose logo looks the most badass scribbled in the margins of your notebook? And, yes, who kicks the most ass?

At first glance, Led Zeppelin seems a more intimidating force than Black Sabbath. They've got more fans than Jesus. And from "Whole Lotta Love" to "When the Levee Breaks" to "The Immigrant Song," Zeppelin's riffs are guaranteed to give you a good pounding. Plus, you've got to give props to John Bonham. He is to drumming what Donald Trump is to comb-overs. Bonham's the master. (Some people claim that Rush's Neil Peart is rock's best drummer, but come on, those people like Rush.) There's a reason every classic-rock station in the country has a nightly Get the Led Out set slotted into their programming. Sure, Zep's tunes are embarrassingly overplayed by coked-out DJs with monikers like the Barracuda and Johnny "The Wild Man" Carnage, but that doesn't change the facts. Led Zeppelin is a nearly perfect rock band.

But Ozzy and his band of demons get beneath your skin. Tunes like "Paranoid" and "Into the Void" can kick your ass with their sheer intensity, but they also have the power to scare the bejesus out of you. There's some demonic, Freddy Krueger shit on those first Sabbath records. And let's cut to the chase, *Ozzy bit the head off a goddamn bat.*

Though it's been nearly forty years since they first assembled, Led Zeppelin and Black Sabbath remain the two most influential forces in the history of Metalhood. In fact, they created the genre. Borrowing generously from Robert Johnson, rock and roll got *heavy* with Led Zeppelin's 1969 debut, a musical adrenaline rush of feedback-drenched blues. The nine songs on their *Hindenburg*-covered masterpiece invented cock rock and whet the budding headbanger's palate for what was to come. Then things got truly *metal* in 1970 with *Black Sabbath,* a release that the Rock and Roll Hall of Fame credits as being the first bona fide heavy-metal record. The era of the power chord, not to mention the mullet, was under way.

But who had the *most* influence? When it comes to ascertaining the "importance" of a band, it's the first question rock historians like to ask.

Led Zeppelin vs. Black Sabbath

Bands like Slipknot and My Chemical Romance may be a lot of fun if you're a cashier at Hot Topic with a pierced lip who sniffs permanent markers, but it's doubtful that the next generation's Kurt Cobain will be citing them as inspiration. Bands like the Velvet Underground, the Replacements, and, of course, Zeppelin and Sabbath will be remembered not just for being great bands but for how they made an impact on rock and roll as a whole.

When the disaffected youth of America heard the angular punches of "Good Times Bad Times" and the frenzied assault of "Communication Breakdown," the strawberry-field hippie pop of the late sixties began to sound antiquated. Pick up any rock record from the early seventies and you'll hear Zep everywhere. Their influence was *immediately* felt. The first Rush album—totally Zep. AC/DC and Aerosmith—that was Zep, too. Thanks to Jimmy Page the seventies became the era of the guitar riff, while Robert Plant ushered in a generation of wailing that persisted until the mid-eighties, when people began to realize that, unless you're Robert Plant, wailing is usually kind of faggy.

More recently, Zeppelin's influence single-handedly enabled the career of Jack White, who otherwise never would have been able to have sex with Meg, Renée Zellweger, or that redheaded supermodel wife of his.

While Black Sabbath's influence took a little more time to simmer than Zeppelin's, their impact is ultimately much more far-reaching. Power chords across the board, repetitious as fuck, making up in attitude what they lacked in talent, Sabbath's sound refuses to fade into the woodwork. Sabbath inspired zillions of knockoffs and new metal-fusion genres including doom metal, black metal, and sludge metal, to name a few, as well as Slayer, Metallica, Motörhead, Iron Maiden, Sleep, Lamb of God, Mastodon, and Godflesh. True, they also bequeathed to us Whitesnake, Rainbow, Great White, and countless other *painful* bands including that abomination known as Korn, but anyone familiar with Hank Williams Sr. and Hank Williams Jr. knows you can't be held accountable for the sins of your progeny.

THE LEMMY CURVE

If you're making *pop* music—like the Beatles, Madonna, or M.I.A.—then being cute is an enormous asset. It's trivial, but sex appeal plays an important role in rock music, and if you ain't got it you should at least get some good outfits and practice your synchronized rock moves. Let's face it: Neither Sabbath nor Zeppelin is going to win any beauty contests (despite Plant's proclivity for keeping his shirt unbuttoned and apparently waxing his chest).

Comparing the two, Zeppelin unquestionably outshines Sabbath when it comes to sex appeal, but this apparent victory holds little weight when you factor in what's known as the Lemmy Curve. If you're playing metal, you want to be fucking ugly. Like Motörhead's lead singer, Lemmy. Motörhead's a great band, but their resonance and sheer *metalness* intensified in direct proportion to the fucking nastiness of Lemmy's moles. Meanwhile, look at the "cute" metal bands like Poison, Skid Row, and Mötley Crüe. They all suck.

Since Page, John Paul Jones, and Plant were all *relatively* cute (Bonham is another story), Zeppelin defies the Lemmy Curve slightly. But still, just imagine how kick-ass they could have been if Robert Plant had Ozzy's stringy, oil-drenched hair or Page had Tony Iommi's disfigured hand. They could have melted your eardrums.

SEX, DRUGS, AND MUD SHARKS: THE BADASS FACTOR

Ever since its inception, rock and roll has been the music of rebellion. Pastors preached that Chuck Berry was playing the devil's music, networks censored Elvis's gyrating hips, and more recently, Linkin Park shocked the world of rock with their patently disturbing suckiness. Thus the Badass Factor plays an equally important role in discerning a band's significance, especially when you're discussing metal, the most testosterone-driven genre of music—with the exception of speed polka, of course.

John Bonham clocked out choking on his own vomit after downing forty shots of vodka. Tragic? Absolutely. It's also *totally* badass, dying at the height of his fame just like Hendrix, Joplin, and ODB. (It's *extra* badass since Bonham was the only band member who didn't have a perm or a snakeskin jacket.)

Misbehaving in hotels is par for the course if you're in a metal band, but Zeppelin took the obligatory hotel trashing to the next level. Things got so out of control on one occasion, the band actually chained Jimmy Page to a toilet to prevent him from going apeshit on the establishment. And who could forget that Zeppelin are the reigning champions of *Spin* magazine's elite "100 Sleaziest Moments in Rock" issue—a rare honor they earned for a 1969 incident at a Seattle hotel that involved a dead mud shark, a female groupie, and lots of sodomy.

On the Sabbath side, anyone who's seen MTV's *The Osbournes* can attest to Ozzy's drug-induced incoherence. The man is fried. Legend has it he once snorted several lines of ants as if they were cocaine. At the height of their fame, Osbourne and drummer Bill Ward reportedly did LSD every day for two years. Ozzy even got kicked out of his own band in '79 for being so far gone.

What's more, while Robert Plant was sewing angel patches onto his overly tight jeans and practicing his "push, push, push" scream in hotel mirrors, Sabbath was tossing pounds of bloody pig intestines and calves' livers onto their audiences. You know you're dealing with a badass band when attending a concert could give you E. coli.

To make a concession to Zeppelin, I'll admit that being badass must be difficult when your guitarist's name is *Jimmy*. To their credit, Zeppelin didn't let that slow them down. No one could write better riffs than Jimmy Page, not even Tony Iommi. Yet when you consider Iommi's backstory, Sabbath trumps Zep once again.

When Iommi was eighteen, his right hand got caught in a machine at the sheet-metal factory where he worked. Tragically, the tips of his middle and ring fingers were sliced off. It was a devastating accident that could have ended his music career before it had even begun. Instead, Iommi decided to improvise a solution:

"I melted down a Fairy Liquid [a brand of dishwashing detergent] bottle," Iommi told *Guitar World* in 1997, "made a couple of blobs of the plastic and then sat there with a hot soldering iron and melted holes in them so they'd fit on the tips of my injured fingers. . . . I ended up with these big balls on the ends of my fingers, so I then proceeded to file them down with sandpaper until they were approximately the size of normal fingertips."

Nothing's more badass than detergent-bottle prosthetics. And when Iommi later ditched them and began down-tuning his guitar to decrease the tension of the strings on his injured fingers, the result was a lower, heavier pitch—Sabbath's signature dark sound.

Snorting ants. Detergent-bottle prosthetics. E. coli. Zeppelin may have been naughty, but Sabbath was seriously fucked-up.

Did I mention that *Ozzy bit the head off a goddamn bat*?

WE SOLD OUR SOUL FOR ROCK 'N' ROLL

Though both bands were obsessed with the occult, Sabbath and Zep have routinely denied allegations of Satanism. You know, just like Lucifer wants them to. How could the Dark One continue to possess the souls of the children if all secrets were to be revealed? Conveniently, Sabbath and Zeppelin say they were just goofing around for shock value.

Naturally, being Satany can add lots of credibility to any band. Think about it: Would anybody really have considered the Eagles to be a "serious" band had rumors not persisted about "Hotel California" being a demonically inspired tune? Of course not.

Led Zeppelin gets a fiendish few points right off the bat since, in the seventies, Jimmy Page purchased a house formerly owned by Aleister Crowley, the iconic occultist who once wrote: "It would be unwise to condemn as irrational the practice of those savages who tear the heart and liver from an adversary, and devour them while yet warm. . . . A male child of perfect innocence and high intelligence is the most satisfactory."

What's more, the alleged backward masking on "Stairway to

Heaven" has traumatized more Baptists than Hillary Clinton. Still, Zeppelin's breed of occultism suffers from heavy doses of Tolkien silliness. The cheesy mystical scenes in the concert film *The Song Remains the Same*—like the encounter with the sword-toting man on the mountaintop—could be outtakes from a more psychedelic episode of *Xena: Warrior Princess*. Sure, it's cool that Page lived in Crowley's house, but come on—you just know he planted an herb garden there and filled it with gnome statues.

On the other hand, Black Sabbath's *very name* conjures images of the Dark One. Sabbath's bass player, Terence "Geezer" Butler, claims to have been visited by a demonic, hooded spirit—the vision becoming the subject of the band's name and breakthrough song.

From the beginning, Sabbath wanted to do more than simply raise some hell; they wanted to terrify. Noting how people shelled out money to be frightened by horror movies, Iommi suggested that the band should be the *Rosemary's Baby* of rock, scaring their fans into submission. Appropriately, they released their debut on Friday the thirteenth. As Ozzy says, Sabbath wanted to "possess people," a fact that shouldn't be too surprising given his nickname: "The Prince of Fucking Darkness."

Unlike Zeppelin, Sabbath never felt the need to cloak their devilish messages in esoteric symbols or with backward masking. Consider, for instance, the lyrics of "N.I.B.," one of countless demonic numbers in Sabbath's catalog:

> *I will give you those things you thought unreal*
> *The sun, the moon, the stars all bear my seal . . .*
> *Look into my eyes, you will see who I am*
> *My name is Lucifer, please take my hand*

You can just picture Ozzy's hair drenched with the blood of some cloven-hoofed beast he's dragged into the studio for a fresh bleeding. In an interview he did with *Hit Parader* in 1984, Ozzy even claimed to be possessed: "Sometimes I think that I'm possessed by some outside spirit.

A few years ago, I was convinced of that—I thought I truly was possessed by the devil." You can't get more Beelzebubtastic than that!

Where Zeppelin's breed of Satanism reeks of hobbits, dragons, and candelabras, Sabbath always kept it real: sporting the upside-down crosses, doing shots of blood, and, of course, kickin' it Old Testament with lots of demon iconography. Admittedly, Sabbath's Satanism has long been reduced to pure camp—one of Ozzy's tour shirts features a parody of the "Got Milk?" ad campaign that asks, "Got Blood?"—but there's a reason frat boys still opt to listen to "The Lemon Song" instead of "Children of the Grave" when they're getting hammered on Molson Ice and talking about poon. Zeppelin's a party band, but Sabbath will haunt your dreams.

GOOD TIMES BAD TIMES AND EMBARRASSING TIMES

Even the great will stumble. Both Zep and Sabbath have unquestionably made some legacy-damaging choices, especially lately. I mean, for God's sake, Plant and Page dabbled with "world music" by recording a live record with a quartet of Moroccan players and strings. Their stint with rockabilly, the Honeydrippers, didn't help much, either. Meanwhile Ozzy is one misstep away from appearing on *The Celebrity Apprentice*.

Here's a rundown of the major blunders tainting their legacies. First, Zeppelin's:

1. Allow P. Diddy to cover "Kashmir" for use in a Godzilla movie.
2. Iconic angel logo doesn't have genitals.
3. Robert Plant becomes Arthurian knight and has sword fight in *The Song Remains the Same*.
4. That "Ooh oh-oh oh, oh oooh" reggae song, "D'yer Mak'er."
5. Plant records a folk record with Alison Krauss.

6. Jimmy Page tours with David Coverdale from White-snake doing Zep tunes.

7. Jimmy Page tours with the Black Crowes doing Zep tunes.

8. "Rock and Roll" is used in a Cadillac commercial targeting baby boomers thinking, "You're right, fellas—it *has* been a long time since I rock and rolled."

9. Allow Phil Collins to play drums in Bonham's absence at a Live Aid reunion.

10. The lyric, "If there's a bustle in your hedgerow, don't be alarmed now."

Now, Sabbath's:

1. *The Osbournes.*
2. Their affiliation with Rick Wakeman of Yes and *Journey to the Centre of the Earth* fame.
3. A disproportionate number of hardcore fans begin growing soul patches and/or neck beards.
4. Ozzy agrees to be the voice of the green fairy in *Moulin Rouge.*
5. Tony Iommi briefly plays with Jethro Tull.
6. "Iron Man" is used in a Nissan Titan commercial targeting baby boomers thinking, "Nice truck. Looks like a gas guzzler, though. Would there be enough room for the kids? And what about the environment? Hey, wait, I don't care about that crap. You know why? 'Cause I AM IRON MAN!"
7. Ozzy donates $25,000 to the SPCA.
8. The inclusion of Limp Bizkit and System of a Down at Ozzfest.
9. The music career of Kelly Osbourne.

10. The lyric, "Fairy boots were dancin' with a dwarf, all right now!"

Looks like a tie, right? Wrong. There's still "Stairway to Heaven" to account for. Nothing could have possibly done more harm to Zeppelin's legacy than this song. It was great the first five and a half million times you heard it, but now when it comes on the jukebox three things are certain:

1. You're in a really lame bar.
2. A middle-aged redneck who has a venison freezer in his toolshed played the damn thing.
3. For the next eight minutes and three seconds of your life, you're going to *hate* Led Zeppelin.

Plus, given the success of "Stairway," Zeppelin holds the dubious honor of popularizing the rock ballad. Remember Extreme's "More Than Words"? It's the bastard stepchild of "Stairway." *Does anyone remember ~~laughter~~ vomiting in their own mouth?* Now every time a metal band pulls out chairs and acoustic guitars and offers to "take it down a bit," you know who to blame.

Sabbath doesn't have a "Stairway," though to be fair Ozzy did do that painful "Bark at the Moon" video. But that was post-Sabbath and it'll be forgotten fifty years from now, when the next generation of cock rockers is slowing-it-down with Zep's "song of hope."

CODA

So, you see, it's just as true today as it was in 1975: Black Sabbath kicks more ass than Led Zeppelin. Whether or not you agree, well . . . I hope you'll at least take my advice on one thing: Keep your kids away from that Dumpster in the parking lot behind the A&P.

When all is said and done, I'll always love both bands, but it's Sabbath that stands to leave the larger cock imprint in the leather pants of rock history.

Abba

vs.

The Bee Gees

Katy St. Clair

Benny. Barry. The similarities do not begin and end with the letters *B* and *Y*. Both men were the driving forces behind two of the most successful groups of all time, Abba and the Bee Gees. Both men sported bilevel hair and full beards. Both men enjoyed the look and feel of white satin against their skin and a measurable grade of trouser snugness across their bums. And both men created some of the finest white-man boogie this side of Justin Timberlake.

The similarities between the two are so striking that some folks have even gone so far as to make the argument that they are not two distinct musicians, but are in fact *the same person*. This hypothesis was first put forth in 1978, when Jons-Jakob Bjönglbjörner-Smitt posited in the

Swedish rock magazine *Rolling Fjord* that both the Bee Gees and Abba had never performed live on the same night. According to Smitt, Abba was actually the brainchild of Atlantic Records founder Ahmet Ertegun, who wanted to corner the Scandinavian market but didn't want to pay all those Swedish taxes. His solution, says Smitt, was to dress Barry up like "a homosexual psychologist with an edge," adding a light-brown wig, some lip gloss, and a playful sidekick, Björn, who was better looking than both Robin and Maurice Gibb combined (which, let's face it, just isn't that hard). From there they amassed a few other Viking folk to round out the group, and the Bee Gees Scandinavia was born.

Smitt never really proved his controversial theory convincingly, but he does point out some rather creepy coincidences. First, there is each band's name. "The Bee Gees" originally came from the first initials of Bill Goode, an early promoter of the band, but later came to represent "the Brothers Gibb." Abba, on the other hand, supposably stands for the first initials of each primary member of the group: Anni-Frid, Benny, Björn, and Agnetha. The Abba logo looks like this: AℲBBA. The fattish, rounded *B*'s, says Smitt, could conceivably be read as medieval *G*'s. It therefore follows that the logo is a clever play on "BG." As for the rest of the Abba logo, which is flanked by *A*'s, it stands for "all the ass we are going to get in Oslo once this thing hits," if *Rolling Fjord*'s unconfirmed quote from Ertegun is to be believed.

The second-most-compelling argument that Smitt makes involves the managers of each band. For the Bee Gees, there was Robert *Stig*wood. For Abba, there was *Stig* Anderson, a somewhat fatter and jollier version of the former—things that can easily be created with stage makeup and some decent acting chops.

The real truth about Abba and the Bee Gees, as with most things, lies somewhere in the middle. The reason that there are so many eerie similarities between the two bands isn't because they are fronted by the same man. No, Benny and Barry are not the same person. Benny, however, desperately *wished* that he was Barry and spent his entire adult life emulating the eldest Gibb in every way.

Oh, sure, Benny would never admit to such things. In his mind he isn't the Salieri to Barry's Amadeus. No, in his mind he is the McCartney to Barry's Brian Wilson. But it goes much deeper than that. In fact, to this very day, if you mention the name Barry around Benny, he will freeze like a lingonberry on a January vine, slowly turn an icy gaze toward you, and then swiftly backhand you across the face.

Benny's so-called emulation of Barry is actually a deep-seated, often painful rivalry that emerged from the early skiffle scene that both of them belonged to before they became famous. It is a story of loss, heartbreak, and twee li'l ditties played with washboards, combs, and wax paper. It is a story that has never been told. Until now.

Skiffle is an ancient and revered form of folk music that first appeared around 1900. It was most notably embraced by British musicians in the late fifties and early sixties. Skiffle is pared-down folk music—if that is even possible—played on just about anything you can salvage from your parents' basement and then drag to the nearest street corner. Many famous musicians got their start in skiffle, including Mick Jagger, Robert Plant, and John Lennon.

Suffice it to say, skiffle was the DIY punk of the mid-twentieth century. Skiffle musicians, or "skiffies," would get together and compete head-to-head in folk-music hootenannies, much as the inner-city kids did during the early stages of rap music, which were themselves an offshoot of Jamaican ska contests, which were themselves offshoots of African call-and-response showdowns, which of course can all be traced back to the Old Testament and the first time a Pharisee used the phrase, "Your mama dons warrior sandals made from a lesser-quality papyrus."

So, yeah. Skiffle was more like "your mum!" played on a milk jug, and the competition was fierce. But no one wanted to win a skiffle contest more than Benny Andersson. Every morning little Benny would get out of bed, stretch, and then get down on his hands and knees and pray. In the next room his mother would be scraping together the last of the porridge, part of their meager diet that consisted of minnows, oatmeal, and jürgen-flergen, a diluted soup made from potato peelings and Absolut vodka. "Dear God," he prayed, "please let me win the skiffle contest tonight. If you let me win and become a success, I promise to always pay at least eighty percent of my income in taxes to sustain the socialist welfare state."

Benny would hum songs to himself on the way to school, often stopping to jot down notes and toot into his makeshift flute made from an old shoe. His band, the Westbay Singers, were poised to win the big prize that evening at the great Hoot Championship, which pitted all the European skiffle bands against one another in a fight to the finish. This year's contest was taking place in Benny's hometown of Stockholm— a sign, he believed, that he was destined to win. Besides, he *had* to win. Not only the contest but the love of a very special girl who would be there that night, the fair Aslög Hüchen. Sure, everyone knew that Anni-Frid was his girlfriend, but to him she was really just a *focka*-buddy. Aslög, on the other hand, was a *woman*. And women like her didn't date losers.

Benny was very excited because he had a secret weapon, something never before tried in skiffle. It would revolutionize the form. People would be talking about it for decades. It would reinvent popular music as we know it. Tonight, in front of all of his peers and the bonny Aslög, Benny would plug in his washboard and go electric.

Across town, another young lad from England named Barry was preparing for the evening's contest. His band, Wee Johnny Hayes and the Bluecats (formerly Wee Willie and the Bluecats, which was changed for obvious reasons) had already cornered the British skiffle kingdom and was now poised to dominate all of Europe. He not only had rugged good looks, but he also had two brothers with him—twins—who would zig to his zag, tweet to his twattle, and strum that ol' badminton racket like a-ringin' a bell.

That evening all the musicians gathered at the arena. The crowd was humming with activity. The celebrated Belgian skiffle band,

Pommes Frites, were tuning up and swapping tour stories with the Spaniards. The Scots were eyeballing the British, who were eyeballing the Irish, who were eyeballing the complimentary glögg table. Barry Gibb was warming up his voice. Benny stood in the back by himself, sizing up the competition. "Belgians?" he scoffed. *"Good luck, Hercule!"* The Spaniards also seemed to lack that certain something. And the British? Please. Sweden not only had a better national dental plan, it also produced a superior musician. No, he thought confidently, this contest is *mine.*

It came time to draw straws to see what order the bands would play in, and Benny was very excited to see that he was to go last—all the better to wow them with his turbo washboard. Better still, the British guy's band, Wee something, was right before him. Even if they reinvented the kazoo with a higher grade of wax paper or made cymbals out of tea saucers . . . nothing would rival his electric washboard.

Aslög entered from a side door. The late-evening haze of Scandinavian half sunlight/half moonlight streamed in and surrounded her like a halo. *Du er min ängel,* said Benny to himself. Her tortoiseshell glasses seemed to shimmer upon her face. She caught his eye and gave him a girlish little wave. Tonight he would kiss her for the first time, right after she hugged and congratulated him onstage, while confetti fluttered around them like doves. He had been planning for this moment his entire life.

The first group took the stage, a trio from Germany, Die Dreien Angeboren. The singer had an interesting twang to his voice, thought Benny, but they were certainly no competition. Besides, it was barely fifteen years after World War II. No one in his right mind would ever let the Germans win.

As band after band performed, Benny's spirits soared in anticipation of his big finish. At one point he thought he saw Aslög talking to that British guy with all the hair, but she was probably just telling him how proud she was of her friend who would be playing that night.

It finally came time for the second-to-last band to perform, Wee

Johnny Hayes and the Bluecats. Benny just hoped that they would finish quickly. He was so excited to perform he could hardly stand it.

The threesome took the stage, the guy with the hair and two others who looked to Benny like the sort of lads who frequently got their lunch money taken from them on the playground. They jumped right into an upbeat number about their dear ol' mum and her champion roses, or some such crap, thought Benny.

The one with the pronounced overbite began prattling on in a high whine about the perfume of his mother's petals, and Benny was starting to think that he should've worn his blue suit and not the black one, as black tends to more readily absorb flashbulbs. He was just bending down to spit shine his shoe when he began to notice some sort of a commotion in the crowd. He looked up and saw that everyone was peering at the stage in anticipation of something. He followed their gaze to Wee Johnny, and what he saw stopped his heart. There, onstage, stood the Englishman with all the hair, carefully plugging a washboard into an amplifier. Benny grew very pale. Wee Johnny then gave it a cursory strum, electrifying the crowd. Then his band lit into a rollicking version of "I've Got a Bird in East 'Ampsted, Tuppence a Dance," and the rest, as they say, was history.

At the end of their set, the applause was deafening. People couldn't believe the genius of the electric washboard. Other musicians in the arena threw down their instruments, never to pick them up again. Women rushed the stage, eager to touch Wee Johnny. One girl in particular was very taken with Johnny, and, gentle reader, I think we both know who that girl was.

Benny forfeited his set in anguish, unable to take the stage. All of his years of preparation and prayer, destroyed in one evening. He stood in the eaves and watched the silly little Brits claim their prize, his backbone stiffening and his gaze hardening.

"And the first prize goes to . . . Barry Gibb and his amazing electric washboard!" exclaimed the announcer.

The words ripped through Benny. He nearly fainted. Gradually his despair turned to anger. Yes, his pain was slowly and surely turning into something that could only be assuaged by *revenge*.

"I'll get you, Barry Gibb," he said with fists clenched and the arch of an eyebrow. "And your little brothers, too."

Now that the real story has come out, it is possible to see the entire history of Abba as nothing but a reaction to all things Gibb. Quite simply, the phenomenal success of Abba can be attributed to only one factor: Benny Andersson's pathological need to "beat" Barry at every turn, all in an attempt to re-create that cold, cold night in Sweden, oh so long ago. His bitterness can easily be seen in Abba hits like "Waterloo" and "The Winner Takes It All," but it is also subtle, showing itself in songs like "SOS," a reaction to the Bee Gees' 1968 sleeper hit "I've Gotta Get a Message to You."

Basically, once Benny rose from the ashes of defeat, he set about putting together the group that would rival "That Band," as he had begun referring to them. The Bee Gees had successfully graduated from what Benny had called "limp-wristed sixties balladry[1] and Beatles rip-offs"[2] to certified funkmeisters with hits like "Jive Talkin' " and "Fanny (Be Tender With My Love)."

Initially he knew that he would have to add siblings to the mix if he really wanted to compete. There is something to be said for bands with siblings—folks who have known each other for their entire lives and speak an unspoken language that carries over into remarkable song-writing. Unfortunately, one of Benny's brothers was tone-deaf and the other had been lost on a Nordic whaling expedition. He'd have to find replacements.

1. He has a point. Benny especially enjoyed ridiculing this early Bee Gees lyric from their first album: "When I was small, and Christmas trees were tall. . . ." "*Idiotisk!*" exclaimed Benny.

2. Again he has a point. One need only listen to the Brothers Gibb's attempt at psychedelia, "Red Chair, Fade Away," to see what he is talking about. "*Crap!*" exclaimed Benny, which is the same word in Swedish.

But he was forgetting one thing. The Bee Gees weren't composed of just any old brothers. The Bee Gees had *twins,* the fraternal bookends Robin and Maurice.[3] How could his new band ever compete with that synergy?

If there was one thing Benny learned from skiffle, it was to make the best of what instruments you had. If life throws you empty herring tins, you bore a hole in both ends and call it a clavichord.

"Hmmm," thought Benny. "Holes in both ends. . . ." Suddenly it hit him. Anni-Frid! And his best friend and Westbay Singers bandmate Björn was going out with this chick Agnetha. That's it! They would ask the girls to be in the band. That would also make up for Barry's falsetto, which, try as he might, Benny just could not duplicate.

Abba of course became an international supergroup, so it can be said that Benny got even. However, like most men with a grudge, fame, money, and success never really took away his feelings of unworthiness. In the movie *Abba: The Movie,* a so-called documentary about their 1977 Australian tour, Benny is quoted as saying that he isn't in it for the money. It came across as the words of a dedicated musician in love with his art, but we now know what he really meant. It's not the money factor, all right. It's the Barry factor. In fact, shrewd music fans will note the film's location as the old Bee Gees stomping ground, the brothers having spent most of their formative years in Australia despite being born in England. As Abba travels from Sydney to Aberdeen to Perth, Benny is metaphorically pissing all over Barry's territory, and loving every minute of it.

Perhaps the best example of Benny's single-minded mission can be seen in a recently unearthed tape from the "Dancing Queen" recording session. Though not as lengthy as the now-famous "Troggs Tape" in

3. "*Skit!*" said Benny.

which the band argues about a two-second drum bit, nor as painful to listen to as Linda McCartney's infamous bootlegged soundboard vocals, it is, nonetheless, quite telling. Here is an excerpt:

> [Björn at the keyboard, beginning to play what he has come up with for Benny.]
>
> "It's at night and the lights are low . . ." he sings.
>
> "*No!*" screams Benny. "*Friday* night and the lights are low. It must be a Friday."
>
> "Why do we need to say what night it is?" asks Björn.
>
> "Who cares?"
>
> "It's the end of the workweek," Benny says. "There is a certain tension that needs to be there. We are all getting off work, and we are going to go dancing. Working stiffs like dock workers will relate. Trust me."
>
> "Fine," sighs Björn. "So, here's the chorus, 'You are the dancing king . . .' "
>
> "*Stoppa!*" yells Benny.
>
> "What now?" pleads Björn.
>
> "It must be a queen, not a king."
>
> "Queen? That sounds gay."
>
> "Does not."
>
> "Does too."
>
> "Does not."

That continues for a while. What can account for Benny's insistence? He never says, but surely it's no coincidence that John Travolta had recently appeared on *American Bandstand,* where he discussed his upcoming movie, *Saturday Night Fever.* "It's about a guy who is king of the disco," Travolta said to Dick Clark. No doubt Benny knew that the Bee Gees were gonna be all over this thing, and as it would be released in 1978, at the same time as Abba's next single . . .

"It's a dancing *queen,* and that's that," says Benny with finality.

"So it's Friday night and she's just gotten off her shift at the docks?" Björn retorts.

"Shut up."

"No, you shut up."

"No, you shut up."

In the end Benny got his song. Björn was right about one thing, though. "Queen" did sound gay. It was intentional. Benny was calling Barry Gibb a poofter. Plus Friday comes before Saturday. So there.

But perhaps Benny's most bizarre attempt at Barryness came in the form of Andy Gibb vs. Ted Gärdestad.

Any true artist needs a protégé. Plato had Aristotle, Phil Spector had Ronnie, Mr. Roarke had Tattoo. Barry had his youngest brother, the "fourth Bee Gee," Andy Gibb.

You could say that Andy was the final piece of the Bee Gees puzzle, for even though they had mad commercial success, the threesome didn't really have the same power that other rock bands of the time had—the power to pull in the really young chicks. In the early seventies, Barry was shrewd enough to figure out how to steal funk from the black man and package it for the honky. With Andy, what he wanted to do was corner what is now called the tween market, those "barmy little harlots with mummy's lipstick on," as he phrased it, from the ages of seven to thirteen, who seemed to go through money like the six o'clock Titfield Thunderbolt into Victoria Station. Barry was, quite simply, a marketing genius. It worked marvelously. Andy Gibb sold millions of singles and had six top-ten hits, all of which big bro had a hand in composing, from "Shadow Dancing" to "I Just Want to Be Your Everything." Plus, to quote Victoria Principal, he was "hella fine."

Abba vs. The Bee Gees

As to be expected, Benny sat back and watched Andy Gibb's success with jealous acumen. He knew that he needed to find *his* Andy. Never mind that Abba was already adored by young girls everywhere; Abba had indeed cornered the global market from kindergarten to retirement. No, Benny had to have *his* own Andy because Barry had one. It was that simple.

It didn't take him long to find one. Ted Gärdestad came to the attention of Stig Anderson at the age of fifteen. He knew immediately that Ted was the kind of young man ten-year-olds would plaster their walls with, teenage girls would lie to their parents to go see in concert, and grown women would dust off their miniskirts for. He had a rather nice singing voice, too. Benny and Björn produced myriad hits for him including his best-known number, "Jag vill ha en egen måne." Ted became huge; a real sensation. Benny had found his Andy.

Ted did get a little nutty at one point, joining the Bhagwan Shree Rajneesh sect in Oregon, headed by a charismatic religious leader (read: kook) of the same name who espoused laughter, sex, and ostentatious wealth in the form of a fleet of over ninety Rolls-Royces, called himself the "rich man's guru," and, unlike other Eastern "sages," claimed that poverty was *not* a spiritual value.

All of this was fine, however, because Benny could capitalize on the notoriety of his protégé. After all, Andy Gibb was dealing with his own rumors of drug addiction and depression, most of which seemed to stem from being dumped by Principal. Yes, thought Benny, every teen idol needs a fatal flaw. It makes him more human. Elvis had a drug problem and even Bobby Sherman was rumored to have had virulent BO. Wearing a Hindi loincloth and hearing voices—Ted's brother publicly claimed he was schizophrenic—just happened to be Ted's Achilles' heel. He could work with that.

Yep, things were going great for Benny and Ted. And then Andy Gibb died. "Jesus," said Benny when he heard the news. "How am I going to top that?" Andy would now be elevated to some sort of legendary status, a beautiful Adonis struck down at the height of his fame . . . well, actually after his fame had waned. But never mind. As Benny saw it, Barry had one-upped him again.

Fortunately for Benny, something fortuitous eventually happened. On an evening in late June 1997, Ted Gärdestad stepped out in front of the queue at a Sollentuna, Sweden, station and threw himself in front of an oncoming train, killing himself and forever drowning out the voices.

Benny couldn't believe his luck—it was one thing to die of a rumored drug overdose,[4] but yet another to commit suicide in such a romantic, courageous way. Score one for the Abba camp!

It was only later that certain eyewitnesses on that fateful day began to report seeing what they described as a "homosexual psychologist with an edge" in dark sunglasses lingering around the station. Some assert that this mystery man appeared to have reached out and *pushed* Ted to his doom, only to scurry up the stairs and into the Swedish night afterward. The story could never be fully corroborated, and the death was officially ruled a suicide.

It is a crisp November evening in 2000, and Benny Andersson is sitting in the audience at the Orpheum in San Francisco. It is the American premiere of *Mamma Mia!,* his coda to the phenomenon that he created known as Abba: his *Saturday Night Fever.*

He is older now, grayer, a bit pudgier and more stooped, but he still holds a healthy Scandinavian presence. The psychologist has lost his edge, you could say, but San Francisco is homosexual enough for the two of them, and tonight they will make sweet love.

His career has been nothing short of sensational. His songs have been covered by R.E.M., U2, and Erasure, and sampled by Madonna. More important, though the Bee Gees have sold more than 100 million

---

4. Not true, actually. Andy Gibb died of heart failure, which was perhaps exacerbated by all his drug use, but was not directly caused by it.

records, Abba has sold more than 250 million albums and singles worldwide.

Besides, thinks Benny as he sits in the audience, soaking up the attention, these days Barry Gibb looks like Wolfman Jack at a tanning salon, lives in a garish Miami mansion, and has seen Barbra Streisand with no makeup on. All in all, thinks Benny, he has ended up doing better for himself, when all is said and done.

If there is one regret he still holds, it isn't losing that skiffle contest four decades earlier. No, his one regret is never seeing Aslög again. His letters to her have gone unanswered all these years; tickets that he mails her to his shows gone unredeemed. Still, he writes.

He can't think about that now. Tonight is the launch of the American tour, which will eventually culminate in one of the most successful Broadway runs in history. The opening strains to "Mamma Mia" begin to trickle through the theater. As the lights fade, a small, elderly woman enters through the side door and takes a seat. She adjusts her tortoiseshell glasses and folds the program across her lap. She is smiling.

The Album vs. The Single

The Album vs. The Single

EVERYBODY KNOWS THE ONLY WAY TO SAY SOMETHING *IMPORTANT* IS TO SAY SOMETHING FOR A *LONG TIME*... AND PREFERABLY TO *REPEAT IT* AT THE END — JUST LIKE ONE COSMIC, NEVER-ENDING LOOP OF MEANING, YOU KNOW?

YES! OF COURSE, 8-TRACK, WE ALLOWED FOR MUSICIANS TO REALIZE THEIR

GESAMTKUNSTWERK!

— OH, THE CONCEPT IN ITS CONTEXT...

...WHO DOESN'T YEARN FOR NARRATIVE ARC OR A *CONTEMPLATIVE* SONG CYCLE?

HA, LIKE THE PROFOUND CONCEPTS OF *SOUTH PACIFIC* AND *SWITCHED-ON BACH!*

...AND IF IT WAS TRULY GREAT...

...IT WARRANTED...

THAT'S WHAT I HATE ABOUT YOU, LP, AND YOU TOO, 8-TRACK— YOU OFFER SO MUCH TIME AND ATTENTION FOR AN ARTIST I WOULDN'T EVEN MAKE A RARE B-SIDE. IT'S ABSURD.

WELL, BACK IN MY DAY, WE DIDN'T EVEN HAVE THAT— IT WAS SINK OR SWIM, NO B-SIDE. IT WAS NOVELTY OR BUST.

I'M NOT ASHAMED TO ADMIT IT! ...NONE OF THESE HIGH FALUTIN' CONCEPTS.

YEAH, BUT YOU WEREN'T A REAL RECORD, JUST A MOMENT DOCUMENTED.

OH, LEAVE HIM ALONE ABOUT ELECTRICAL RECORDING. IT WAS AFTER HIS TIME. AND CYLINDER, DON'T DRAG GENRES INTO THIS.

BUT MUSICAL GENRES HAVE BEEN INSEPARABLE FROM US FORMATS. ROCK WASN'T RECORDED ON A SINGLE, IT WAS A SINGLE. AND LP, YOU HAD A SECOND LIFE AS A 12", BECOMING A WHOLE NEW THING AND MAKING A NEW MUSIC IN THE PROCESS. WHY DO YOU THINK CLASSICAL HATED US SO MUCH?

FOR THOSE FOLKS, SCORES WERE ARCHIVED FORMS BUT NOT A FORMAT IN AND OF ITSELF. LONGER WORK? ADD MORE PAPER. WHEN WE FIRST CAME ALONG, THEIR EXTENDED FORMS DIDN'T FIT US.

CLASSICAL. YEAH, I COULD ONLY FIT FOUR MINUTES, SO THERE WOULD BE SIX OR TEN OF US TOGETHER FOR A SYMPHONY. THEY CALLED THOSE COLLECTIONS AN "ALBUM."

HEY LP, REMEMBER GETTING STARTED IN POP, HOW AT FIRST YOU WERE JUST A COLLECTION OF SINGLES CULLED BY SOME GOONS IN A&R?

EVERYBODY STARTS SMALL.

BUT I BECAME TRULY GREAT— THE MUSICAL FORM OF THE CENTURY FOR SERIOUS POPULAR MUSICIANS ...AND ALL WAS WELL UNTIL IT CAME ALONG...

The Album vs. The Single

AWW, SUCK IT UP, LP. YOU HAD AT LEAST 30 YEARS, AND ME? HA! NOT EVEN 20!

BUT FOR A WHILE, I WAS ON TOP.

AND YEAH, SONY/PHILLIPS MADE ME BIG ENOUGH TO FIT ALL OF BEETHOVEN'S 5TH ON ONE DISC, BUT I WAS SO MUCH MORE THAN THAT — 74 MINUTES OF POSSIBILITY.

I THOUGHT YOU LOOKED *GREAT* IN A LONGBOX.

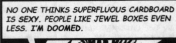

SHUT UP, CASSINGLE.

NO ONE THINKS SUPERFLUOUS CARDBOARD IS SEXY. PEOPLE LIKE JEWEL BOXES EVEN LESS. I'M DOOMED.

WELL, HELLO THERE, LONG TIME NO SEE. WHAT CAN I GET YA?

NOTHING, REALLY... THOUGHT I'D STOP BY TO SEE YOU ALL...

— YEAH, IT'S BEEN A WHILE. I'VE BEEN OFF DOING MY OWN THING.

HEY, COME AND SIT DOWN HERE WITH ME AND TELL ME A BIT ABOUT IT.

WHY DON'T YOU ALL COME IN, WE CAN GO IN THE BACK AND HAVE A LONG CATCH-UP.

GEE, THANKS, BUT WE DON'T REALLY DO THAT KINDA THING ANYMORE.

WHADDAYMEAN?!

The Album vs. The Single

WE JUST...NEEDED OUR SPACE TO GROW AND YOU ALL WERE... HOLDING US BACK. ACTUALLY, WE JUST DROPPED BY TO PAY OUR RESPECTS.

YOU CAN GO YOU CAN CALL IT... YOUR OWN WAY ANOTHER LONELY DAY

WE OWE YOU ALL A LOT FOR TAKING US THROUGH THE OLD TIMES, BUT NOW WE'VE JUST GOT TO GET MOVING ON.

YOU'LL NEVER SOUND AS GOOD WITHOUT ME.

I SAID THAT SAME THING TO SONG WHEN IT LEFT ME FOR CD!

THAT'S TRUE, FOR NOW. BUT I JUST HAVE TO BELIEVE THAT I'LL BE BETTER OFF WITHOUT YOU IN THE END.

I GAVE YOU SO MUCH SPACE— HOW COULD YOU WANT MORE?

I'M SO SORRY, CD... WE'LL STILL BE TOGETHER...

IN THE USED BINS.

Radiohead
vs.
Coldplay

Matt Diehl

Amid alt-rock royalty, perhaps there is no greater rivalry than that between Coldplay and Radiohead—especially among the bands' fans. "Coldplay or Radiohead?" is a typical title for a debate on a message-board thread—one of thousands similar if you Google their names together. Indeed, the two groups are positioned to be competitors for almost everything, even beyond music: One headline about a poll run by the People for the Ethical Treatment of Animals nominated "Coldplay vs. Radiohead for World's Sexiest Vegetarian."

No disrespect to PETA, but with Radiohead and Coldplay it's sort of a chicken-egg situation, their destinies fused since the beginning. "Who will be the next Radiohead? In England, the answer on everyone's lips is

Coldplay," I mused in a review for *Rolling Stone* of Coldplay's 2000 debut album, *Parachutes*. Proximity is as key as any aesthetic similarities. For years, each was not only signed to divisions of EMI (both to EMI's Capitol imprint in the U.S.), their efforts were considered bellwethers indicating the success and failure of the company. Radiohead was EMI's flagship signing, serving a similar role for the label as Pink Floyd did in the seventies: a band that emanated credibility despite global-superstar status. As major-label fortunes dwindled in the digital era, it was seen as a death knell when, in 2007, Radiohead left EMI to self-release music on the Internet and indie imprints. As well, EMI saw its stock price tumble precipitously when Coldplay—who had already sold more than twenty million copies of their first two albums combined—delayed the release of their third long-playing effort, 2005's *X&Y,* for a few months.

Throughout, the press has been the primary instigator of any rivalry between the two bands. "In its early days, Coldplay could easily be summed up as Radiohead minus Radiohead's beat, dissonance or arty subterfuge," Jon Pareles wrote in his crushingly dismissive 2005 *New York Times* article "The Case Against Coldplay." While in Alex Ross's 2004 *New Yorker* feature on Radiohead ("The Searchers: Radiohead's Unquiet Revolution"—probably the best writing ever done about the band), Ross describes a scene that demonstrates the humorous but real tension between the two. In it, MTV News reporter Gideon Yago sent Radiohead members into hysterics when he asked a question sent in by a Radiohead fan named Stanley from Coney Island: "How do you guys feel about the fact that bands like Travis, Coldplay, and Muse are making a career sounding exactly like your records did in 1997?" According to Ross, Radiohead front man Thom Yorke self-consciously avoided the question, "[cupping] his hand around his mouth and [calling] out, 'Good luck with *Kid A*!' "

Yet Yorke plays his part to fuel the fire, too. In interviews, he isn't afraid to wax poetic about his fave bands, typically giving effusive support to the likes of underground Pitchfork faves like Clinic or Deerhoof or Autechre. In the case of the last, mainstays of the Warp label's "Intelligent Dance Music" brand of esoteric electronica, it is seemingly as much the outlaw elitism of the IDM scene that appeals to Radiohead as it is the music's revolutionarily dissonant grooves. That becomes clear in Yorke's dismissal in a *Time* magazine interview of Coldplay as mere "lifestyle music," best suited for soundtracking yuppie boutique consumerism, TV commercials, and sentimental movie trailers. Elsewhere on the subject, Yorke has displayed a sort of patronizing paternalism reeking of noblesse oblige. "I really worry about other people like Coldplay and the Strokes," Yorke told Jon Wiederhorn of MTV.com, " 'cause the sort of success they've had really screws with your head. It's like, what do you do next?"

Coldplay also feel the sting, yet choose to confront their standing-in-shadow status head-on. "We're like an eager dog just yapping around their heels, and they're trying to kick us away," front man Chris Martin joked to *Newsweek* about the rivalry. "It's like unrequited love. I'm in love with a lot of things. Some of those things love me back. And some of them don't—and one of them is Radiohead." In response to a plagiarism lawsuit with a Dutch songwriter over Coldplay's massive hit "Clocks," Martin stated, "We used to just be able to steal off Radiohead. Now we can steal off everybody." And in a recent interview in *Q* magazine with comedian Ricky Gervais, Martin bittersweetly summed up his band's debt to Radiohead this way: "Ah, man, it's tricky. I don't think we'd be anywhere if Radiohead didn't exist. I think we're like why Diet Coke was big. Because some people couldn't handle Coke. That's how I see Coldplay."

Whether Thom Yorke likes it or not, however, there's much both bands share. For one, there's how they began their careers, resisting easy categorization. When Radiohead started to appear on the industry radar in the early nineties, they were caught between eras. Neither their music nor their persona was entirely representative of the shoegaze movement that preceded their arrival (shoegaze legends Ride coincidentally also hail from their Oxford, England, hometown). Nor were they particularly nationalistic and Britpop enough for popular taste. Instead, especially in England, they were considered a variation on nineties grunge-era alternative—an interpretation, granted, they themselves fed, as press photos from Radiohead's early days display an embrace of now-dated alt-rock signifiers like floppily stylized hairdos, dramatic rock-star sunglasses, polka-dot shirts, pseudo-U2-style poses. "A lily-livered excuse for a rock band," the famously bitchy *New Musical Express* derided them as.

Coldplay seemed equally misplaced when they debuted at the tail end of Britpop's baroque hangover phase; *Parachutes* landed just a few months within Oasis releasing the bloatedly ambitious, out-of-it *Standing on the Shoulder of Giants.* Just as Radiohead had nearly a decade earlier, Coldplay seemed meek and stoodentlike next to those whose throne they'd inherit: too populist for snobby Blur, and strangely fey and posh-seeming next to sodden hooligans like Liam Gallagher. Chris Martin didn't even do drugs or drink—unthinkable in a British rock star!

Both bands feature piano-playing vocalists who, however you slice it, feel like guilty pleasures because their melodic charisma is so compelling. Yorke and Martin can turn any phrase into a hook; despite their infectiousness, there's something tentative and dissonant about their melodies. Both inevitably come off as ethereal yet melancholic, regardless of any other emotions seemingly being expressed. And when they make choices that are unexpected, it's thrilling and cathartic. (R.E.M.'s Michael Stipe—a huge fan of and influence on both bands—is perhaps the closest parallel in terms of a sensitive, moody front man whose eerily unique, expressive voice embodies both masculine and feminine.)

While often defined thusly in the media by their front men, Coldplay and Radiohead are both bands above all else, dependent largely on their collective interplay. One suspects a Chris Martin solo album wouldn't be as good as a Coldplay album, and Thom Yorke's sketchlike 2006 solo effort, *The Eraser,* proved the significant debt he owes the other Radiohead members. Alone, Yorke's sound doesn't have the heft, dimension, and contrast that guitarists Ed O'Brien and Jonny Green-wood bring—O'Brien typically providing a more direct connection to rock and roll while the classically trained Greenwood does the opposite, adding crucial ambient tonal color and rigorous compositional variance. In Coldplay, the guitar playing also serves as Chris Martin's essential foil—Jonny Buckland's six-string reverberations acting as a sort of Greek chorus, much as the Edge does for Bono in U2. Indeed, much of the band's compellingly atmospheric quality is due to Buckland's tex-tures, flourishes, and, above all, a melodic sense as keen as his vocalist's. Buckland's guitars can contrast Martin's vocal line with an elegant, min-imalist line or assemble chiming tones into a wall of sound that owes as much debt to symphonies as it does to shoegaze. Without Buckland, one imagines that Martin just might morph into an unrestrained piano man at any point.

The rhythm sections in each band are just as primary, fulfilling similar functions to expand their sounds. Drummer/percussionist Phil Selway may be Radiohead's secret weapon, lacing the band's material with rock's most deceptively complex rhythms. Coldplay stickman Will Champion, meanwhile, is perhaps the least musically trained in his band, but he works his limitations to his advantage à la Ringo Starr of the Beatles. Champion's humble restraint keeps Martin and Buckland's sonic overreach in check; often using brushes instead of sticks on the band's early material, his jazzy, tentative feel emphasizes the sense of wide-open space in Coldplay's music, the very human pulse adding an even greater approachability.

Radiohead and Coldplay also stand out together amid today's popu-lar music due to their shared classical-music influence. This plays no small part in both bands being considered "important." One paradigm to be taken seriously by critics is when a band—say, Pink Floyd—approaches rock with the meaningful intent, scope, and literary themes of a classical composer, resulting in a unified artistic statement like a "rock opera" rather than just a collection of hit singles. In Coldplay, the classical influence reveals itself as romantic, more Mozart, perfect and grand, with hints of the irresistible bombast of Orff in the dramatic dynamics. It's proven to be a crucial element of the Coldplay sound—the resonant, one-finger major-chord progression in "Speed of Sound," the hymnal organ figure announcing "Fix You," the infectious piano arpeggios that announce "Clocks" so distinctively. Radiohead, on the other hand, look to challenging contemporary composers to underpin their own compositional strategies. When I interviewed the band's members back in 1997 about the impact of their artistic breakthrough album, *OK Computer* (their first, ahem, rock opera), all they could talk about was the influence of Eastern European avant-garde composers like Górecki and Penderecki, whose experiments with unlikely tonalities and minimalism proved revelatory. (Ross, in his piece, also convincingly details Radiohead's debt to Messiaen.) Both bands' embrace of classical helped them dispense with any notion of the rock band as a working-class vehicle for expression (regardless of either's actual class status), reiterating that this is music of the mind as much as it is pure expression.

Both bands aspire to the astral plane, a higher state of consciousness where the quality of the soul and intellect eclipses class status in any hierarchy of existence. Quite simply, they float above such banal frays for the most part via the helium balloon of sophistication. Banality is the antagonist, the gas in the motor that powers both bands' stories—the thing that must be avoided at all costs, that will corrupt the art so that it is no longer recognizable. But with popularity, banality trailed both Radiohead and Coldplay at every corner, their respective abilities to elude it being their mark of success.

Yet despite these deep similarities, is the Coldplay vs. Radiohead rivalry really a fair fight? Radiohead remain so revered they are almost beyond reproach, pulling off rock's ultimate tightrope walk: venerated for their iconoclasm, yet catchy enough to be beloved by the masses. In terms of both street and critical credibility, outside of Fugazi or, say, Steve Albini, Radiohead remain distinctly resistant to pop's sellout siren call toward filthy lucre—laughing all the way to the bank on their own terms. They are the ideal of independence, able to exist above the mainstream while dipping down to enjoy some of its benefits without injury. Radiohead personify the true artist; fame is an afterthought, for once a by-product seemingly of quality, not marketing. There is ambition, yes, to Radiohead's game, but it is an ambition to push beyond borders. Yet when they get those borders open, they let even more and more into the Radiohead diaspora; *Kid A,* Radiohead's most difficult album, entered the charts at number one.

Coldplay, meanwhile, receive some positive notices but are just as often derided as "Radiohead lite" following Pareles's critical lead. How could they be the real thing, the peanut gallery of critics and hipster bloggers concludes, with such sheer populism, such shameless hooks, such sentimental themes? Coldplay are inevitably punished in their attempts to reach the widest audience possible even if they wish to do so because they feel that what they have to say has an urgent need to be communicated. This has allowed Coldplay to be wildly underestimated, much as U2 initially were for their earnestness. However, Coldplay bring far more depth, integrity, and sophistication to pop forms than they are given credit for. As well, Radiohead's Kevlar reputation has caused a blind eye to be turned to their own missteps and stagnant dips.

Such dualities and dichotomies imparted a frisson to the alternative scene that produced both bands—the same way Nirvana was seen as the apogee of all things genuine while their successful U.K. imitators Bush were perceived as plastic Satan personified. But just as Coldplay is perceived to bogart wholesale from Radiohead's repertoire, the loud-soft dynamics and disturbed protagonist of Radiohead's first hit, 1992's "Creep," displayed a slavish debt to the Pixies, causing them to be considered "Nirvana lite," as Andrew Smith pointed out in a 2000 *London Observer* review. It didn't help that the producers of Radiohead's inconsistent 1993 debut album, *Pablo Honey,* Paul Kolderie and Sean Slade, had also produced the Pixies, Dinosaur Jr., et al., or that the title comes from a Jerky Boys sample. And while "Creep" is a classic of sorts, it hasn't entirely lost its novelty status. More golden oldie than timeless (or *Loveless*), it sounds slightly dated today, sharing its very nineties slacker ennui ("I'm a creep, I'm a weirdo / What the hell am I doing here?") with another supposed-to-be one-hit wonder, Beck's "Loser."

Radiohead didn't really reach godhead until their next album, 1995's *The Bends.* Not only filled with classic songs—"Planet Telex," "My Iron Lung," "Street Spirit (Fade Out)," "Just"—it showed how much potential the band actually had, showcasing a new tendency to experiment and innovate alongside anthemic pop tracks like "High and Dry" (sometimes derided by the band as a sort of sequel to "Creep" in an attempt to get another alt-rock hit). Yet at the same time they were becoming known as the greatest band in the world, Radiohead began to grow too content in their own iconoclasm, and so did their fans; even if they had made an album of themselves farting through a vocoder, a large segment of their following would've declared it a masterpiece. 2000's *Kid A*—a truly expansive, genre-redefining masterwork in the style of *Dark Side of the Moon*—was followed up by *Amnesiac,* primarily comprising tracks taken from the *Kid A* sessions. While *Amnesiac* featured some amazing songs like "Knives Out" and "Pyramid Song" (as well as a growing free-jazz influence), it still imparted the feeling that you were getting tasty, but ultimately reheated, leftovers.

Radiohead didn't improve matters much with their next release, 2001's *I Might Be Wrong: Live Recordings,* a fairly superfluous concert album; it's certainly no *Live at the Apollo.* The band's next studio album, 2003's *Hail to the Thief,* seemed to follow this progression of complacency. Recorded in just two weeks, *Hail to the Thief* featured some indelible songs, yes, but it was no boundary-smashing masterpiece—and Radiohead had set themselves up, intentionally or not, as the go-to guys for masterpieces. *Hail to the Thief* heralded what was now the "Radiohead sound," familiar instead of surprising. "What once seemed impossibly outré is starting to sound orthodox," Alexis Petridis wrote in a review of the album in *The Guardian.* "However, *Hail to the Thief*'s big drawback has less to do with its similarity to its predecessor than the sense that Radiohead's famed gloominess is becoming self-parodic."

At the same time, other bands started to pick up the baton Radiohead had left on the track. TV on the Radio, for example, came out of nowhere with their own take on Radiohead's antiformula formula; melodic, soulful, yet deeply experimental, they were one-upping Radiohead at their own game. In addition, nearly simultaneous with Radiohead's slight decline, Coldplay, following U2's (and Radiohead's) lead, were pushing harder than ever to prove that they were more than just a mere pop band, trying their best to make important music, albeit with an earnestness post–*OK Computer* Radiohead have studiously avoided. Smartly, they used their increasing popularity to become better and more forward in their choices. *X&Y* featured more angular, challenging noises, Brian Eno—rock's most brilliant vanguard figure—guested on keyboards, and "Talk" even sampled Kraftwerk!

The height of Coldplay's edgier sophistication came on *X&Y*'s title track. "X&Y" floats into intergalactic regions on a melody of almost Floydian grandeur, while its hallucinatory atmosphere and eerie harmonies suggest a vital connection with rave-culture electronica (someone in the band must've inhaled the Orb's "Little Fluffy Clouds"). The compositional structure also avoids the obvious verse-chorus-verse contraption of the typical pop song. Instead, the song offers up a series of mini-suites in slow motion; building in their symphonic intensity, they climax on a beatless orchestral passage of great beauty. "X&Y" was as complex and ambitious an epic as Radiohead might attempt, but with one key difference: It no longer sounded like Radiohead—it sounded like Coldplay.

Coldplay were also becoming a better and better live band, with rapturous concerts creating an even deeper bond with their audiences. Their ambitious stage production grew increasingly sophisticated and high-art influenced—equal to that of Radiohead's similar multimedia stage spectacles. Radiohead's performances, on the other hand, grew increasingly erratic. Radiohead can be truly the greatest live band ever, but they can also descend into jazzbo self-indulgence with the best of them. During this period, some Radiohead shows proved transcendent while others seemed like the five individuals onstage were playing only to themselves, barely interacting with one another, let alone the audience. Sometimes when you go to a Radiohead show, you wanna hear "Street Spirit," not Sun Ra, y'know?

Coldplay's next album (to be titled *Viva la Vida or Death and All His Friends*) is due out in 2008 and is being produced by Brian Eno. The album will be the band's fourth studio long-player, which is a not-insignificant number: Eno also produced U2's fourth album, 1984's *The Unforgettable Fire,* which took the Irish foursome into both more adventurous material and even greater superstardom than ever before. By turning to someone like Eno, driving themselves to go beyond what they were previously capable of, Coldplay are following the most important tenet in Radiohead's template: be yourself, by any means necessary. In being true to themselves (with Eno's expert guidance, of course), it seems possible that Coldplay just might catch up artistically with Radiohead.

Well, it *did* seem possible—before the release of *In Rainbows,* that is. Radiohead's seventh studio album proved to be the cultural event of 2007 on many levels. Most notoriously, freed from their contract with EMI, Radiohead initially self-released *In Rainbows* on the Internet with no major-label involvement; shockingly, they allowed consumers to pay whatever they wanted for the download—even nothing. Not content to rewrite the rules of rock music, Radiohead demonstrated through the marketing of *In Rainbows* that they wanted to rewrite the rules of the entire decaying music industry in their own image. Thank God.

That *In Rainbows* set a new paradigm for artists to release music nearly overshadowed a most salient fact: Radiohead were in the business of making masterpieces again. Easily on a par with *Kid A* and *OK Computer, In Rainbows* might actually come to eclipse them regardless of how people came to hear it. As Andy Kellman wrote in a review of the album at allmusic.com, "*In Rainbows* will hopefully be remembered as Radiohead's most stimulating synthesis of accessible songs and abstract sounds, rather than their first pick-your-price download."

Radiohead vs. Coldplay

Accessible is the key word here. "The most surprising thing about Radiohead's seventh album turned out to be neither the method of distribution (e-mail) nor the suggested retail price (whatever you want) but the fact that when the damn thing finally materialized . . . it was a Coldplay record!" Josh Tyrangiel wrote in *Time*'s year-end roundup. Yorke's words on *Hail to the Thief* had begun to edge toward the predictable: What had once been a surprising lyrical persona was now seemingly written by an actual paranoid android. His musings on the dystopia of modern life were still beguiling in their alienated expressionism, but his themes didn't feel as fresh on the umpteenth listen; the line between actual literary profundity and adolescent sci-fi angst had grown dangerously thin. On *In Rainbows,* however, theme doesn't seem so important as feeling and emotion, though if there is a theme here it's more about the importance of human relationships rather than the individual being crushed by ye olde techno-horror of everyday existence. On hypnotic slow jams like "All I Need" and "House of Cards," Yorke and Co. come off dark, yes, but also erotic and playful; Selway's percussive, echoey rhythms on "Reckoner" prove surprisingly funky, subtle, and unexpectedly hypnotic in their mandala-like repetition; "Faust Arp" exudes a lullaby loveliness recalling, say, "Blackbird" by the Beatles; and "Videotape" fuses Penderecki minimalism with undeniable passion. "I'm an animal trapped in your hot car," Yorke moans on "All I Need"; it's one of his most powerful, succinct, and perverse metaphors, with the crafted, brutal elegance of a Raymond Carver sentence. As such, *In Rainbows* proves Radiohead to be as ambitious as ever, but their ambition seems to be to discover what's going on inside us—and that intimacy is what gives it power.

In Rainbows still represents many of the pros and cons of late-period Radiohead's tendency toward self-indulgence. The lack of thematic linkages, not to mention the fact that some of the songs have been popping up in Radiohead live sets and bootlegs for years, makes *In Rainbows* feel a bit like an odds 'n' sods wrap-up; the ersatz Squarepusher-style beat of album opener "15 Step" certainly suggests a time warp back to Warp Records' mid-nineties heyday that Radiohead alchemized so brilliantly on *Kid A.*

But what incredible sods! While *In Rainbows* works perfectly as an album listening experience, it's also great to go through it and pick your favorites at random; either way, it sounds just as strong. The entry on *OK Computer* in Continuum's 33⅓ book series by Dai Griffith suggests rather inanely that that album was among the first to self-consciously design itself as a CD listening experience; *In Rainbows,* in truth, may be the first Radiohead long-player sequenced with the iPod generation in mind. (It's also the only Radiohead album ever to be sold track by track on iTunes.)

So once again Radiohead raised the bar for followers like Coldplay, right as they were starting to truly nip at their heels. They will inevitably stay one step ahead of the competition, finding new ways to both create and distribute even greater songs: Their next album will probably be even better than *In Rainbows,* but all people will talk about is how it lodges directly into our cerebral cortex Philip K. Dick–style, bypassing even the Internet in Radiohead's quest to dislodge every aspect of the music industry.

This aspect of the Coldplay-Radiohead rivalry is probably what keeps bands like this vital; in the end, comparing them isn't exactly a draw, but the competition makes all of them better. We are lucky to have two bands trying so hard not to suck, and either way, both will remain contenders for Best Band in World. What a blogger named Max from Sydney, Australia, wrote in a message-board forum sums up the whole thing with perfectly apt eloquence and incoherence: "stop arguing about coldplay and radiohead they are both good . . . except radiohead is better."

Van Halen
vs.
Van Hagar

Mick Stingley

It was the best of times, it was the worst of times: Smack-dab in the middle of the roaring eighties and exploding with color, Van Halen was on top of the world. With five sensational records behind them, Van Halen released *1984* to critical acclaim and mainstream radio acceptance; Michael Anthony, Alex Van Halen, Edward Van Halen, and David Lee Roth were household names and fixtures on MTV; and all was right with the world. But as if foreshadowed by the coda of the "Hot for Teacher" music video, in 1985 "Diamond" David Lee Roth left Van Halen. Whether he was fired or whether he had quit simply didn't matter: The party was over, and the world was plunged into total darkness.

Soon after, Wilson Phillips, Vanilla Ice, and Milli Vanilli would top the charts. Boy bands (who didn't play *instruments*) would proliferate, and Sweden would unleash a plague of locusts called Ace of Base. Thug rap would flourish in the suburbs, and every Long Island Lolita with a Hot Topic gift certificate and Auto-Tune would pole dance into America's tabloids. Rock bands would become angry, vocalists would start growling, nobody would play leads, and lead singers wouldn't do anything onstage. MTV would stop showing music videos. Most of the Ramones would die, along with Dean, Sammy, and Frank. There would be famine and disease on every continent. Enron. Tommy Lee rapping. Jimmy Page playing guitar for Puff Daddy. 9/11. *American Idol.* War. Global warming. Paris Hilton. Hurricanes. Ozzy Osbourne would have a TV show. Everything would be *fucked.* But back in the summer of '85, no one could have known the catastrophic and demoralizing domino effect that would take place when Roth left.

The band had etched into history an unassailable catalog of six now-classic recordings: *Van Halen* (or *Van Halen I* if you prefer), *Van Halen II, Women and Children First, Fair Warning, Diver Down,* and *1984.* Eddie Van Halen single-handedly (sometimes quite literally) conjured rapturous sounds, and reinvented the idea of what could be done with a guitar with his sleight of hand. Bassist Michael Anthony and drummer Alex Van Halen gave good rhythm. But it was the boozy, risqué crooning and goofy yelping of a lovable motormouthed madman that made Van Halen so irresistible.

From the very first words uttered on the opening song on *Van Halen I,* "Diamond Dave" set the tone for what Van Halen was all about: "I live my life like there's no tomorrow . . ." It was 1978. Disco ruled the charts, punk had yet to capture the attention of anyone but scenesters and journalists, and California mellow rock had all but emasculated the previous generation. Shaped by the raw, uneasy edges of the Kinks' Ray and Dave Davies and thrown on the wheel forged by the Who, Van Halen brought riffs and harmony and bombast to the occluded world of FM radio, and that song, "Runnin' with the Devil," as well as others including but not limited to "Ice Cream Man," "I'm the One," "Beautiful Girls," "Dance the Night Away," "And the Cradle Will Rock . . . ," "Could This Be Magic?," "Unchained," "Little Guitars," "Big Bad Bill (Is Sweet William Now)," "I'll Wait," and "Hot for Teacher," were a triumph because they gave swagger to apathy, tossed fear aside in favor of frolicking. Teenagers coming of age in an ever-frightening Cold War nuclear-missile buildup suddenly had party music and a shepherd to lead them.

Roth was a bluesy everyman guys could look up to and girls could swoon over. Part California surfer, part Hugh Hefner, he was a comic foil and ringmaster for the ceremonies at hand, a blissed-out Louis Prima on a gakk binge with a shtick ripped straight from the borscht belt and a manner both cocky and self-deprecating. He might not always have been talkin' 'bout love, but that blowsy delivery rendered his womanizing largely innocuous. A Sinatra in spandex. A David Niven cad. The lifeguard who wanted to give mouth-to-mouth to girls who weren't drowning.

By the end of 1985, Van Halen's search for a new lead singer was over, and though lamented by many, Sammy Hagar, a proven arena-rock staple, seemed an excellent choice. The former semiprofessional pugilist had recently captured America's attention with his scathing social commentary on automotive highway speed restrictions and his own inability to conform to them. His favorite color was red. He played guitar. He liked to party. Also, he sang the title songs on the soundtracks to both *Heavy Metal* and *Fast Times at Ridgemont High*. Plus he and Eddie shared the same auto mechanic who worked on their Ferraris or something. So there was *that*.

When the Sammy-led incarnation of Van Halen released *5150* in 1986, the result was pretty spectacular: a number one record with a slew of hit singles. But there was a problem. The record was light on the rock—only "Best of Both Worlds," "Summer Nights," and "Get Up" (essentially a "Hot for Teacher" rewrite) provided the understood Van Halen dynamic—and heavy on the keyboards and ballads. Which, of course, the girls loved. The instrumentation, anyway. As for the lyrics . . .

Where Roth had been nuanced and clever, relying on double entendres and sexual innuendo, Sammy was ham-fisted and cloying and just downright embarrassing. On the opener, "Good Enough" (following his sketchy Big Bopper take on "Chantilly Lace"), Sammy sings, "U.S. Prime Grade A stamped guaranteed / Grease it up, turn on the heat / Throw it down and roll it over once, maybe twice / Then chow down . . . she's good enough / Good enough to HUH!" Gross. Where was the romance, the mystery, in a misogynist representative for the Meat Council of America telling you to "grease it up"? Ick. Later in the song he sings, "I like to open up / C'mon, gimme six on the half shell / Cuz it's 3-6-9 time!" More ick, and not exactly leaving anything to the imagination. Then again, this was the guy who had written "Dick in the Dirt" on his last solo record (not about Watergate).

Sammy Hagar would record three more studio albums with Van Halen. First the largely unimpressive *OU812* (1988), which gave the world "When It's Love" (keyboard-driven ballad), "Feels So Good" (another keyboard-driven ballad), "Finish What Ya Started" (notable for being a ballad rendered *without* keyboards), and "Black and Blue," a midtempo "rocker" that sounded as slickly overproduced as anything Def Leppard had coughed up after the drummer lost his arm.

Then, in a seeming capitulation to all the grumbling, Van Halen reenlisted producer Ted Templeman, responsible for the Roth-era records, and released 1991's *For Unlawful Carnal Knowledge* (or *F.U.C.K.*). Heralded as a "return to rock," it yielded the band four singles—"Top of the World" (a ballad), "Right Now" (a keyboard-driven ballad), "Poundcake," and "Runaround"—but did little for the legacy. "Poundcake" was okay, though too much was made of Eddie's power-drill intro. Here was a guy who had navigated the world of rock like a fretboard Magellan only to have been so entranced by keyboards that he was now reduced to pushing a shopping cart through the aisles of Home

Depot in search of inspiration. It smacked of novelty and desperation and was far from exhilarating. Likewise Sammy's sex/food lyric dementia: "Homegrown and down-home . . . let me get some of that . . . uh-huh, uh-huh huh!" (Will someone please give this guy a show on the Food Network already!) "Runaround" was a little better, but still burdened with Sammy's by-the-numbers date-rape lyrics ("I got her in my sights but just outta reach . . . here we go round, round, round . . ."). "Right Now" was a pretty big hit but mostly thanks to the innovative video. Incredibly, VH would license the song to Pepsi, only driving home the fact that this lineup was *not* the Real Thing.

Live: Right Here, Right Now (1993) seemed little more than a contractual obligation, and two years later the band released its last full-length studio record with Hagar. *Balance* yielded two minor hits, "Can't Stop Lovin' You" and "Don't Tell Me (What Love Can Do)"—ballads, unsurprisingly—but if the guys couldn't see the coffin for the nails, the fans sure as hell could. One last track with Hagar, "Humans Being," would chart thanks to its placement on the *Twister* soundtrack, but that song really, really sucked.

And then there was a sliver of hope. In 1996, a major fuck-up of a press engagement yielded Roth reuniting with Michael, Alex, and Eddie at the MTV Video Music Awards to promote *Best Of: Volume 1,* the first of two hits collections Warner Bros. would issue. It featured two new efforts with Diamond Dave on vocals, but in spite of the appropriate song titles, neither "Can't Get This Stuff No More" nor "Me Wise Magic" had the abracadabra that made the original Van Halen great. Roth was out before the year was done.

1996 to 1999 marked a curious period in the history of Van Halen. With both Roth and Hagar out of the band, VH reached out to Extreme singer Gary Cherone to take the mike. While many would agree that Nuno Bettencourt, the guitarist for Cherone's former band, was Eddie Van Halen's heir apparent, no one could see how Cherone filled the lineage of Roth/Hagar. The resulting *Van Halen III* was a flop, critically and commercially, and Cherone took the blame for it in the public eye. Time has been kind to Mr. Cherone, as everyone seems to agree that however inspired a choice, he was the wrong man for the job. In the end, the best contribution Gary Cherone made to Van Halen was to leave.

By 2004 Hagar was back, and that summer the band hit the road in support of the second hits collection, *The Best of Both Worlds* (which favored Roth compositions). But even the suits at Warner Bros. must have seen the spray paint on the wall. A couple of years later Sammy announced a solo tour and during interviews made it clear that he was no longer in Van Halen (though this was hardly shocking). He would go on to write more songs about food while the Dave rumors once again began to fly.

Finally, after twenty-two years and countless delays, Van Halen reunited with Roth for its 2007 tour. And though Eddie's son Wolfgang ended up replacing Michael Anthony and it was not an official reunion, very few people seemed to care. For the world had stopped spinning horribly out of control. Britney Spears completely lost it at the 2007 VMAs, heralding the death of vapid pop-music manure harvesting. Shortly after, a cure for all STDs was announced. Universal health care was implemented and taxes lowered for all (and eliminated for guys with long hair). Hope and prosperity had been restored. And so long as Van Halen stay together and tour every summer for the rest of eternity, we might stave off the apocalypse after all.

Patsy Cline

vs.

Kitty Wells

Laura Cantrell

There it was, in the list of CD titles I'd brought up
on the Web: *Queens of Country Music: Kitty Wells and Patsy Cline.* And
there on the cover, in that hand-colored look of old photographs, were
the two women's portraits. Both dark haired and fair skinned. Their
rouged lips curled in winsome smiles. Laurel wreaths adorning their
heads as if they were important women of Rome. Well, they were important women of a world capital, all right. "The Athens of the South."
Nashville, Tennessee. Music City, U.S.A. It was only a cut-rate reissue,
but the designation of both singers as "Queens" irked me. Though their
music is now more than forty years old, and one of them is long dead, I

thought to myself as I clicked to another window, "There is only one Queen of Country Music, and it ain't nobody but Kitty Wells."

My father introduced me to the great lady Kitty Wells. I was about five or six, taking a drive with my family through the suburbs of East Nashville. We lived on Saunders Avenue, which was bisected by Ellington Parkway. On the other end of the avenue was the home of Kitty Wells, and that evening he drove us by and pointed it out. I don't remember the house so much, my face reflected in the backseat window as I looked out at a summer-green lawn. What stuck in my memory was my father's tone of voice: elevated, impressed, and imploring us to "look." It seems he slowed the car down to a roll so we could all get an eyeful of a tidy split-level. This was my first impression of Kitty Wells—the owner of a nice house in East Nashville, and my father's voice rising in excitement to note it.

I grew up at a time when Nashville looked a lot like the set of Robert Altman's film of the same name. Country-music artists were not especially rare to see on the street or in a restaurant. Johnny Cash picking up his Sir Pizza, the Judds shopping at Dillard's—almost everyone I knew growing up had one sighting or another. But despite how close we lived to her, the only time I ever saw Kitty Wells was on TV, on the many now-forgotten local country-music programs that, along with Lawrence Welk and *Hee Haw*, filled Saturday afternoons. At that time Loretta Lynn, Tammy Wynette, Dolly Parton, and Barbara Mandrell were the most prominent of country music's female stars. But Kitty—in her black bouffant, strumming her guitar in her stately dresses, her soft speaking voice and modest demeanor belying a lifelong urge to entertain—held me in sway. She seemed like my father's mother or sister, a member of our extended family.

I had no idea then that Wells was a real pioneer of the country-music industry, that the success of her song "It Wasn't God Who Made Honky Tonk Angels" in 1952 would signal the commercial arrival of the "girl singer" in Nashville and usher in a new era of candor in country song. Kitty's hit was controversial for its frankness about marital infidelity, and the sensation only added to its success. She quickly abandoned the more traditional fare she'd previously sung and recorded—songs that now seem quaint, like "I'll Be All Smiles Tonight"—and instead became the voice of the perils of country womanhood in the 1950s, a time of quickly changing social mores, honky-tonks to go wild in, and the rise of divorce. Both restrained and emotionally piercing, her high vibrato was the perfect instrument for this period in the postwar South during which women struggled to gain solid ground. In the late 1950s Decca Records would offer Wells a lifetime recording contract, unheard of for most artists and certainly for female country singers. And in her moment of commercial supremacy, she and husband Johnny Wright considered trademarking the term "Queen of Country Music" for her exclusive use.

I wouldn't begin to learn any of these things until I was eighteen, when I took a summer job as a tour guide at the Country Music Hall of Fame and Museum and had to learn a few facts to tell the crowds. This was my first experience of thinking about country music as anything other than the sights and sounds of my hometown. I was surprised to find myself drawn to the history of country music; it was both interesting and familiar. If you traced the evolution of the music from the Appalachians across the country, you could also trace the trajectory of my family across North and South Carolina to the hills of northwest Tennessee.

The realization that some studied country-music history with a scholarly purpose was exciting, and I took my newfound interest with me as I packed my bags and headed for college in New York City. Once there, I parlayed the few country-music facts I knew into a hosting gig at WKCR, the campus radio station. And I started collecting records and learning as much about country music as I could in between my studies. I took on an attitude that many newcomers to classic country music do: that the music was a pure and unaffected expression of Southern culture until the music business tampered with it in order to sell more records in the late 1950s. This is a simplistic view that incorrectly casts some artists as heroes and others as villains, but it served me at the time. One fact I accepted without question: Kitty Wells was the Queen, and I her liege.

One weekend during my junior year, I trekked with two classmates to see her perform out in the wilds of New Jersey, at the Hungarian American Citizens Club of Woodbridge. The place was more a community center with a function room than a music venue, but it had a stage, a velvet curtain, and colored lights. Though most watched the show from neat rows of folding chairs, I sat cross-legged on the wood floor near several children in the audience. Kitty, in her late sixties, gazed down on us several times, looking fondly as if we were her own grandchildren. Her show was the product of another time and, being in my "pure country music" phase, I swallowed it whole. She performed with Wright, who did songs from his days as the leader of Johnny & Jack and the Tennessee Mountain Boys. Her son, Bobby, who played a country-bumpkin character on the 1960s TV show *McHale's Navy,* did a few songs from his brief recording career. Kitty finally came onstage and Johnny mugged and distracted behind her. She played a guitar that was not plugged in and seemed to strum every song in the key of C. Her performance style was sweetly reserved, a collection of her fans' favorite songs for their aural scrapbooks. I couldn't have been happier as I approached her afterward to comment that she didn't do my favorite song, "I Gave My Wedding Dress Away." She smiled and said, "I'm sorry, we'll have to do it for you next time," in the same reflexive tone that my grandmother would say, "Well, God bless you, honey." The Queen had brushed off one of her subjects with courtly grace.

Looking back, I realize that show, even twenty years ago, was a living artifact of a type of country program that had its heyday in the pre–rock and roll era. The idea that she was the star of the show was a formality; she was just like the rest of us. There was little drama in the performance; it was more a display of one family's musical history via the songs they came to perform. The tone was light, even as those old cheating and heartache songs unfurled one by one: "It Wasn't God Who Made Honky Tonk Angels," "I Don't Claim to Be an Angel," "Making Believe," "A Wedding Ring Ago." Unlike the Decca recordings of these same songs, made in the 1950s and early 1960s, the rueful, haunted undertow of the music was absent. Perhaps almost forty years of playing these family-style shows had worn the emotional content of the songs down to a fine consistency. Perhaps Kitty had enjoyed the performing so much that the irony of a long-married, family-loving, churchgoing woman singing about cheating and going wrong was lost.

Kitty Wells and Patsy Cline shared many things. Obviously they both loved country music. (Patsy even loved yodeling and cowboy garb.) They both recorded for Decca, home of Ernest Tubb, Red Foley, Webb Pierce, and Loretta Lynn. They both made memorable music under the guidance of Owen Bradley, one of Nashville's legendary A&R men, producers, and business leaders. They both played the Opry and crossed the country in cars playing schoolhouse concerts and dances.

Yet for all their similarities, they were effectively of two different generations. Kitty was thirty-three in 1952 when "Honky Tonk Angels" sent her career into high gear. Patsy's first real success came in 1957, when the singer was twenty-five years old. Wells, along with Wright and the Tennessee Mountain Boys, joined the Opry in 1953. Cline moved to Nashville and joined in 1960.

It wasn't just when they got their break, but how—more specifically, through what medium. Kitty and Johnny and the Boys endured the typical dues-paying of country-music artists of the era: using regional radio as a platform to generate an audience for their live shows. They performed on stations in Raleigh, North Carolina, Knoxville, Tennessee, and Decatur, Georgia, before joining Grand Ole Opry rival KWKH's Louisiana Hayride in Shreveport in the late 1940s. Patsy, on the other hand—coming of age as she did in the mid-1950s, as country's post–rock and roll bust left artists and labels scrambling for new formulas for commercial success—got an opportunity that many country entertainers fight for even today: a shot at establishing herself on national television.

The program was *Arthur Godfrey's Talent Scouts,* a weekly talent contest in which the studio audience rated performance by applause—a sort of *American Idol* of the 1950s. Godfrey gave a boost to many up-and-coming performers such as Pat Boone, Tony Bennett, and Steve Lawrence. The format was that a "talent scout" from the TV audience would present an artist for review. In Patsy's case, the "scout" was her mother, Hilda Hensley, and the song presented was one of her first Decca singles, "Walkin' After Midnight."

In just a few minutes of listening to this particular rendition or viewing kinescope performances of the same era, one can see why Cline's star rose so quickly. She had poise, grace, and an incredibly supple voice that conveyed heartache and humor, swung knowingly, and made full use of her time on camera. She was a presence, her stated wish to "be the best singer anyone ever heard" no idle daydream.

For television, the country music Cline performed was smooth: piano, upright bass, cool electric guitar—gently jazzy in the way of late-1950s pop music. The television appearances themselves, though performed live and recorded simply without embellishments like background singers, could have been the template for her early-1960s hits. This country music was understated in its regional flavor and refined by the supremely confident person of Cline herself. When she came to Nashville in 1960, no doubt Bradley planned to use this "countrypolitan" approach to advance her pop-crossover appeal. But what began with the relatively straightforward goal of selling more records resulted in a new sound that would redefine the art of country recording.

It was just this expansion of country music's signature sounds and identity—Cline's hits regularly crossed over to the pop-airplay and sales charts—that gave me pause in my earliest days as a record collector and amateur country-music historian. Some years later

Patsy Cline vs. Kitty Wells

I was grousing about the excesses of the "Nashville Sound" to Tony Maimone of Pere Ubu at Studio G in Brooklyn where I made two records. I thought I was preaching to the choir when this new-wave pioneer from Cleveland took me to task for arguing *against* the value of Patsy Cline's music.

Tony was right. I couldn't say that her art wasn't important, because the opposite was true. Even with my intellectual reservations about the "commercial" aims of her recordings, I had my favorites. I started to think about other things that made Cline interesting besides that big voice. She got the benefit of a new breed of country song, like Willie Nelson's "Crazy" and "I Fall to Pieces" by Hank Cochran and Harlan Howard, updating the classic country-heartbreak formula with touches of dark humor, irony, and a sense of the world beyond country music. Eventually I had to concede that the combination of these songs, Owen Bradley's innovative production, and the voice and presence of Patsy Cline elevated the craft of country record making in the early 1960s. It was a moment when country music was reinventing itself, and one brassy, pantsuit-wearing country sweetheart superceded the demure lady singer previously crowned the Queen of Country Music.

Patsy Cline's death in a plane crash in the cold west Tennessee woods on March 5, 1963 (along with Opry members Hawkshaw Hawkins and Cowboy Copas), instantly deified her. Hardly ten years from the premature death of Hank Williams, country fans felt deeply this too-early end for a beloved artist. As Patsy ascended into hillbilly heaven, a flower gathered for the Master's bouquet, her relatively small body of work became a touchstone. Repackaged and rereleased for more than forty years, Patsy Cline's records have dominated country-music catalog sales, her songs a staple of every jukebox and tastemaker's record collection.

But what of my Queen, Kitty Wells? Truthfully, her records during the "Nashville Sound" era have the same elements—vocal choruses, strings (not banjos, either), luscious reverb, all administered by the sure hand of Bradley—that I'd objected to in Patsy Cline's work. The results are at times overglossy, but often wonderful. I could list dozens of great songs, like "Amigo's Guitar" from *Seasons of My Heart,* "Dark Moon" from the *Kitty's Choice* album, or "The Ways to Love a Man" from *Kitty Wells Bouquet of Hits.* Whether or not they were chart records (and many of them were), they are lovely—Kitty's voice, the songs, and setting ringing true.

Wells persisted through the sixties and early seventies, recording at least two albums a year until her lifetime contract with Decca was canceled by parent company MCA in 1973. I haven't done an official count of every country recording artist, but I'd say that at fifty-seven albums for Decca alone, she's one of the most prolific in country-music history. Sadly, in the digital age most of that music is not officially available, limited to the 150 tracks on iTunes (and many of these are duplicate titles) or the wilds of online auctions and collectors' sites. Though certainly not the only CD available, the cut-rate one I started this journey with, *Queens of Country Music: Kitty Wells and Patsy Cline,* is a good example of the oftentimes thoughtless way Wells's music is presented in the marketplace.

In recent years I had one last great Kitty Wells discovery. Since she released so many albums on Decca, I still don't have them all. So I must look through the *W* bin in used record stores, and was doing just this at the great Jerry's Records in Pittsburgh a few years ago. I stopped in disbelief as I encountered a title I'd never seen before. An acid-green background framed a picture of Kitty sitting in a regal chair, her lap and torso filling the photo. She's wearing a gown made of golden fabric with her dark hair worn down and pulled to one side. She smiles beatifically, as if so happy to assume the role rightly hers—the Queen of Country Music, anyone's country music, not just the old-timers who'd danced to jukeboxes and leaned in close to old radio speakers, but those who'd heard her music on their parents' record players, mamas humming along as dinner is prepared, daddies tuning the car radios to hear their girl on the Opry. The gold-and-red type across the cover proclaimed, *Kitty Wells: Forever Young.*

I flipped the album over. The label was Capricorn, the year 1974. Among the players were members of the Allman Brothers and Marshall Tucker Band, and the songs included covers of Otis Redding and Bob Dylan. The jolt of finding this was so exciting, perhaps only record collectors could know it—finding a title by their favorite artist that they'd not known existed for a meager four dollars in a dusty record bin in gray Pittsburgh. On the album's best moments, particularly the title track, Wells twinkles through the sometimes awkward folk-rock trappings and manages to sing a Dylan chorus as well as any ever have.

Wells has lived and performed long enough to go out of fashion, get old, and fade away. (Kitty and Johnny continued to perform their family show until their retirement in 2000. She has split her retirement between homes in Nashville and Hawaii.) Though *Forever Young* would not be her last album or charting record, it is perhaps the moment that we know the Queen had finally left the castle to her maids and ladies in waiting. Those maids were busy anyway, wearing spandex, flirting, and warbling their way through their own nationally televised variety shows. Eventually they'd prance and caper in videos, tone their midriffs, and pawn off 1970s soft rock as the "new" country of today. The coal miners' daughters and redneck women would find their own sounds and make the music new again. But none would ever carry the crown with such grace as my Queen, Kitty Wells.

Bob Dylan

vs.

Bob Marley

Vivien Goldman

BOBOB

O O O

BOBOB

Now squaring off,
it's Bob vs. Bob.
Bob against Bob.
Bob confronts Bob.
Will one Bob win, the other lose,
having made a . . .

Bob Dylan vs. Bob Marley

B

BOB

BOOBOO

BOB

B

Boo-hoo!

??????????????

Bob M. is wearing red, green & gold.
Bob D. is in the red, white & blue . . . sometimes just red,
sometimes white & blue,
sometimes he's tangled up in blue,
cos of which way the wind blew.

So we have our two opposing players. Both quite short and slight singer-songwriters and guitar pickers (though in BD's case, the chords come in more of a *skanga* chop), both weighing in at some 160 pounds. Born three years, three months, and eighteen days apart, in very different circumstances . . . chilly Hibbing, Minnesota, U.S.A., and sweltering Nine Miles, Saint Anne's, Jamaica. And, of course, both called Robert, an old Norman name which most appropriately means "bright fame." This international synchronicity can be explained: Robert was the most popular name in the anglophone world right before the two Bs were born.

Pitting one Bob against the other is hardly something either of them would go for. Bob Marley sure wouldn't. That I know, because I worked with him for years, first as his PR rep for seven tumultuous months round *Rastaman Vibration* time, and then as his frequent chronicler. In my journalistic capacity, I remember when I tossed him that old "influences" question. He looked at me, very earnest. The kind of artists he admired, he insisted, were those with integrity, whose sincerity and thought touched him, "inna me chest," as he put it, smiting his heart with his hand for emphasis.

But Bob Dylan I only have a sense of, like anyone sentient in the 1960s, when I was a would-be feckless teen who actually spent most of her time studying in the local library. Still, even then I understood Dylan as a tousle-haired, impish agent provocateur. Though spiked with the odd ravishing smile, sullen insouciance was his way of siding with the outsiders, the Rimbauds, James Deans, and Jack Kerouacs.

Bob 'n' Bob are evenly matched on several points. They're both Voices of a Generation, particularly the 1960s–1970s crew called boomers. But BM is also famous for being beloved by babies and toddlers (Gwyneth Paltrow cited BM as her baby's fave, and it's a given in playgrounds), a fan base that I don't think BD's yet penetrated.

Both starting out in the 1960s, each Bob drank deep from that old, cold wellspring of roots music—BD, Appalachian mining songs; Rastaman chants for BM.

Both Bobs reinvented their form. BD was unusual in cutting cohesive, if not actually concept albums as early as *Highway 61 Revisited.* All tracks were strong meat, no filler. (Okay, let's give that one a soy option—both BD and BM have major hippie-crusty cred.) And every Wailers fan knows that with Chris Blackwell's backing, the Wailers cut *Catch a Fire,* which, as the most rounded, resolved album out of Jamaica to that date, was a landmark that transformed reggae from being a strictly singles market.

But
One
Bob
Only
Beats

Bob Dylan vs. Bob Marley

Other

Bob

On

Babies

Marley has thirteen with nine women; Dylan a respectable six, five of whom are with one woman, his ex-wife Sara.

Something else the two Bs share—a faith. Every BD aficionado knows that his birth name is Zimmerman, which, for the uninitiated, is a big blip on the Jewdar. However, BM was a Jew, too. His *sist'ren* and lawyer Diane Jobson once remarked to me that, "You call yourself Jewish. I am a Jew," and Bob was of the same mind.

There is some talk about his father Norval's family having originally been Lebanese Jews; but certainly for most of his bodily existence, BM belonged to the Twelve Tribes of Israel, a Rasta organization. Specifically, Bob was a member of their tribe of Joseph, the Biblical avatar of a visionary, gorgeous, envied rock star who tries to do right, which BM perfectly embodied. Very unusually for a rock star, BM used to tell me he didn't want to talk about himself; he'd much rather reason about Rasta.

Unsurprisingly, BD displays the typical ambivalence of his generation toward his faith—sometimes it's a yarmulke, other times a cowboy hat. But my paternal second cousin once removed, Ellen Simer, née Baker, remembers Bob remarking how much he enjoyed the atmosphere in a Jewish home. I drop this exclusive *haimische* factoid because Ellen constitutes my inside track on the Dylan/Zimmerman persona, having been officially anointed as BD's first girlfriend in various biographies. She even sang with him at local folk clubs before he made it to the Village and Woody Guthrie's hospital ward.

Now living in Switzerland, Ellen reminisces, "I don't know if you could say we were dating—I don't even think I dated my husband! But we spent a lot of intense time together."

So chez Baker, BD got to eat good chicken soup and also devour my uncle's serious collection of Folkways albums—that being the leading blues and roots label of the time.

On another sort of spiritual note, Ellen clearly remembers one prophetic pastime: the way the radio was their inspiration and education. "There was only one record store," Ellen recalls. "Otherwise we all listened to blues and R&B radio programs from the South. There was no FM, but somehow at night that Southern AM radio used to travel. Must have been something about how the night sky beamed the radio waves. Anyway, that's where we used to order our records from."

And that's where we see a lovely arc in BD's development, as he has sagely made an excellent satellite-radio series, *Theme Time Radio Hour.* He gets to share the songs that inspire him, and link them with cute observations in a voice you're happy to hear at your table or fireside.

BM never got to mellow into trading places with the media, but he did publish a newsletter and fund Earl Chin's long-running cable TV reggae show, *Rockers.*

So far, so synchronicitous.

The way Bob and Bob handled their names is intriguing. Shucking the glaring pointer to his Jewishness for that of a "cooler" guru bard, Welsh poet Dylan Thomas, BD wove himself a new persona.

Rather differently, BM reinvented the resonance of the "slave name" he inherited from Norval Marley, the mostly absentee father whose name he kept anyway, even though his family continued to rebuff Bob after Norval's death. (They're sorry now, I bet.)

Both Bobs made their names so large that they could be heavy to bear. Round about the punk era in the late seventies and early eighties, just when BM was hitting yet another peak, BD went through a fallow period of self-doubt. BD had OD'd on the attention, and the Prophet's robe felt more like a straitjacket. With impressive candor, in the first volume of his autobiography, *Chronicles,* BD recalls the time when, albeit briefly, "It had become monotonous. My performances were an act, and the rituals were boring me. . . . It was time to break it off."

Bob Dylan vs. Bob Marley

But BM had no choice—once the musical ball started rolling, it spun faster and faster. He had to be the Messenger, no time off for good behavior. In his uptown Kingston home on Hope Road, BM aimed to make a commune where opposing downtown political dons could reason and stop the savage ghetto wars. He risked his life to make the ideal reality. Though he was warned that assassins were gunning for him, before the shoot-out aimed at him happened in his little kitchen, BM stayed put. And went on to alchemize his brush with death into the glorious *Exodus,* an album of escape and triumph.

Not to have some vulgar pain contest here, but really the worst Dylan faced was the possibility of lousy reviews and disappointing sales. One of the big differences between the two masters' careers is that BD got recognized pretty early on and mentored by the best in the business—legendary Columbia A&R man John Hammond, the courtly musical connoisseur. Round the same time BM's crew had to beat up DJs to get the Wailers' music played on the radio; as ghetto rude boys, they'd get no respect from anyone in the hierarchy of the establishment. Despite his persona as the plaintive, caustic outsider, BD had it comparatively easy, wrestling more with self-doubt than with the industry.

Thus when things became too overwhelming, BD could take time off from being the Prophet. He got to duck out to Woodstock and Jerusalem and be a family man. But BM never stopped working, constantly on the road or in the studio. Evasive, a trickster by trade and inclination, BD was wont to don some sort of costume—whether heavy kohl makeup à la Rudolph Valentino or a scarf flung over half his face. He experimented with movies and guested in underwear ads. But BM spent his life baring his beliefs on disc, getting more naked and direct with his communiqués on every record.

As on "Hurricane," BD can be a straight-up reporter-balladeer, but he also delights in being the Great Poet whose evocative yet ambiguous words can undermine empires. However, BM's creative grail was a quest for clarity. His songs were increasingly pushed toward maximum (sophisticated) simplicity and directness, each word calculated to communicate as clearly as possible with as many as would listen. He always said he didn't have much time to do his job.

BM never had the luxury to write, as BD did on "Things Have Changed," from his most recent album, *Modern Times,* "I used to care but things have changed." Even if BD means it facetiously, or as a role—and who knows, with that master of masks—BM couldn't even put out a suggestion like that in a lyric. He had to keep on caring and making people care. The urgency just grew greater for BM, to the point where he pushed himself to do the final shows on the 1981 American tour knowing that each night might be his last. And one night in Pittsburgh, it was.

Which brings us to one area where BD certainly beats out BM—length of years alive on the planet, in bodily form. Rastas don't believe in death as such, but there's no denying that we don't see BM playing football in the yard much anymore. Except in dreams.

The challenge facing BD, then, has been how to reinvent himself and maintain the creative quality control over such a sustained career. In which he is succeeding handsomely, with films like Martin Scorsese's *No Direction Home* and Todd Haynes's *I'm Not There* exploring his enduring mystique.

BD is blessed that he got to explore the aging of his instrument. Admirers may even love his new old voice more than the cynical panache of the slightly bratty nasal intonation that first enchanted them, down in our collective basement, thinkin' 'bout the government. After all, they've known BD's voice intimately for years, longer than most lovers'. Grown up with BD's changes.

Enjoying listening to *Modern Times,* I found that the scrape of his low vocals was attractive, like a three-day beard when it's just right. With a pang I caught myself wondering how BM's voice might have matured, how the rusty groan he affected on songs like "Running Away" might have come to dominate the ringing vigor that summoned a movement in "Exodus," or the tenderness with which he implored us to "Turn Your Lights Down Low." That would have been good to hear.

The way it worked out, though, BM just got to stay on message, on the job, all the time.

So.

Two bantam-size heavyweights.
When it comes to artistry—
It's a draw! They're both winners!
Really, there's no contest.

When it comes to affecting the whole world, particularly the developing world, with galvanizing, healing songs that gain potency over the years, even after his physical departure, brothers and sisters:

BM is Number One.

And for a love like that, you know BD should be glad. Frankly, it's saved him a whole heap of stress.

THE OUTRO

OK, now let's go get stoned. BD says everybody must do it and BM, he's got to have Kaya. But BM says you shouldn't get stoned just to get high! Oh, well, rules should be flexible, right? Or maybe we'll just think deep thoughts. Right, that'll work.

Elton John
vs.
Billy Joel

The Harvard Lampoon

When the *Lampoon* was asked to decide which rock-star pianist, Elton John or Billy Joel, was better, we were pretty confused. We're a comedy magazine. We don't judge music, we judge humor—like how many butts should be in a joke. So we did the most logical thing any person would do in this situation: judge these two rock greats using that most hallowed of measuring systems, the National Football League scouting combine.

You'll find John and Joel's ratings in seven NFL combine events, each of which was adjusted to acutely measure rock performance. Of course, there were some kinks at first—like New Orleans Saints running back Reggie Bush somehow ranking higher than Mick Jagger—

but eventually we worked everything out. So let's see how these two legends stack up!

PHYSICAL MEASUREMENTS

You can tell a lot about a football player just by looking at him. Bigger arms translate on the field into more forceful pushing; larger shoulders equal larger slamming; bigger hands mean bigger crunching. And where big muscles and limbs are the currency of football, panache and style are the currency of music.

Before we move forward comparing the physical looks of Joel and John, it is important to note that neither of the two is attractive. Both have been seriously losing hair and putting on the pounds for the last ten years. Truth be told, Joel never looked good. Anyone who is willing to dispute this should check out the album cover to *Cold Spring Harbor,* which features Joel with shoulder-length disheveled hair and a chin-length mustache. A fan throwing undergarments onstage at a Joel or John concert is like somebody throwing a friendship bracelet onstage at a Led Zeppelin concert.

With all that said, they both have some charm. Joel, for example, somehow seduced Christie Brinkley, a real-life supermodel, to marry him. And John has a handsome partner, David Furnish, who looks like a cross between Guy Ritchie and Adam Levine of Maroon 5. But we are not going to make our final ruling based on the attractiveness of lovers because money and fame complicate everything, especially love.

When one actually looks at the stage presence of these two artists, though, it becomes clear who the winner of this category is. Joel once accurately described his stage presence as "dopey." He looks like a bumbling man in jeans, a man taken out of your neighborhood deli and implanted awkwardly on the stage. John, on the other hand, outlandish and bawdy, has a kind of odd elegance and energy about him. From his wild handstands on the piano to his oversize glasses to his flamboyant-ostrich Mozart and Statue of Liberty wardrobes, he commands your attention. While his five-thousand-dollar spectacles with "Elton" written on them may be considered over-the-top by some, he somehow is able to pull it all off with a kind of sophisticated grace.

> *John: 1*
> *Joel: 0*

DRUG TEST

Drugs are bad. Don't do them.

Okay, now that we've satisfied the teetotalers and they've already moved on to reading the next rivalry, let's get something straight: Drugs in rock are essential, part of the holy awesome trinity of sex, drugs, and rock and roll. (At least that's *our* holy trinity; we're Episcopalian.) Unlike the NFL, which punishes players who do drugs yet pays them loads of money so that they can buy more drugs, the rock world unequivocally says go for it.

For this drug test, the question isn't simply who did more drugs: It's who did drugs *better.* Here, Sir Elton gets a slight nod. Sure, he got hooked on coke and other drugs in the seventies, but that's par for the course in glam rock, and his recording pace never slackened—unlike Joel's, which abruptly ended in 1993.

Shit first got real for Joel in the early seventies when he attempted suicide by downing furniture polish. Furthermore, 80 percent of his songs take place in or mention bars, and he only bothered checking into rehab in 2002 after all those years of alcohol abuse. And, of course, the guy clearly was on something when he decided to release 2001's *Fantasies & Delusions,* a disc of original classical compositions. By comparison, John pretty much went clean after rehab in 1990, replacing his drug addiction with an even healthier and more rockin' spending habit (cf., his one-million-pound stag party in 2005). However, for massive rock stars, both Joel and John deserve credit for never falling too hard to the dark side. It's not like they were sticking poison up their butts or anything. And for that we salute both of them (but we salute John a little more).

John: 2
Joel: 0

WONDERLIC TEST

In 1937, psychologist Eldon F. Wonderlic created a condensed aptitude test that required little testing time and delivered valid and reliable results. Wonderlic's aptitude test revolutionized the game of football, giving NFL coaches and fans the opportunity to see through players' helmets, pads, bruises, cuts, hair, cartilage, fat, bone, and muscle straight through to the brain, more specifically the synapses of the brain.

The challenge of comparing John and Joel on a cognitive level is especially difficult because we do not have nor do we know how to purchase a Wonderlic test. However, we have seen a lot of players' scores, most notably that of Daunte Culpepper, the *Lampoon*'s favorite football player. (When we go out to dinner with Daunte, he always offers to take us out for dessert afterward.) So we have a pretty good sense of what the Wonderlic test is all about—Daunte creativity and Culpepper memory.

An amateur observer might throw him or herself behind John, pointing to his variety of musical creations. From pop ("Your Song") to disco ("Victim of Love") to glam rock ("Bennie and the Jets") to rock and roll ("The Bitch Is Back") to croc and roll ("Crocodile Rock") to the straight-up whimsical (*The Lion King*), John's diversity of styles and sounds make Joel look like a one-trick, "Piano Man" pony.

Not to be overlooked, however, is the fact that Joel can play a whole lot of instruments: acoustic guitar, ARP, Baldwin piano, banjo, clavichord, Clavinet, electric grand piano, Farfisa, Fender Rhodes, Fender Stratocaster, Fender Telecaster, Gibson Explorer, Gibson ES-335, Gibson Firebird, Gibson Flying V, Gibson Les Paul, Gibson L-5, Gibson SG, Gretsch 6120, Hammond organ, harmonica, harpsichord, mandolin, melodica, Mellotron, Moog synthesizer, Pianet, Rickenbacker, RMI 368 Electra-Piano and Harpsichord, Wurlitzer electric piano. We at the *Lampoon* don't even know what an ARP is, unless, of course, we just misspelled "harp."

In addition to his ability to play nearly any instrument one can find in a music store, Joel also writes his own lyrics. John does not; Sir Elton is busy reapplying glittery feathers to his favorite Donald Duck costume while Bernie Taupin is very fashionably chained to a desk in the basement of John's Old Windsor mansion, scribbling away.

John: 2
Joel: 1
Culpepper: Infinite points

TWENTY-YARD SHUTTLE RUN

The combine shuttle run is not your typical presidential-fitness version. Instead of having to frantically run in front of all the pretty girls in your middle school, you have to frantically run in front of prospective coaches. Instead of wearing jeans because you accidentally left your shorts at home that day, you must wear uncomfortable, aerodynamically designed uniforms. The twenty-yard shuttle is a grueling event; only the toughest players do well.

When it comes to comparing the toughness of Joel and John, the winner is obvious. Where John is a diva, Joel is as macho as a piano-playing singer can be. Where John would be played by Philip Seymour Hoffman, Joel would be played by Bruce Willis. Where John attended the Royal Academy of Music in London, Joel went to public Hicksville "Hard Knocksville" High School, where he was picked on so much for his love of music that he learned to box in order to defend himself. He won twenty-two bouts on the Golden Gloves circuit, punching twenty-two self-conscious, blossoming musicians in the face. Elton John does not know how to box.

In that same vein, Joel, in 1982, was sidelined—hit by a car while riding his motorcycle through Huntington, New York. There are a couple highlights from this story that one should keep in mind: First, he was riding a motorcycle. Second, upon being hit so hard that he flew over the windshield and landed on his back on the pavement, he got up with his broken hand and wrist and checked to make an inventory of his belongings. Straight out of an action movie, he was then airlifted by helicopter to a hospital.

Likewise, while John simply whines, Joel is not afraid to knock shit over. In one concert in Russia, the lighting crew had too much light on the audience. He yelled three times in the middle of the song, "Stop lighting the audience, for God's sake." When nothing changed, he threw his keyboard onto the ground. When later asked about it, he said, "That's what rock and roll is all about." This is a real story. We have no jokes to write.

John: 2
Joel: 2

BROAD JUMP

Broad jump is an antiquated track event that the NFL still uses in the combine because it's really fun to do. Because our combine-rock metaphor is falling apart, we're just going to say we're using this event to measure career longevity.

There's absolutely no contest here. Other than his 2007 iTunes single "All My Life," Joel's written zilch since '93, while Elton continuously gets his groove back despite nearing both retirement age and three hundred pounds. He's remained hip enough to share the stage with and melt the hearts of alleged homophobes like Axl Rose and actual homophobes like Eminem. Very recently he collaborated on albums by the Scissor Sisters and Timbaland. And from Joel? "All My Life" is five minutes of faux-Sinatra theatrics featuring a video where he's dressed like the villain from *Road to Perdition*. Sure, he's rehashed a lot of his peak material into some lucrative tours and even a Broadway musical, but Elton's simply too powerful, penning the critically acclaimed *Aida* and pushing new material with hip videos starring Justin Timberlake and Robert Downey Jr. To Joel's credit, though, he has married more hot twenty-three-year-old food writers than John has.

John: 3
Joel: 2

THE BENCH PRESS

The bench press is the combine's best measurement for sheer strength. Joel beats John by repping 185 pounds once to John's zero.

John: 3
Joel: 3

FORTY-YARD DASH

We were having lunch with one NFL scout (who's chosen to remain anonymous), and he told us that the forty-yard dash is the most important test at the NFL combine. Then we had dinner with Indianapolis Colts quarterback Peyton Manning, and he said the same thing. This led us to think the same is true in rock. Chart-topping hits are like running a 4.2, and shitty songs are like tripping and falling on your face.

John has racked up nine number one hits and fifty-nine top forty singles. He even won an Academy Award for "Can You Feel the Love Tonight." Joel's no slouch, either, with three number ones. Forget the sales figures, though—the easiest way to measure this is by tallying how many times we've seen a man drunkenly cry while singing each performer's songs. Joel's got "Piano Man" (obviously), "Just the Way You Are," and "Uptown Girl" (though the guy claimed he just "had something in his eye"). Elton, however, has too many tearjerkers to count. "Goodbye Yellow Brick Road," "Daniel," "Tiny Dancer," "Can You Feel the Love Tonight," "Your Song"—there are just too many to list, though somehow Wikipedia does list all of them. You should probably just stop reading this and go there.

Elton John vs. Billy Joel

Bottom line is, Sir Elton's a bona fide hit machine, so much so that he even somehow recorded a sack in a 1975 NFL game, thus further complicating our combine-rock metaphor.

John: 4
Joel: 3
Winner: Elton John

The Four Tops
vs.
The Temptations

Sean Howe

Friday, March 25, 1983: At the Pasadena Civic Center, *Motown 25: Yesterday, Today, Forever* is being taped for a May broadcast. Smokey Robinson's voice—a sound that's familiar but for its degree of shrill excitement—echoes within the auditorium, washing over the studio audience of three thousand: *"The Four Tops! And the tempting Temptations! Here to battle it out, just like in the old days!"*

The Tops take the stage in gold lamé; the Tempts are in black tuxedos. The contest consists mostly of the groups alternating choruses of their biggest hits, in leaden arrangements that incorporate the pit orchestra's best idea of contemporary jangle-funk. "Reach Out (I'll Be There)" cedes to "Get Ready," "It's the Same Old Song" to "Ain't Too

Proud to Beg." An awkward faux cockiness emerges, with exaggerated arm folding, eye rolling, and back turning yielding to it's-all-good smiles. The Temptations trot out their famous dance steps, while the Tops make do with a lot of clapping and snapping. "Baby, I Need Your Loving," "My Girl," and "I Can't Get Next to You" follow, before the Tops really heat things up with . . . "I Can't Help Myself (Sugar Pie, Honey Bunch)"? What kind of fool brings a song about a honey bunch to a knife fight? The Temptations respond with "I Know I'm Losing You," and the house band—not the legendary Funk Brothers, though James Jamerson watches from the cheap seats—signs off, everybody hugs, and the camera crane swoops over the audience.

Like the lyric says, it's the same old song, but with a different meaning now: It's all showbiz. The songs that make up this murderer's row of classics have been clinically excerpted, delivered in key, and forgotten. The performers leave the stage, never having inhabited the songs tonight in the way they did decades ago (how can you inhabit a medley?), and gather across the street for a party at the Plaza Pasadena. When the special finally airs, the sing-off will be fondly received and the two groups will tour together for the next few years, re-creating the playful tussle for the oldies circuit. But the television audience will pay most of its attention to former child star Michael Jackson and his funny new backsliding dance step.

Among that audience is a sophomore at Buffalo State named Bill, who catches the NBC broadcast in the study lounge of his dormitory building. It's a week before finals start, and though anxiety looms, it's eclipsed by the acute infatuation he's experiencing with Elizabeth, a redhead in his art-history class. They've had four dates. It's too bad that Liz missed that show. She loves "Billie Jean."

Inspired by the Motown special, Bill goes to a record store the following day and spends $10.19 on a double-length cassette compilation entitled *Motown: 25 #1 Hits in 25 Years*. He'll listen to it several times in the next few weeks, and then frequently all summer, most memorably on an August trip to visit Liz in New Hampshire. She teases him for preferring the sentimental journeys of Motown to the *Flashdance* sound-track and Men at Work's *Cargo,* but they sing along to "My Girl" and "Endless Love" and "I Heard It Through the Grapevine" while they drive around. The visit lasts four days. Before he leaves, she breaks up with him, as gently as possible. When he listens to the tape on the drive home, he gets the feeling that he's being taunted by the sweet nothings of Smokey Robinson and the Temptations and the Four Tops and Mary Wells and Marvin Gaye and the Commodores. (Rick James, on the other hand, is just doing his own thing.)

In September, Bill and Liz go (as friends, just friends) to see *The Big Chill,* and he experiences a quiet satisfaction in seeing these songs pre-sented as sacred. He buys a stack of used Four Tops and Temptations records, but after a few months Van Halen's *1984* rules his world, and the Motown records stay in their sleeves.

Bill graduates and moves to the Boston area. He works as an adver-tising manager for a newspaper. When he's twenty-nine, he sees Liz at a party of a mutual friend. He asks her out to dinner, and within a year they're engaged. Their wedding song is "The Way You Do the Things You Do" by the Temptations.

In October 1963, the month Bill is born, Smokey Robinson is asked to write a song for the Temptations; he comes up with "The Way You Do the Things You Do." At the time, the group consists of Otis Williams, Paul Williams, Melvin Franklin, Eddie Kendricks, and Al Bryant, but before the group gets around to recording it, baritone Bryant is gone. Despite the last-minute lineup change, the harmonies on the record weave seamlessly. The parade of similes is clever, Marv Tarplin's guitar figures shimmer, and the rhythm demands that fingers snap along. The Temptations have their first hit.

Also in October 1963, the Four Tops—childhood friends Levi Stubbs, Duke Fakir, Obie Benson, and Lawrence Payton—appear as backup singers on the Supremes' "When the Lovelight Starts Shining Through His Eyes." It's the first Supremes 45 from the songwriting-producing team of Brian Holland, Lamont Dozier, and Eddie Holland. The Tops had been playing gigs and recording (mostly Drifters-style R&B) for half a decade before signing to Motown for four hundred dollars. They've just finished recording *Breaking Through,* an album of upbeat vocal jazz, for the label.

"When the Lovelight Starts Shining Through His Eyes" becomes the Supremes' first hit. The Tops, however, remain backup singers; *Breaking Through* is shelved.

Seven months later, after midnight on May 7, 1964, at a club in Detroit, Brian Holland approaches the members of the Four Tops and tells them he has a song for them. They are in the studio by three A.M., laying down the vocals for "Baby I Need Your Loving." (The instrumental track had been recorded a few weeks prior, the first of many times Holland-Dozier-Holland would work with the Detroit Symphony Orchestra. It was so tightly packed in the studio that Motown founder Berry Gordy had a wall torn down afterward.) The record is as sweeping as anything that's been attempted by Phil Spector. In fact, after Cynthia Weil and Barry Mann hear it, they hole up in the Chateau Marmont and write "You've Lost That Lovin' Feelin' " for Spector and the Righteous Brothers, which will go on to become the best-selling song of 1965.

David Ruffin, the singer who replaced Al Bryant in the Temptations, eventually gets a chance to sing lead on another Smokey Robinson song, this one called "My Girl." His voice, at once fluid and sandpaper rough, transforms the song from wistful to exuberant after the bridge ("I don't need no money, fortune or fame"). You listen to the song now and you realize you know every note—not just the guitar intro and all the words. You can sing along with the violin arrangement and the ad-libs on the fadeout. The Temptations can handle the dance-party stuff, but here they tug at your heartstrings.

"My Girl," the Temptations' first number one song, appears on *The*

Temptations Sing Smokey in April 1965. Also that month, the Four Tops release *their* first number one song, "I Can't Help Myself (Sugar Pie, Honey Bunch)." And Bill turns eighteen months old.

It's "I Can't Help Myself" that plays quietly just after the lunch rush at Charter's, a family restaurant overlooking the lake. The place is nearly empty, so Andrea (six) and Phillip (four) run for a seat by the picture windows. They sit down and look out at the choppy waters and dark skies before the kids realize that the paper menus have word hunts and pictogram puzzles. The sounds of tables being cleared are louder than the sounds of Levi Stubbs singing, "Sugar pie, honey bunch, you know that I love you." Lost in his thoughts, Bill realizes that Andrea is saying, "Daddy!" He looks down to see Phillip knocking over water and dropping parts of his sandwich on the ground and throwing curly fries. The waitress glares from a distance. Bill starts to pick up the mess, wishes Liz were here, and finally notices the song on the oldies channel because Andrea starts singing it to Phillip. This is a surprise. I guess kids just absorb some songs from the air, he thinks. Or else it's in a commercial for detergent, or in that movie where Robin Williams dresses up as a nanny. The kids love that one. Bill watches them singing. Andrea knows all the words. "In and out my life, you come and you go, leaving just your picture behind, and I've kissed it a thousand times." Bill had never realized until now, a couple hours after he and Liz explained the separation to the kids, that it was a sad song.

At Motown the Supremes famously got first dibs on the best songs, with the Marvelettes and the Vandellas vying for scraps. But this kind of competition wasn't a problem between the Four Tops and the Temptations. At their peaks, they each had their compositional patrons: Holland-Dozier-Holland and Norman Whitfield, respectively. The Four Tops were stewarded by HDH until 1967, when the songwriting team, in a royalties dispute with Gordy, left Motown. It was a tough split, since HDH had found Levi Stubbs to be the perfect voice for their most personal songs. Eddie Holland would lock the door, close his curtains, unplug the phone, and spend weeks on the lyrics. Lamont Dozier would run through the chords with the band. Levi would carefully handwrite all the lyrics as they were taught to him. Brian would turn off all the lights and kick everyone out of the studio when recording the Tops' vocals.

Despite Gordy's mandate that all Motown songs be written in the present tense ("Make it sound like it's happening now!"), there's a past loss that haunts most of the great Four Tops narratives; the present, accordingly, is a sham. The eponymous first album is entirely about this despair, and it all spins from "Baby I Need Your Loving." When Stubbs starts to get agitated ("empty nights . . . echo your name!"), everything feels like it's about to break open. But he quiets down again for the last verse, and reveals—

> *When you see me smiling,*
> *You'll know that things have gotten worse*
> *Any smile you might see*
> *Has all been rehearsed*

—and you realize that at some point drummer Benny Benjamin's insistent beat has invisibly turned from a steady calm to a nervous pulse, and Earl Van Dyke starts hitting his piano harder, and the Tops start to overtake Stubbs:

> *And I need you baby and I want you baby and I love you*
> *baby*

At least on "Baby I Need Your Loving," Stubbs feels "half alive"; on the very next song, "Without the One You Love," the situation's deteriorated: "I'm not living . . . I only exist." They've found a theme: The album also includes "Where Did You Go," "Ask the Lonely," "Sad Souvenirs," and "Love Has Gone."

In a few years it would get even sadder. Nothing else on Motown—or all of pop radio—would approach the effusive candor of their 1966–67 songs: the possessive paranoia of "Bernadette"; the disbelieving anger of "7 Rooms of Gloom" and "Standing in the Shadows of Love"; the harrowed anxiety of "Shake Me, Wake Me" and "You Keep Running Away." At first it's surprising that the same men wrote "Baby Love," "You Can't Hurry Love," and "I Hear a Symphony." But that's less a difference in lyrical content than in the singing of Stubbs and Miss Diana Ross.

The greatest Supremes songs create emotional truth by capitalizing on the way that Ross obediently serves the melody and the momentum of the song. It's perfect casting for songs about an individual still in denial, shocked and unable to fully register heartbreak—on "My World Is Empty Without You," her benumbed voice, the aural equivalent of a hundred-yard stare, mixes with baritone saxophones and a relentless beat to stir strong feelings in the listener. (One of several Four Tops songs she was given to cover on *The Supremes Sing Holland-Dozier-Holland* was "I'll Turn to Stone." But she couldn't convincingly pull off the metastasis—her voice was already calcified and cold. So they had to write a song that was, essentially, "I *Have* Turned to Stone." Of course, the lonely masterpiece "Love Is Here and Now You're Gone" falters only when Ross attempts to simulate a sob after the first chorus.)

When Levi Stubbs sings, on the other hand, he sounds like he's fighting everything around him.

Bill sits in his empty house with a dwindling bottle of scotch and no plans. Liz has the kids for the weekend. This will be the first extended time they'll be spending with Jim, Bill thinks. Unless he came around before when Bill wasn't around, and Liz introduced him to them as a coworker . . . better not to dwell on that. Bill starts thinking instead about how she always used to get the Motown singers confused.

He'd say that the Miracles sang in falsetto about what they would do to make a girl happy, and the Temptations sang in falsetto about how a girl made them feel. And the Four Tops were the ones where the guy always sounded like he was in a bar shouting over the music. And then Bill would play them back-to-back for her and quiz her and she'd get bored pretty quickly.

Tonight he puts on "Ain't Too Proud to Beg" and starts singing along, and before long is thinking about the ridiculousness of the idea that begging Liz would do any good at all. As if life was anything like a Motown song. And at the part where Ruffin sings about a crying man being "half a man, with no sense of pride," Bill can't sing along anymore. Ruffin is hitting way too many high notes to be nearly as upset as he claims, and Bill begins to get furious at the record. It feels like some kind of cruel facsimile of pain. The way the other four Temptations buoy Ruffin at every turn, he's not alone, not by a long shot; his buddies have his back, and he's still dancing. Bill thinks that maybe *The Big Chill* had it right, and that "Ain't Too Proud to Beg" is simply a way to make doing the dishes more enjoyable. He tries not to think about how he is now older than the Kevin Kline and Glenn Close characters.

As soon as side one of *Gettin' Ready* ends (with "Too Busy Thinking About My Baby"—someone's idea of a joke?), he takes off the record, washes down some Tylenol PM, and stretches out diagonally in the big, empty bed.

More than anything, the Temptations could make exuberance contagious. True, many of their early songs—including "The Way You Do the Things You Do," "It's Growing," "You've Got to Earn It," and "Get Ready"—retain the stamp of their writer, Smokey Robinson; Eddie Kendricks's falsetto even sounds like Smokey's. But songs cut by the Miracles always had a hazy melancholy that the Temptations' voices (and hand claps, and, in person, the seven-step "Temptation

Walk" routine) cut right through. And if "Girl (Why You Wanna Make Me Blue)" and "I'll Be in Trouble" seem ridiculously ebullient given their lyrics, well, ridiculous ebullience isn't something to sneeze at. The world needs to feel goofy sometimes.

The exuberance could also serve as an ironic twist—the joyful call-and-responses of "Since I Lost My Baby" underscore Ruffin's clouds-on-a-sunny-day plaint. In a sad-sack inversion of "My Girl" (the coda even quotes the earlier song's string arrangement), Ruffin leaps into the hopeful bridge section ("Inclined to find my baby / Been looking everywhere") and steers the course back to misery ("Determination is fading fast / Inspiration is a thing of the past").

And then there's the greater irony that hangs over so many of the songs: the unhappiness behind the scenes. The subject of the majestic, generous "You're My Everything" was the wife of lyricist Roger Penzabene. She repaid his generosity by cheating on him. He then wrote "I Wish It Would Rain" and, completing a tragic trilogy, "I Could Never Love Another (After Loving You)," before putting a gun to his head on the last day of 1967. David Ruffin, meanwhile, began riding in a separate limo to concerts, and was finally voted out of the group in 1968. "He was never comfortable in the Temptations," said his brother, Jimmy. "In his heart of hearts, he was a [solo] artist." But his solo career was only sporadically successful, as were attempts at sobriety. He died of an overdose in a Detroit crack house in 1991. Eddie Kendricks left acrimoniously in 1971, after repeated clashes with Otis Williams. Paul Williams, battling depression, alcoholism, and sickle-cell disease (he kept an oxygen tank backstage), also left the group in 1971; a year later he sat in a parked car a few blocks from the Hitsville studios, wearing only swimming trunks, and shot himself in the head.

Liz is at her parents' house. Speaking with them, she's found herself in the peculiar position of alternately defending herself and defending Bill. She calls home every night to talk to the kids and says she'll be home soon. On Tuesday Liz starts crying on the phone and tries to regain her composure before Andrea hands the phone to Phillip. But Phillip needs to go to the bathroom and starts tugging on Andrea's arm, telling her to hand over the phone because he needs to pee and wants to talk first.

> *Soon we'll be married, and raise a family*
> *In a cozy little home out in the country*
> *With two children, maybe three*
> *I tell you, I can visualize it all*
> *This couldn't be a dream, for too real it all seems*

The last song that Paul Williams and Eddie Kendricks sang on before leaving the Temptations, "Just My Imagination (Running Away With Me)," is without a doubt the group's greatest post-Ruffin recording. Kendrick's sad falsetto floats over swirling strings, horns, and the group's dreamlike legato backing.

> *Oh how I hate to wake up, 'cause that's when we have to*
> *break up*
> > —"Is There Anything That I Can Do"
> > (The Four Tops, 1965)

After the success of the Four Tops–Temptations team-up on the *Motown 25* special, the groups record "Battle Song (I'm the One)"; it appears on the Temptations' 1983 *Back to Basics* LP. Really, nobody—not the Tops, not the Tempts, not the listener—wins. Sometimes a whole is less than the sum of its parts.

> *If I've ever, ever dreamed before, somebody tell me I'm*
> *dreaming now*
> > —"Shake Me, Wake Me (When It's Over)"
> > (The Four Tops, 1966)

• • •

After Bill drops the kids off with Liz, he comes home and tries to continue with the Tempts. But he still can't shake the idea that Ruffin is just too in control to be sharing any kind of grief. "I've been unfaithful, darling, I've caused you misery," he sings jauntily on "All on Me," with all the self-reflection of a sailor on leave. Bill finds his old cassette of *Motown: 25 #1 Hits in 25 Years,* gets in his car, and listens to "I Can't Help Myself" over and over. But every time he rewinds the tape, he hears the end of "My Girl," and David Ruffin's triumphal fade-out mocks Bill just like it did in the summer of 1983: "I've e-ven got . . . the month . . . of May . . . with my girl . . ."

Trent Reznor

vs.

Marilyn Manson

Melissa Maerz

There are two kinds of people in this world: those who want to raise children and those who'd rather eat them. Those who love animals and those who'd prefer to sodomize them. Those who treat others with respect and those who may or may not have surgically removed a rib in order to give themselves blow jobs more easily. There is the brotherhood of man and there is Marilyn Manson. At some point Trent Reznor had to ask himself, *Whose side am I on?*

Granted, the difference between Manson and Reznor wasn't always so stark. Like all great archenemies—Superman and Lex Luthor, God and the devil, Paris and Nicole—they started out on the same team. In 1992, when Reznor signed a then-unknown Manson to his Nothing label, they were just two miscreants brought together by a shared fascination with Charles Manson and a shared distaste for human decency. Reznor coproduced Manson's debut, 1994's *Portrait of an American Family,* which borrowed some lyrics from a song Charles Manson wrote. The two men toured together—and, by Manson's account, shared groupies. Manson appeared, sans makeup, in the video for an alternate version of Nine Inch Nails' "Gave Up," which was recorded inside the house where Charles Manson murdered Sharon Tate. Both skinny, long nosed, black haired, vomiting their inner demons into separate microphones, the two artists even looked alike. By the time Manson released his second album, they were industrial goth's golden couple: Mr. and Mrs. God of Fuck.

What caused their friendship to degenerate between 1997 and 2000—the year they officially made up during a Nine Inch Nails show at Madison Square Garden—is still up for debate. Depending on whom you ask, the falling-out was either caused by (a) Manson's indifference to the death of Reznor's grandmother; (b) deliberations about who would write the soundtrack for David Lynch's *Lost Highway;* (c) Manson overlooking Reznor as the producer of his third album, *Mechanical Animals;* or (d) the day Manson videotaped himself doing drugs all day while wearing nothing but a blonde wig, a Burger King crown, and a paper-towel tube around his penis. ("I think [Trent] felt unable to deal with it, and it crumbled our relationship," Manson told *Spin* magazine.) Suffice to say, from that point on industrial goth has been a house divided. Have mothers disowned their daughters? Have men battled their brothers? Okay, maybe not. But teenagers who dyed their hair jet-black definitely stopped speaking to teenagers who dyed their hair blue-black, all because they couldn't agree, and eventually everyone has to choose sides. Reznor or Manson? Chicken or steak? Drunk or high? Masochism or sadism? With nuts or without? Your answer will determine your innermost feelings about Satanism, second-person pronouns, and naked photos of small children—but we'll get to that later.

First, let's start where most good rivalries begin, with an origin story. As any comic-book fan knows, all good antiheroes have a reason why they crossed over to the bad side—a freak accident, an experiment gone wrong, some grave injustice that sets them on a path to world domination. For Marilyn Manson, that journey began in his grandfather's cellar. As the story goes, a young Manson—then known by his birth name, Brian Warner—creeps into the old man's basement, finding his secret stash of bestiality porn, a rusted can of feminine deodorant spray, and dildos caked in "a hardened orange slime." Oh, and watches the old man masturbate. As Manson so generously offers in his autobiography, *The Long Hard Road out of Hell*, "His yellow, wrinkled penis [was] like the insides of a squashed cockroach." Shamed by that experience and other early acts of childhood deviance, Manson later finds himself believing that he's damned. Listening to his very religious elementary school teacher describe Judgment Day, he pictures his own future. "I was constantly haunted by dreams and worries about what would happen if I found out who the Antichrist was," he says in *The Long Hard Road*. "Would I risk my life to save everyone else? What if I already had the mark of the beast somewhere on me where I couldn't see it? What if the Antichrist was me?"

Has there ever been a better existential question to sum up rock and roll? From Robert Johnson to the Rolling Stones to Black Sabbath, sympathy for the devil has become the best symbol for rebellion. But Manson took that trope even further. From the very beginning, he didn't believe Satan was just some goat-hoofed guy who eats kittens or rocks out to death-metal albums. He knew the true essence of Satanism: the belief that God does not inspire you toward good or evil, because you are ultimately responsible for your own choices. You are your own Jesus or Lucifer. "I believe I am God," Manson says in his autobiography, and anyone who doesn't think the same of themselves is among the faithful. Why do fans hold up lighters at rock shows? Because Jesus said, "I am the light of the world," and kicked off the tradition of lighting candles at places of worship. When you hold up your lighter, you're winking at the idea that God is among us, that he is both human and divine, and that he may be persuaded to play "Baboon Rape Party" during the encore. True Satanists don't worship the devil. They worship themselves.

Reznor, well . . . he's not really one for that world-domination stuff. He's more of your run-of-the-mill industrial-S&M everyman. This is, after all, the guy who once inspired *People* magazine to speculate: "Is Nine Inch Nails' lead singer fury incarnate or just a hardworking guy with a gig?" In that 1995 article, Reznor's grandfather, who raised him, reveals that Reznor was a Boy Scout; his former piano teacher admits, "[He] always reminded me of Harry Connick Jr."; the high school band director who taught Reznor tenor sax in Mercer, Pennsylvania, recalls, "I considered him to be very upbeat and friendly. I think all that 'dark avenging angel' stuff is marketing." In a 1997 interview with *Spin,* Reznor himself does little to negate that idyllic portrait of his upbringing: "I'm boring . . . and I kind of made this pact with myself that I would just be honest," he says. "I am thirty-one. I was born in Pennsylvania. I wasn't a male prostitute. I'm not gay. My tongue is my own. It's not like a Marilyn Manson situation."

Now, if Trent Reznor were an indie-rock singer, or a country singer, you might regard this authenticity as a form of strength: *He puts his pants on one heterosexual leg at a time. Dude's rockin' the realness!* But think back to Nine Inch Nails videos. There's "Happiness in Slavery," where Reznor watches from inside a cage while Bob Flanagan straps himself into a machine that pleasures, tortures, and kills him. And "Closer," where Reznor appears blindfolded, chained, and apparently unable to watch the bald, naked woman who's walking around the joint. And "Pinion," where a toilet flushes directly into somebody's mouth. Now, if Reznor's upbringing was relatively trauma-free, why would a nice suburban Boy Scout give his music those connotations? Why should he have issues? You've gotta ask yourself, *Would Harry Connick Jr. do that?*

If there's one thing that destroys Reznor's whole theater-of-pain drama, it's his deep-seated normalcy. Every time he tries to reinforce the idea that rock should be deviant, he ends up proving that he's just an average guy. Case in point, in a 1997 interview with *Rolling Stone,* Reznor explained why he thinks a certain shock value is important in rock: "Being a rock and roll star has become as legitimate a career option as being an astronaut or a policeman or a fireman. . . . Death to Hootie and the Blowfish, you know what I'm saying?" But what could be less shocking than hating Hootie in 1997? Why not at least endorse rubbing his genitals against a Gila monster or something?

In the same interview, Reznor returns to his favorite theme—raging against rock's quest for authenticity: "[The music scene] doesn't need more Pearl Jam rip-off bands. It doesn't need the politically correct R.E.M. telling us 'We don't eat red meat.' . . . We need someone who wants to say, 'You know what? I jack off ten times a night and I want to fuck groupies.' It's not considered safe to say that now, but rock shouldn't be safe." But nothing could have made Reznor sound less threatening. How many men in America jack off ten times a night and want to fuck groupies? Refusing the deliciousness of red meat is way more messed up. More important, why give us that message in such straight terms? Marilyn Manson might agree with what Reznor says, but the difference is, he doesn't waste much time *talking* about danger. He's more likely to give a demonstration.

One of the reasons it's hard to side with Reznor is that no one can take him as seriously as he takes himself. And, in fairness, he's probably earned that right. He's a much better musician than Manson. Having written, coproduced, and played every instrument on *Pretty Hate Machine,* he's responsible for creating what was probably the first industrial album to sell a million copies. And the car-crash pulse of his best songs is so gripping that its message has a ridiculously diverse crossover appeal. You haven't really grasped Reznor's range until you've seen dozens of sorority girls sing "I want to fuck you like an animal" at a Nine Inch Nails show. Problem is, Reznor's lyrics never feel as weighty because he so often tells the same story. The typical Nine Inch Nails song goes as follows: "You" screws Trent over, Trent rages against "You," both parties wrestle for control, hurting ensues. Even Nine Inch Nails' concept album, 2007's *Year Zero,* reads like a first-person diary entry. Though the record imagines how current U.S. government policies will affect the world in the future, lines like "The longing that you feel / You know none of this is real," sound like Trent's breaking up with his girlfriend, only this time his girlfriend's George Bush.

Reznor seems to view his entire career as a contest with the Yous of the world. "I beat you, fucking Soundgarden!" Reznor said when *The Downward Spiral* outsold *Superunknown.* "Fred Durst can surf a piece of plywood up my ass," he famously proclaimed after falling out with the Limp Bizkit front man. Billy Corgan, Courtney Love, Tori Amos—few popular artists have escaped Reznor's wrath, yet his rage often sounds like martyrdom. "I don't have many friends," he told *Rolling Stone* in 1999. Which might be why every "fuck you" on his records sounds like a plea to be loved. "My best friends turned on me," he explained in another interview with *Rolling Stone* later the same year. When asked who those friends include, he offers, "Their name has two words in it, and they start with the letter M."

Paradoxically—or perhaps predictably—Manson shares a key quality with Pearl Jam, R.E.M., Hootie, and other musicians whose authenticity Reznor rages against: All of them want to erase the difference between their onstage personas and the lives they lead offstage. True, Manson's not exactly known for being down-to-earth—this is, after all, a guy who claims he once smoked a human bone. And, yes, the artist born Brian Warner has repeatedly insisted that he created his alter ego Marilyn Manson as a caricature of a rock star. But now that caricature has become indistinguishable from Manson's actual personality. You get the sense that he feels a moral responsibility to live out the crazy mythology he cooks up for his legend. That's never been more clear than during the making of *Mechanical Animals.* When, for that 1998 album, Manson reimagined himself as an androgynous, cocaine-addicted space alien named Omega, he claimed the character was not Marilyn Manson but rather "a satirical picture of a rebellious rock star." After the album was released, Manson's girlfriend Rose McGowan left him—allegedly because of his cocaine addiction. Maybe also because he wouldn't stop dressing like an alien clown in public. Who knows? Whatever the issue, he'd become exactly what he was parodying: a satirical picture of a rebellious rock star.

There's no more relentless commentary on Marilyn Manson than the existence of Marilyn Manson himself. And that's precisely what makes his songs so complex. If there are first-person pronouns here, you can't read them as a straight manifesto of his—or anyone's—beliefs. You have to listen closely to determine who the narrators are and decide whether or not they can be trusted. Take "Irresponsible Hate Anthem," a song reviled by right-wing Christians:

> *I am so all-American, I'd sell you suicide*
> *I am totalitarian, I've got abortions in my eyes*
> *I hate the hater*
> *I'd rape the raper*
> *I am the animal who will not be himself*
> *Hey victim, should I black your eyes again?*
> *Hey victim, you were the one who put the stick in my hand*
> *I am the ism*
> *My hate's a prism*
> *Let's just kill everyone and let your God sort them out*

Yes, that could be Satan singing, but that's too predictable. This is a song about enforcing Biblical justice, getting in touch with your animal nature, recognizing that the culture around you is sick and needs to be destroyed. So whose perspective is Manson really singing from? Hard to say. It could be anyone from a serial killer to an evangelical Christian. But the antagonist is clear: Self-righteousness is the enemy of Americans. And when right-wing Christians blamed the song as evidence that American morals were declining, they only helped prove Manson's point.

You have to be smart to listen to Manson. You can enjoy Nine Inch Nails for purely sonic reasons, but you have to think critically about Manson's constructions in order to enjoy his music at all. His work is a litmus test for his listeners' own beliefs. When he was planning the cover booklet for his debut album, Manson originally wanted to use a naked photo of himself when he was a very young child—he claims Interscope protested that the photo was child pornography. In his autobiography, Manson recalls telling the label that they were missing the point: "I said, 'This is a photograph that was taken by my mother, and it's extremely innocent and normal. But if you see it as child pornography, why am I the guilty person?' " Later, he hits on the essence of his message: "People's morality is so ridiculous. If they get turned on by it, then it's wrong."

Because Manson leaves any moral judgment up to his fans, his detractors—and even his disciples—often take him far more seriously than he takes himself. Not many people give Manson credit for being genuinely funny. (Accused of spending his bandmates' funds on the skeleton of a four-year-old Chinese girl, Manson told MTV: "I would never spend my money on a Chinese girl skeleton. That would be crossing the line. It's a Chinese *boy,* for the record.") The critics who've blamed him for everything from the 1996 suicide of a North Dakota boy to the Columbine massacre don't really get the absurdist message behind his lyrics—and his career. Marilyn Manson can't be blamed for corrupting Americans. His mere existence suggests that we're already living in a semi-moral society. The day that Marilyn Manson no longer shocks anyone—when snorting Sea Monkeys and having threesomes with conjoined twins has become passé—will be the day that we really do need to worry.

Which makes you wonder: What would be better, a world without Manson or a world without Reznor? Life with the earnest original or the reactionary duplicate? Well, you could argue that Reznor created Marilyn Manson—pioneering Manson's style of music, signing Manson to his label, and catapulting Manson into the spotlight. But in embodying the business that created Reznor and everyone who came before him, Manson did something far more important. He's a total fake. A copy of a copy of a rock star. Yet that fakeness challenges his fans not to be passive interpreters of his art, and it's helping him do something more honest than Reznor. To paraphrase Oscar Wilde, man is least himself when he talks in his own person, but give him some wicked vampire geisha makeup, and he will tell you the truth. So let the naysayers say Trent Reznor is a better artist. That might be true. But ultimately the most interesting art Reznor has ever created is Marilyn Manson.

Bruce Springsteen

vs.

Bon Jovi

Russ Meneve

Not to begin on a sour note, but I honestly can't even believe how absolutely necessary this critique is. I've really had it with this Springsteen-can-do-no-wrong, knee-jerk hero worship that has been going on, seemingly forever. It's about time someone took a stand for what's right. What I'm about to do pains me. But like everything else, the dumb public has to be led by its fat, monkey, buffalo-wing-and-Cinnabon-eating hands to anything that takes thought to get there. I just hope I have the patience to last the required amount of writing I signed on for before I smash my computer out of disgust for all of you.

Bruce Springsteen vs. Bon Jovi

Jon Bon Jovi is a musical megagod whose prolific and extremely versatile genius has made him one of the greatest artists of all time. His songs are not only awesome, but he sings like a nightingale—a nightingale with a giant, hormone-filled nutsack hangin' off it. He's got kick-ass hair, good looks, and monster, MONSTER style. Bruce Springsteen, on the other hand, not only looks like but should *be* a guy bein' worked over in the back of a saloon. I wonder if a trucker's fist propelled deep enough into his hairy, blue-collar gut would cause him to produce a sound outta that gullet any better than the Cro-Mag, tone-deaf yells his one-chromosome-deficient musical instinct has green-lit as singing—which is almost always in praise of his New Jersey roots and in praise of how proud he is of the state. I'm from Jersey. *I prays* I never have to go back to that shithole.

Slippery When Wet. . . . It is a fact that this title was inspired by the state of the global vagina population anticipated upon its release. The record sold over twenty-six million copies worldwide. Experts agree, gravelly screeches referencing Jersey would have certainly hindered such worldwide secretion. The album included two number one hits: "Livin' on a Prayer" (title actually inspired by Bruce Springsteen's singing) and "You Give Love a Bad Name" (title also inspired by Springsteen—*love* being a code word for *music*). But it's the third single, "Wanted Dead or Alive," that kicks serious ass. How anyone calling himself a man can fight the urge of wanting to tear his shirt off and wrestle a bear when he hears it is beyond me. And once beating that bear into submission, which you easily will on your Bon Jovi pump, make sweet, sweet love to it. Partially to teach it a lesson that any man listening to "Wanted Dead or Alive" (and has father issues, whatever) is not to be fucked with . . . EVER! And partially out of bringing a moment of loving species solidarity to the world in honor of the great humanitarian that is Jon Bon Jovi. And upon the start of a very confusing, questionably legal orgasm, look into that bear's eyes, reach over, and hit play on the fourth hit on that record, "Never Say Goodbye." And as the sound of the park bloodhounds draws closer, and the intense feelings/raging erection(s)[1] make it too difficult to actually *say goodbye,* completely destroy the loving moment and return to flaccidity by popping in *Born in the U.S.A.,* Bruce Springsteen's most commercially sucksessful album—an album in which Bruce's horrific screams could make Gandhi skeet-shoot babies in little pink hats or compel Santa to force himself on a dolphin's blow hole.

Born in the U.S.A. was released in 1984. Big Brother may have been watching but he sure as hell wasn't listening to this disaster. Its most famous song, of the same name, depicts the hardships of returning Vietnam veterans. I am extremely supportive of any and all war veterans, which is why I'm thankful this song was released well after the actual Vietnam War. I shudder to think of that war going on any longer due to mass reenlistment—anything to get as far the fuck away as possible from this song.

"Dancing in the Dark" was Springsteen's biggest hit single, reaching number two on the Billboard 100. Prince's "When Doves Cry" kept it out of the top spot. It is common knowledge that birds do not have tear ducts. However, "Dancing in the Dark" got so close at number two that they wept uncontrollably, hence the name of the Prince song. I remember when it first came out I was confused over the title "Dancing in the Dark." Then I saw the music video and understood. I think we can all agree the dark is the best place for Bruce Springsteen to dance. He does pull off a truly amazing feat, however: somehow making a young Courteney Cox look totally unhot, pulling her up onstage from the crowd to have a controlled epileptic seizure with him. At first I thought it was Ralph Macchio.

"Cover Me," another hit from the album, was based on racial and economic tensions in Springsteen's hometown of Freehold. In one of the most historic, powerful, and moving outcomes due to artistry ever, all ethnicities were able to set aside their differences and unite for a com-

---

1. Scenario does not specify male or female bear.

mon cause: making sure this song is readily available at the Freehold poison-control center.

Why is it when an artist is good-looking, critics want to take his artistry down a few notches? It's just the way it is. If young chicks dig you, you're ripe to be called an idiot. They totally did it to Bon Jovi. Nerd critics who can't get laid really need to get over it already. If Newman from *Seinfeld* was singing those Bon Jovi songs, the critics would bow down and write glorious, legendary tales of the great four-eyed, man-breasted wonder who wrote and sang like a miraculous divinity from the heavens above. I'm tellin' ya, all other things being equal, repulsive equals a better critiqued artist. I ain't sayin' Bruce is ugly, but he ain't Jon Bon Jovi—or Richie Sambora, for that matter. I mean, Bruce has those big dumb arms he likes to show off onstage. They're cool, right? Yeah, maybe in Belmar circa '85.

No disrespect, Mr. Springsteen—whenever someone starts off a sentence with "No disrespect," you know it's not gonna end well. Whenever I hear those words, I know to put my helmet on, 'cause the bomb is a-comin'—but you know what? I really, truly mean it when I say, Mr. Springsteen, no disrespect . . . you are a legend. But in the Battle a da Jerz, when that thick chemical-waste smoke clears and the overly sprayed mall hair parts, the Jov man is the last man rockin'.

Parliament

vs.

Funkadelic

Ben Greenman

In the mid-1950s a teenager named George Clinton, then living in Plainfield, New Jersey, got together with some friends and formed a doo-wop group called the Parliaments. Vocal groups were extremely popular at this time among urban teens, particularly those with Italian-American and African-American backgrounds. The Parliaments were named for Parliament cigarettes, a popular brand manufactured by Philip Morris.

Singers came and went at first, but within five years or so Clinton had a stable lineup of vocalists: himself, Stingray Davis, Fuzzy Haskins, Calvin Simon, and Grady Thomas. In 1964 he added a backup band of Plainfield musicians, and shortly thereafter moved the entire band to

Detroit to pursue soul stardom with the Motown empire. Instead he ended up signed to Revilot Records, a smaller label owned and operated by LeBaron Taylor and Don Davis. (The label was supposedly named after the reverse spelling of Taylor's middle name, Toliver.) With a harder-soul sound than most Motown records, the band had one moderate hit, "(I Wanna) Testify." Then Revilot folded, taking the Parliament name along with it, and some of the backup musicians left the band to enlist in the U.S. Army.

Clinton hired a new band—guitarists Eddie Hazel and Tawl Ross, bassist Billy Nelson, drummer Tiki Fulwood, and keyboardist Mickey Atkins—and reemerged on the local Westbound label as Funkadelic. In Funkadelic, the instrumental talent was brought to the fore and Clinton's songs began to pursue a more rock-oriented sound. Three albums were released in 1970 and 1971: the eponymous debut, *Free Your Mind and Your Ass Will Follow,* and *Maggot Brain.* The early years saw frequent shifts in personnel: Ross departed due to drug issues; Hazel took a break for financial reasons; keyboardist Bernie Worrell became a mainstay; bassist Bootsy Collins came to Funkadelic from James Brown's band, helped to record *America Eats Its Young* (1972), and then left.

At this point in the history, Parliament was reborn. In 1974, frustrated by Westbound's lax promotion of Funkadelic, Clinton shifted gears and—with Hazel and Collins back in the fold—recorded *Up for the Down Stroke* under the Parliament name for the Casablanca label. Though the first record did not attract much attention, Parliament soon added two key veterans of James Brown's bands, the saxophonist Maceo Parker and the trombonist Fred Wesley, as well as the singer Glen Goins.

The Parliament-Funkadelic empire was now in place. Both bands continued to record and tour. Parliament released *Chocolate City* (1975), *Mothership Connection* (1976), *The Clones of Dr. Funkenstein* (1976), and *Funkentelechy Vs. the Placebo Syndrome* (1977). Funkadelic released *Cosmic Slop* (1973), *Standing on the Verge of Getting It On* (1974), *Let's Take It to the Stage* (1975), and *Tales of Kidd Funkadelic* (1976). On the face of it, the distinction was clear. Parliament leaned more toward horn-based soul and long funk chants and enjoyed more chart success. Funkadelic emphasized guitars and a more politically charged rhetoric and earned more critical praise. But anyone listening to any of the records knew, of course, that both bands were identical. After Funkadelic moved to Warner Bros. in 1976, the two main bands continued to release records, and there were many spin-offs and side projects as well, including Bootsy's Rubber Band, the Horny Horns, the Brides of Funkenstein, and Parlet.

This history is incomplete, of course. It does not mention later Parliament records such as the excellent *Motor Booty Affair* (1978) or the less-than-excellent *Gloryhallastoopid* (1979). It does not mention the disco phase of Funkadelic, which produced the huge hit "Not Just (Knee Deep)" and a collaboration with Sly Stone on 1981's *The Electric Spanking of War Babies*. It does not mention George Clinton's solo career, particularly the gigantic hit "Atomic Dog." Still, it brings us to the question at hand: Parliament or Funkadelic? On the face of it, this seems like an impossible question, and yet it is perhaps the only question.

Choosing between Parliament and Funkadelic first begs the question of whether they can be separated. If the two were truly one, the choice would be barbaric—like Solomon halving the baby in the Bible. In fact, Parliament and Funkadelic are best thought of as identical twins from different fathers. James Brown and his superbly tight, brass-heavy funk spawned Parliament, while Jimi Hendrix and his outer-space guitar explorations spawned Funkadelic. They exist independently, with absolutely no substantive difference.

This independent existence resulted in a strange conjunction. During both bands' heyday, there was no presiding intelligence that felt compelled to resolve the Funkadelic identity with the Parliament identity; in fact, the intelligence that presided, George Clinton, seemed perfectly happy to let them exist side by side. This is almost unprecedented in popular music. There are cases, of course, of established artists recording under pseudonyms: David Johansen became (memorably) Buster Poindexter; Garth Brooks became (less memorably) Chris

Gaines. There are cases of bands experimenting with alter egos without quite committing to the idea (the Beatles and Sgt. Pepper's Lonely Hearts Club Band) and bands committing, if only briefly, to another version of themselves (XTC and the Dukes of Stratosphear, Sly and the Family Stone and Abaco Dream). There are dozens of examples in literature, from classic doppelgänger tales such as Dostoevsky's *The Double* and Poe's "William Wilson" to stories of assumed multiple identity like Dickens's *Our Mutual Friend,* in which John Harmon, learning that he has been presumed dead, mints two new personalities, Julius Handforth and John Rokesmith. There is the distance, or lack of distance, between Tony Clifton and Latka Gravas, or between Ali G and Borat. But Parliament and Funkadelic are a special case in that they are both the same and different. In addition, since the late eighties, the two bands have recombined almost entirely, touring and even recording as the P-Funk All Stars or Parliament-Funkadelic. Whether this marks a brilliant integration of the two identities or a sad abandonment of a profitable separation is another issue, but it is unquestionable that in this dialectic, thesis and antithesis eventually synthesized.

So, Parliament or Funkadelic? The first thing I did with this question was the least scientific or analytic: I posed it to twenty acquaintances. This got me nowhere. Most of the respondents—about half of whom knew that they were the same band and about a quarter of whom suspected it—blurred the question with psychology. "Depends how you feel," one woman said. "They're two sides of the same personality." This nonanswer frustrated me to no end, in part because it has some truth to it.

Consider the bands' mythologies. Except for the Pedro Bell cover art, Funkadelic had a darker ethos that reached deeper into sexual politics and social criticism. You need only a cursory look at the song titles from *America Eats Its Young:* "You Hit the Nail on the Head," "If You Don't Like the Effects, Don't Produce the Cause," the title track. For a superficially comic band, Funkadelic was dead serious. On a mix tape I have somewhere, I called the band "The Mothership of Invention," a nod to Frank Zappa's satiric rock band the Mothers of Invention. Like Zappa, Funkadelic used a host of strange instrumental effects, distorted vocals, and willfully outré music to frame its arguments. Parliament was more of a commercial concern—more aware of its status as entertainment and less visibly preoccupied with art. Songs like "Bop Gun," "Flashlight," and "Night of the Thumpasorus Peoples" could not have been Funkadelic songs, just as songs like "March to the Witch's Castle," "No Head, No Backstage Pass," and "Cosmic Slop" could not have been Parliament songs. Later on, as Funkadelic made its peace with disco and pop and released highly popular if somewhat less distinctive albums like *One Nation Under a Groove* (1978) and *Uncle Jam Wants You* (1979), the difference became blurrier, though *Electric Spanking* brings it into sharp focus again—"Icka Prick," a filthy outer-space chant, and the left-of-left-field two-part "Funk Gets Stronger" don't have the radio sugar of Parliament.

Could any songs have belonged to both bands? Sometimes now, in the era of the iPod, I'll dump both bands' music into a giant playlist and try to guess within the first five seconds whether a song belongs to Parliament or Funkadelic. In most cases it's easy. And, as I said, there's some truth to the argument I got in response to my poll question. If you're in a violently antiauthority mood, you'll probably lean toward Funkadelic. If you're in a happy mood, you'll probably prefer Parliament. If you're feeling highly individualistic, Funkadelic—with its endless instrumental solos and sometimes overwhelming demonstrations of personality—is likely to be your pick. If you're feeling communal, go for Parliament, with its chants and its massed horns. Except that neither is particularly feminine, Funkadelic is clearly the yin and Parliament clearly the yang.

As I've said, this is a dodge. And yet even in Dodge City there were showdowns. About fifty hours into reviewing the relevant materials, I felt that I had to give an answer. Parliament or Funkadelic? Who wins? To settle the question, I turned to Karen Horney. It probably seems wrongheaded, or at the very least pretentious, to introduce the work of the pioneering German psychoanalyst into the debate. But Horney's work on the self, and particularly the way in which neuroses prevent subjects from being honest about their self-identity, is useful here.

In such works as *Our Inner Conflicts* (1945) and *Neurosis and Human Growth* (1950), Horney argued that if an individual possesses a realistic self-concept, then he or she can activate the self properly and achieve appropriate goals. Whether or not a self-concept is realistic depends on the distance between what she called the "real self" and the "ideal self." These are used fairly commonsensically in Horney. The real self is the person as he or she actually is, complete with flaws. The ideal self is the dreamed-of self, which is almost always more powerful than the real self. When people become intoxicated by the ideal self, they move between a false sense of elation (in which they believe that they can achieve that ideal) and an equally false sense of self-hatred that results from the realization that the ideal is impossible. In language that veered close to self-help parlance, Horney called this self-hating self-aggrandizement "the tyranny of the shoulds," and suggested that it touched off a cycle of neurosis fueled by a futile "search for glory."

With that highly reductive summary of Horney, let's return to Parliament and Funkadelic. Though the names are only labels, the band we know as Funkadelic was the fullest flowering of George Clinton's early plan. The trio of albums that marked their arrival on the music scene were conceived as revolutionary documents. *Maggot Brain,* the strongest of those early records, contains Eddie Hazel's epic title track, a retro message song ("Can You Get to That"), menacing minimalist funk ("You and Your Folks, Me and My Folks"), hard soul ("Hit It or Quit It"), hard rock ("Super Stupid"), a muzzy acid-trip ballad ("Back in Our Minds"), and a pyrotechnic sound-effect orgy ("Wars of Armageddon"). In only seven songs, the record attempts to capture and reflect all of the chaotic aspects and energies of America in 1971. It's an impossible proposition. In fact, the most sprawling of Funkadelic's early songs (not just "Wars of Armageddon" but "Free Your Mind and Your Ass Will Follow" and "America Eats Its Young," among others) are the sonic equivalent of attempting to live inside an ideal. It's a negative ideal, granted, more dystopian than utopian, but those early works are nothing if not intoxicated by the possibility of achieving total understanding. In fact, you could even suggest that the neurotic condition into which their albums are sometimes plunged is the direct result of trying for that ideal and falling short.

Parliament, on the other hand, was less defensive, looser, and more self-possessed, in part because its ambitions were at once narrower and more universal. Like Funkadelic, Parliament frequently addressed social issues, but from the start Parliament's approach hovered on the edge of parody. Take "Chocolate City," which lampooned political campaigns while making a serious point about the growing African-American populations in U.S. cities. *The Clones of Dr. Funkenstein, Funkentelechy Vs. the Placebo Syndrome,* and *Mothership Connection* absorbed science-fiction motifs alongside references to current celebrities, and they had as much in common with comedy records like those of the Firesign Theatre as they did with Sly and the Family Stone. They were records with a growing cast of characters, but above all else they were records made *in* character, from Starchild to Dr. Funkenstein to Mr. Wiggles the Worm. Parliament epics like "Sir Nose D'Voidoffunk" or "Funkentelechy" settle into a groove, appropriating advertising slogans or nursery rhymes as they go; they are a far cry from Funkadelic's intense alienation effects. The opening track of *Mothership Connection,* spoken by Clinton's hip character DJ Lollipop Man, is perhaps the best example of this; Lollipop Man raises, and then does away with, the spectre of white funk artists such as David Bowie, Blue Cheer, and the Doobie Brothers.

More authenticity does not always make for more brilliant music, but it does make for a more comfortable existence within the limited brilliance that can be safely illuminated in a pop context. It makes for less filler and a higher rate of success. And, finally, it makes for a narrow victory for Parliament over its twin Funkadelic.

John Lennon

vs.

Paul McCartney

Joe Donnelly

I had to pull over and weep.

Let me explain. I was driving up into the Hollywood Hills on a burnished Sunday afternoon, one of those early fall days when everything in Los Angeles shimmers with hope and desolation. I was on my way to visit my dear friend and his two kids, whose godfather I am. My marriage was falling apart and the local classic-rock station was playing the "Golden Slumbers/Carry That Weight/The End" medley. Then and there, in a canyon in the Hollywood Hills that used to be the home to hunting lodges where early Hollywood royalty carried out illicit trysts, thus earning it the nickname Bordello Canyon, I felt the immense weight of knowledge, the knowledge of how even the greatest loves, in this case the love between Paul and John, the love that made the Beatles' magic, *their* marriage, can end. And in the end they were going to have to carry that weight. And yes, I knew that in my case, too, boy, you're gonna carry that weight . . . a long time. The weight can be crushing. And as I listened on the side of the road, the full heaviness of ending came down on me. By the time the song suite reached the guitar freak-out that climaxes "The End," the one in which John, Paul, and George air their grievances, plead for understanding, and, yes, tell one another that they will always love one another, I was a puddle.

Nothing like this has ever happened to me when a John Lennon song played on the radio. I mean, like anyone with any grasp, I'm always blown away by "Strawberry Fields Forever," which may be the greatest rock and roll composition ever assembled. Even Brian Wilson pulled to the side of the road upon hearing that one for the first time. Only he didn't start crying, I don't think. Instead, so the legend goes, he put *Smile* on the shelf and admitted to himself that the Beatles had gotten to the promised land first. Even so, "Strawberry Fields" has never made me weep. But McCartney's epic cycle of dissolution that closes out *Abbey Road* has and did. And will again, I'm sure.

In the long-running Paul vs. John debate, there are no winners, only casualties and stupidity. It's a ridiculous question and yields only ridiculous answers, and is, therefore, ultimately meaningless. But it makes for good sport if taken with more than a grain of salt. In the end, of course, John, Paul, George, and Ringo *were* the Beatles, and that lightning in a bottle never would have happened without any of them, despite Lennon joking—when asked if Ringo was the best drummer in the world—that "he isn't even the best drummer in the Beatles." He was referring to the possibility that McCartney was supposedly the best drummer in the Beatles. He was also, supposedly, the best guitar player, piano player, Mellotron innovator (with which he composed the haunting opening passage to "Strawberry Fields"), and, of course, bassist. But does that make Paul the best Beatle? Of course not; virtuosity in and of itself can be as banal as ineptitude if it's possessed by an empty vessel (e.g., Toto equals Grand Funk Railroad). Fortunately Paul's came with a searing, soaring heart. It also came in a madly ambitious package whose reach often met his grasp. It didn't hurt any, either, that Paul also had a soul as open and wide as his formidable partner's, the man who is often referred to as the heart and soul of the Beatles. I guess that's the point on which I beg to differ. See, Paul had soul to spare. It just came across in a less obvious way.

The main difference between the two, for me, is that while John Lennon practiced the art of telling, mostly in plain English (save for a few stream-of-consciousness blasts—*goo goo g'joob*), Paul, a practitioner of the art of showing, spoke in metaphors, imagery, and ultimately in parables. His best songs told stories that had classical narrative arcs, while John, one of the original and all-time-best shoegazers, was all about the id, putting his insides out. Paul, more mature, perhaps, and more empathetic, absorbed everything around him and took the outside in, which is why so many of his songs resonate universally and why he, more than anyone in rock history (including, I'll say, Bob Dylan), expanded the vocabulary of the form.

Take, for instance, "Penny Lane" and the aforementioned "Strawberry Fields." McCartney's "Penny Lane" is often dismissed as a sentimental ditty while "Strawberry Fields" is considered holy. Hell, a section of Central Park across the street from the Dakota, where Lennon lived and on whose sidewalk he was shot dead, is even named for the song. But while the music in "Strawberry Fields" (at its core, like most Lennon compositions, a folk-blues number) is viscerally haunting and has the feeling of a breakthrough, that effect is primarily a feat of radical studio engineering—editing and overdubbing that were generations ahead of their time and about which treatises have been written[1]— not to mention some well-placed Harrison guitar licks, Paul's Mellotron, and, most of all, Ringo's genius drumming. Take all this away and

---

1. Joseph Brennan, "Strawberry Fields Forever: Putting Together the Pieces" (New York: 1996), http://www.columbia.edu/~brennan/beatles/strawberry-fields.html.

simply look at the lyrics—concerning a Salvation Army orphanage near Lennon's childhood home in Liverpool that held an annual fair he would eagerly attend with his Aunt Mimi—and the whole thing falls apart. Consider the following:

> *Always no sometimes think it's me*
> *But you know I know when it's a dream*
> *I think I know I mean "Yes," but it's all wrong*
> *That is, I think I disagree*
> *Let me take you down, 'cause I'm going to Strawberry*
>   *Fields*
> *Nothing is real and nothing to get hung about*

These lyrics, likely rooted in a psyche that was shaped by the early death of his mother, obviously mean something to Lennon. But what do they mean to you? The combination of the abstract lyrical and musical expressionism sets a tone and mood, for sure, but are these abstractions profound, or just abstract? For me, the lack of telling detail stops the song just short of evoking anything tangible. We can sort of get how Lennon feels about Strawberry Fields, but the song doesn't allow us to get *to* Strawberry Fields ourselves.

On the other hand, strip away the music to the seemingly upbeat "Penny Lane"—which could easily stand on its own in its symphonic completeness—study the words, and the effect is devastating. Like a lot of McCartney's best work, the song tells a story. Not his story, necessarily, but a universal one of loneliness and longing. It's a story of a day in the life of nowhere men, suspended in time and space; of people left lingering in absence, sorting through the remains of the day. It's a place where a fireman keeps an hourglass and a portrait of the queen in his pocket, where the children laugh behind the back of the banker who never wears a mac in the pouring rain.

These characters seem to be waiting for something. What is it? Of course, it's the same thing that Beckett's Estragon and Vladimir are waiting for—the thing that will never come. It is the proverbial Godot that they hope will bring meaning to their lives. And you realize, too, that for these characters that hoped-for meaning and release from that doomed hope will only come with death, and even then, none too soon. It's a heartbreaking piece, despite the melody that makes you whistle for the rest of the day, because we can see Penny Lane so clearly. It is a tangible brand of nostalgia McCartney is plying, but it is also a cautionary one. Things never were as easy or as simple as you might have thought they were (not even this melody). Not only can you never go home again, but upon closer look, you probably wouldn't want to. It's a very adult reckoning delivered with the hummability of a nursery rhyme.

Other examples of this sort of rich storytelling quickly come to mind. Of course there's "Yesterday," the stark ode to regret that the precocious McCartney wrote at the tender age of twenty-three, though the words seem fired from the belly of a grizzled bluesman. It's also the first solo Beatles recording, just him and George Martin. The song—pretty much regarded as one of, if not the best brokenheated ballads in the pop-music canon—again, too, is an exercise in brilliant simplicity and succinctness. Nothing about it is tangled or inaccessible, and yet how deeply it probes. How did that happen? Even McCartney doesn't quite know, saying it came to him, basically, in a dream.

A couple years later he wrote "Eleanor Rigby." One could view it and "Tomorrow Never Knows," off the landmark *Revolver* album, almost as an earlier parallel to "Penny Lane" and "Strawberry Fields." As far as I'm concerned, the most mind-blowing song on that album, and one of the most mind-blowing ever in terms of innovation, is "Tomorrow Never Knows." It's a total freak affair, with its tape loops, overdubbing, nasty guitar licks, crazy drumming, et cetera—a sonic assault heralding a new paradigm of what's possible with a great band that has mastered the new powers of studio technology. If it came out today, it would still be revolutionary. But it's revolutionary in terms of style more than substance. I'll never know what it means beyond the platitudinous exhortation to

> *Turn off your mind, relax and float downstream,*
> *It is not dying, it is not dying*
> *Lay down all thoughts, surrender to the void,*
> *It is shining, it is shining*

Okay, I get it. And?

"Eleanor Rigby," which McCartney wrote when he was twenty-four, is something else. It is a classic. I'm not sure any pop song has told such a perfect narrative of loneliness and isolation, of dashed dreams, and, again, of the unrelenting wait for deliverance.

> *Eleanor Rigby picks up the rice in the church where a*
> * wedding has been*
> *Lives in a dream*
> *Waits at the window, wearing the face that she keeps in a jar*
> * by the door*
> *Who is it for?*
> *All the lonely people*
> *Where do they all come from?*
> *All the lonely people*
> *Where do they all belong?*
> *Father McKenzie writing the words of a sermon that no one*
> * will hear*
> *No one comes near*
> *Look at him working, darning his socks in the night when*
> * there's nobody there*
> *What does he care?*

Once again the song's lyrics could be stripped of the music and still stand as compelling narrative. McCartney again proves deft at using relatable imagery in the service of a larger meaning. This ability to juxtapose contradictory images and musical movements to get to a more nuanced and profound level of meaning always seems to escape the more egocentric approach of Lennon. John is interested in telling us what to do, how to feel—or, rather, how he feels. McCartney is interested in showing us what people do and how they live. The difference, I believe, is that while John's best songs are singular and emotive, Paul's best are universal and emotional. For that reason, they stay with you.

There are exceptions, of course, to the universality rule. John's "In My Life" and "Norwegian Wood" come immediately to mind. But those are modest affairs, though they benefit from their modesty. And, again, they come from the inside out. I'd also argue that neither of those Lennon compositions reaches the grand scale of songs like "Yesterday" or "Eleanor Rigby" or "Hey Jude." Paul swung for the fences, and when he connected, he really connected.

Not that it's gospel or anything, but *Rolling Stone* magazine's top five hundred rock songs of all time has four Beatles tunes in its top twenty. They are, in descending order, "Hey Jude" (which even Lennon loved, though he thought McCartney was singing about the strains his relationship with Yoko was having on the band), "Yesterday," "I Want to Hold Your Hand," and "Let It Be." Leaving out "I Want to Hold Your Hand"—a true collaboration written by Lennon and McCartney "eyeball to eyeball," as Lennon put it—they are all strictly McCartney compositions.

The three songs make for an interesting study. Two of them are fortifying gifts that have become part of the pop firmament for their ability to touch deep chords within anyone who has experienced loss and sadness; the other is just a plain lament with no consolation other than knowing we've all been there. But, oh, how we've been there.

There are plenty of other arguments to make in this ridiculous postulate. Wasn't "Helter Skelter" one of the hardest rock songs ever recorded when it came out in 1968? Wasn't it really the first punk-rock song, or maybe even the first heavy-metal song? I remember reading somewhere that Paul McCartney felt challenged by the Who's "I Can See for Miles" and decided he was going to write a song that was even harder than that one. He succeeded. So much so that Lennon is said to have been both taken aback and a bit disturbed that McCartney could write something so brazen without him.

Paul has one of the greatest growls in rock and roll. You can hear it in "Helter Skelter" and "Hey Jude"—*Judey, Judey, Judey, owwwww*. All this from the "light" side of the Lennon-McCartney partnership. And of course there's *Sgt. Pepper*. Not my favorite Beatles record by any means, but it is a testament to his vision, ambition, and, well, it has some of the sickest bass playing ever laid down. The spots where the album bogs down, songs like "Being for the Benefit of Mr. Kite!" and the plodding nonsense of ".Lucy in the Sky With Diamonds," were primarily Lennon's doing. (Of course, to his credit, so was, for the most part, the standout track "A Day in the Life.") All in all, though, nothing like *Sgt. Pepper* had ever been done before, and it was primarily Paul's doing.

A good marriage, though, is a case of the sum being greater than its parts, and clearly a listen to either John's or Paul's solo work argues that they were better together than apart. In the Beatles John pushed Paul, to whom everything seemed to come so easily, to dig a little deeper. Paul added musical genius to John's rather rudimentary palette. After the breakup, John seems to have gotten lazy without Paul, who was known as a bit of a dick for the way he pressed the other band members. Seriously, can you think of one standout track from John's solo career? And don't hit me back with "Imagine" or "Give Peace a Chance," both of which are exercises in limp banality that work better as bumper stickers than as great songs. John would have had a field day with Paul had he written either of those. On the other hand, Paul kept striving even post-Beatles (when he wasn't writing silly love songs, that is), and he has had some shining moments. "Jet," "Maybe I'm Amazed," most of the *Band on the Run* album—all hold up as classics.

Having said all that, it could be argued that Lennon was the more important cultural figure. His greatest art, in the final analysis, may not have been his music but his life. His politics, his courage, and his willingness to be controversial may have made him the more important human being. Maybe. But that's an entirely different argument and one that is likely as ridiculous as this one. As for who was the more important Beatle, well, let's go back to "Penny Lane" and "Strawberry Fields" one last time.

There was a bit of controversy when the two singles came out. Lennon wasn't happy that his magnum opus was relegated to the B-side while "Penny Lane" took the A-side. "Penny Lane" reached number one in the United States and U.K., while "Strawberry Fields" took numbers eight and two on the respective charts. This wasn't the first or last dispute Lennon and McCartney (or Lennon and Brian Epstein) would have about which of their songs should take which side of the single, and such indignities prompted Lennon to remark after the Beatles' breakup, "I got sick and tired of being Paul's backup band."

On another day, I'm sure I'd argue the exact opposite. But for now I'm going to put on *Abbey Road* and allow Paul to help me carry that weight.

Nirvana

vs.

Metallica

Gideon Yago

Twenty years ago, if you took the train ten miles from Times Square, beneath the trash-choked East River, past the slag-pit graveyards that bank Queens Boulevard, you'd have landed smack in the heart of Outer Borough Metal Country: a Jurassic burg of Polish, Italian, and Colombian kids fighting the advance of hip-hop by cranking their sound systems and blasting Testament, Megadeth, and Queens's own Anthrax. They moved in packs, these wasted teenage metalheads with Zakk Wylde hair and puberty 'staches, smoking dirt weed at the White Castle and casing the local Catholic schools for jailbait—the kind Lemmy Kilmister howled for on "No Remorse." At dusk, should you happen to walk by the right garage, you could hear them shredding till their fingers bled, wailing like banshees. They were the coolest.

Before I hit puberty, I knew nothing of metal. "Hard Rock" was my parents' copy of *The Best of Bread*. My older brother was into rap. I watched the metalheads from afar, fascinated. I was convinced they knew some secret alchemy capable of changing cheerful boys like me into badass adolescents like them, and I wanted in.

The sound, the look, the culture of metal fascinated me in part because it terrified my mother. One afternoon, when we were walking home from shul, two dudes, one dressed in a Metallica *Metal Up Your Ass* jean jacket, cut in front of us on the street. Metallica's signature graphic for that demo was simple, beautiful: a knife and fist reverse plunging a toilet next to the band's insignia. Streaks of blood poured down the anonymous, sewer-born wrist. Metal up your ass indeed.

My mom shook her head and muttered, "Vulgar." One of the metalheads turned and sneered.

"Fuck you, lady," he said in a thick Queens drawl.

I was floored. That guy just told my mom to go fuck herself, I thought. And she was too paralyzed to react! It was raw power. I swore then and there to find out just who this Metallica really was.

My social circles at the time were solely my Boy Scout troop and the regular D&D game I played at my friend Mark Ringel's house. Somewhere between the two, I figured someone had a Metallica cassette. I would road test the music before blowing my allowance at Sam Goody.

Boy Scouts proved a success. A kid named Shin Nakayama, known for his knife collection and ability to start fires, was a die-hard fan and gave me my first taste of thrash. I started with *Kill 'Em All* and *Ride the Lightning*. After school, I ran to my kitchen to nick my mom's cassette-radio and play the tapes over and over again, conspicuously letting "Seek and Destroy" play out even though my mother had already called me down for dinner . . . twice! But *Master of Puppets* was by far my favorite. From the thud and chug of "Battery" and "Damage, Inc." to the epic tragedy of "Sanitarium" . . . I *felt* it. *Master of Puppets* was where I *got* metal, where I understood what the older kids knew, where I didn't just pretend, where I fucking *loved* it. For weeks I played *Puppets* over and over. Then I went to the local costume-supply-cum-head shop and bought a *Master of Puppets* patch for my jean jacket. Despite her protests, I made my mother iron it on.

After that, Metallica was my favorite band. I told everybody. At junior high. In summer camp. I learned how to drop D on a guitar and shredded along with the tape recorder, my own vaguely retarded solos an anemic counterpoint to Kirk Hammett's recorded virtuosity. And when I walked past the roosts of other teenaged metalheads getting high near the train station, they saw my Metallica jacket fitting impossibly largely on my prepubescent frame and they gave me the greatest compliment bestowed in rock and roll.

"All right!" they said.

Then came *Justice*.

One late-night D&D session at Ringel's, after I took my Ranger/ Thief to level 4 in both classes, I sat around with my friends eating snacks and watching *Headbangers' Ball*. Onscreen came the first few cathodic flickers of the video for Metallica's "One." It was a watershed moment. Here was this twinkling, foreboding guitar duet kicking off a ballad that ended in an epic, tack-sharp shred session that filled me with the will to destroy. And it had these twisted Dalton Trumbo clips. And those lyrics: "Hold my breath as I wish for death"? I mean, believe it when I say that there was no going back after that. My life was irrevocably changed.

"That's the new one from Metallica," said Riki Rachtman. "And their new album . . . *And Justice for All*!"

For me, *Justice* was the high-water mark of artistic achievement in my lifetime. Not because any of its songs rocked harder or sounded better than, say, "For Whom the Bell Tolls." But that bone-dry sound and those doom-stained lyrics, like on "Harvester of Sorrow" and "Blackened"— it was titrated teenaged angst. It felt just like all the weirdness and rejection that I knew at school. Nothing had *Justice*'s precision. Nothing had its rage.

Like the rest of Metallica's fans, I would have to wait three years for their follow-up. In that time I grew my hair and started my first band (Metallica covers, but some Rush to appease our drummer). I was still playing D&D at Ringel's. But tapes had given way to compact discs, and naturally the first three CDs I bought were all Metallica.

They say that all bands (with the exception of the Beatles and the Stones) only have three great albums in them. Unfortunately, for Metallica that translated to *Kill 'Em All, Master of Puppets,* and—arguably—*Lightning* or *Justice.* When their eponymous black album came out, I didn't expect it to ... well ... suck. I just assumed that, like *Master of Puppets* and *Justice* before it, Metallica's *Metallica* would only raise the bar. I mean, for Christ's sake, it bore their fucking name!

But when you're fourteen years old you don't know about turning points, or entropy and failure. You have no knowledge of what it is to really, truly try and wind up short. You're just potential. So when I listened to *Metallica,* I heard something I had never heard before: the sound of the end. Now, I'm willing to grant that maybe I was outgrowing the music. Or that my taste was changing, that it was somehow my fault and not theirs. But I defy any true Metallica fan to point to the history of that band and not look at that album as the beginning of a long and fatuous decline that would later include jam sessions with the San Francisco orchestra, Andrés Segovia–inspired classical-guitar digressions, and group therapy. Part of me got that. I heard it in that record. I had been so excited to bring it over to Ringel's. But we stopped the album halfway through and decided to play more D&D. It was a letdown.

But fortune snuck opportunity behind disappointment that night. Ringel had an older brother who was a freshman in college. He wore Doc Martens and used big words like *syphilitic* and *albeit.* He was chubby, weird, and none of us knew what to make of him. His favorite band was the Dead Milkmen. I'm not sure what his motivation was, but occasionally he would trudge down to the basement in his English boots to fuck with us. Maybe he was bored. Maybe he couldn't get a date. Maybe he actually gave a shit. Who knew. That night he thumbed through the CDs that lay spilled out next to our *Monsters Compendium* and *Dungeon Master's Guide*. Picking up the jet-black copy of *Metallica*, he made some crack about *Spinal Tap*.

"Is it good?" he asked. We all didn't know what to say.

He asked which song he should play and someone suggested "Sad but True." I knew by the look on his face that my suspicions about the record had been right.

"You guys listen to Nirvana?" he asked afterward.

"Like, the Robert Plant album?" I said, trying to appear sophisticated.

"No, jackass. Nirvana. From Seattle. Hold on a second."

He darted back up the stairs. We rolled our twenty-sided die at a band of orcs and waited for him to return.

I remember looking at the inside of the CD jacket when the music came on: that blurry photo of three guys, impressionistic and dark. Then came the drum fill of "Smells Like Teen Spirit." Ringel's brother turned up the volume. "This is for your own good," he said.

Here is why Nirvana will always be a better band than Metallica. It's not because they hit harder (they do). It's not because they are tighter (they're definitely not). It's not because tracks like "School" and "Frances Farmer Will Have Her Revenge on Seattle" are tougher and more bone jarring than anything in the entire Metallica catalog (please send hate mail to Gideon Yago c/o Three Rivers Press Editorial, The Crown Publishing Group, 1745 Broadway, New York, NY, 10019). It's because Metallica is fundamentally about respecting rules—of metal, of production, of technicality—and Nirvana is about breaking those rules down in the pursuit of innovation. Metallica was metal. Nirvana was something *else*. Over the next forty-plus minutes, three dudes put together a patchwork of weird songs about fetuses, guns, rape, pain, fertility, drugs, isolation, and paranoia. It was blues, it was pop, it was metal, it was hardcore. It was disturbing and it was real. It made everything about my love of metal seem cheap and monodimensional. And it blew my fucking mind.

I suddenly realized that, even though it was dark and scary and edgy, loving Metallica was no different than rushing a fraternity. I had been trying to fit in, to learn metal's secret code, playing with established tropes and themes other people wrote, never really looking into myself, always looking outward at the rest of the pack for external validation. Metallica fit into metal. Nirvana was just . . . weird, creative, new, and next to it, Metallica . . . *all of metal* . . . felt like an operatic act of deliberation. What Kirk Hammett strove to achieve with technical virtuosity, Kurt Cobain attained in a saw-toothed pursuit of noise. Metallica was one thing. Nirvana was many things. Metallica was craft. Nirvana was art. It was, is, and will remain the central difference between metal and punk.

When I heard that first howl, that fucking howl, it told me that everything I had been doing for the last three years was all wrong. Real pain wasn't spooky, scary lyrics about apocalyptic destruction. It came from deep within; it was your own and you had to exorcise it. That's what I heard in Nirvana. Fuck the metal rules. It was time to go it alone.

I retired my Metallica jean jacket to the back of my closet after that. I started writing and painting and got a job in a record store so I could follow Kurt Cobain down the rabbit hole his music led me. Nirvana opened me up to the Velvet Underground and Ornette Coleman, Sonic Youth and Beat Happening, Robert Johnson and Hank Williams, the Buzzcocks and the Misfits. I dyed my hair purple and wore a Nirvana T-shirt until holes appeared in the sides. I started a zine at Kinko's. I took the subway into the city late at night to catch live bands in empty rooms. I swore to be an artist. And I did it all alone.

By the time Kurt put his toe on the trigger, I was a bona fide alien in my town, slaking a hunger for weird shit, weird sounds, outsiders. There were no girls, few friends, and absolutely zero fellow travelers in the fringe Nirvana taught me to seek. But it was real. It was true. I felt exhilarated and alive because of those things I could call my own, each its own buzzing promise of truth never exceeded by that first spin of *Nevermind*.

The metalheads, naturally, turned their backs on me. I stopped trying to hang out. I didn't buy their records. Right after Cobain's death I walked past a pack of them, crowded on the subway steps, getting high and flicking cigarette butts at stray cats.

"I heard your favorite fag just shot himself in the face," one said as the others chuckled on cue.

"Fuck you guys," I said in my Queens drawl, and I skated off to the record store.

N.W.A.
vs.
Wu-Tang Clan

Jonah Weiner

For all of N.W.A.'s antagonism, egotism, and rage, the only rappers they ever feuded with were themselves. To find a comparably fierce case of band infighting, knife wielding, and betrayal, you need to leave hip-hop altogether: In terms of acrimony, they were rap's Police, rap's Supremes, rap's Guns N' Roses. Still, when the subject arises of hip-hop's all-time greats, it makes sense to bracket N.W.A. off against the Wu-Tang Clan. The former were kaput for a year—four years if you count from Ice Cube's departure—by the time the latter debuted, but the two crews are, in several regards, fun-house-mirror images of each other. Each originated off the rap map, as its borders were drawn at the time, and turned that isolation into an asset; each put a premium on 'hood verité before going on to articulate that ideal in dramatically different ways; and each was a gang of contentious, combustible, and brilliant personalities, such that a showdown between them splinters into hotly contested one-on-one beefs. Who's the more visionary producer, Dr. Dre or RZA? Who was the more brilliant madman, Eazy-E or Ol' Dirty Bastard? Whose solo debut was worse, MC Ren's or U-God's?

Today gangsta rap's metamorphosis into a billion-dollar marketing come-on is nearly total, so it's important to remember that when N.W.A.'s 1988 sophomore set, *Straight Outta Compton,* came out, it was intended—and taken—as a threat. Their name, typically decoded as the slur-flipping "Niggaz with Attitude," also shared initials with the phrase *No Whites Allowed.* These threats doubled, of course, as invitations, and when the album started selling to younger, suburban whites, there was parent-group outcry, pundit bile, and, famously, a scolding letter rattled off to Ruthless Records courtesy of the FBI. This five-man crew from Compton pumped many things into the pop mainstream, but near the top of the list is the Parental Advisory sticker.

Their achievement is stunning: With *Straight Outta Compton* (the only N.W.A. LP that features the group's core lineup), N.W.A. created the gangsta-rap persona as we know it—icily Darwinist, gleefully misogynist, violently antiauthority—and made it hip-hop's normative perspective. Earlier MCs—Schoolly D and Ice-T among them—had floated similar positions, but this was where gangsta rap took on the proportions of a worldview. Today N.W.A. are venerated in hip-hop as the gold standard of sawed-off, street-certified rage, and one thing they have over the Wu-Tang in buckets is influence: The narrative they put forth almost twenty years ago has since been refined and amended (Tupac added pathos, Biggie virtuosity, Jay-Z capitalism), but its basic terms have held firm.

When we think of *Straight Outta Compton,* we typically recall its opening one-two punch: the deafening drone of the title track followed by the squealing "Fuck Tha Police." These are chest-thumping taunts and wild-eyed frontline dispatches set to breathtakingly brutal noise; in two five-minute bursts, N.W.A. introduced Compton as a vivid slice of American hell and minted an AK-47 radicalism that made rap's reigning agit-propstas of the moment, Public Enemy, seem like fusty pamphleteers.

But how dangerous was the World's Most Dangerous Group? One of the most remarkable things about listening to N.W.A.'s records today is the reminder of how goofy these gangstas were willing to get; the group's self-proclaimed "reality rap" was heavily theatricalized from the jump. Following Ice Cube's lead, Eazy-E, MC Ren, and Dr. Dre rap in precise, actorly booms (in this regard, Cube's future as a Christmas-movie titan isn't that hard to square with his origins); there are numerous stabs at gross-out humor, which reach a ridiculous extreme on Eazy-E's 1988 solo bid, *Eazy-Duz-It;* and, on *Straight Outta Compton,* Dr. Dre and DJ Yella's apocalyptic blares alternate with rubbery, comical funk and, finally, a *Mighty Mouse*–sampling electro jam—"Something 2 Dance 2"—that sounds as though it popped and locked its way into the wrong part of town. Today it's accepted wisdom that gangstas don't dance, but Dre, who began life in the club-oriented World Class Wreckin' Cru, has always nursed an instinctive desire to get everyone on the floor.

Beyond "Fuck Tha Police," N.W.A. never advanced anything quite so coherent as an agenda, but they were unquestionably political. They needed only to scowl into a camera and it was an act of radical dissent— the phenomenon of five loud, malevolent, hypersexualized African-American men was more than enough to provoke, frighten, and, in significant numbers, entrance mainstream audiences. N.W.A. were well aware of this. In one of their most striking press photos, they stand fully dressed on a beach, rubbing their palms and staring at two oblivious white women; the image crackles with tension, not the least of which stems from a discomfiting sense that, if you feel a surge of protectiveness toward these pale, two-dimensional sunbathers, you have fallen into a trap, laid craftily and cannily, to catch AmeriKKKans.

N.W.A.'s evocation of rageful inner-city otherness was so powerful that when the L.A. riots broke in 1992, many observers referred back to their music as the smoke before the fire. This literally incendiary aura distracts, though, from how tedious much of N.W.A.'s music can be. Time is rarely kind to radical gestures, but listening to their three albums back to back—beginning with 1987's *N.W.A. and the Posse* and ending with 1991's *Niggaz4Life*—you hear them regularly cross the line between shock and its stale, calculated imitation. They'll push a button, then keep jamming on it until their thumbs bleed.

N.W.A.'s woman hate, which they typically play for yuks, grows especially tiresome. On "Straight Outta Compton," when Eazy-E brags about murdering a woman who "got the last penetration" and letting out "a gust of wind" at the crime scene, it's a disturbing mishmash of sex, violence, and scatological comedy; by the time Ice Cube announces, "I think with my ding-a-ling," on the gleefully boorish "I Ain't Tha 1," it doesn't matter how much or how little irony he intends, he's just embarrassing himself.

Despite Dr. Dre's drive-by funk, there is a frustrating feeling of stasis to many N.W.A. songs: the staccato declaratives pitched into tracks like stakes, the sense of a mission statement being laid out again and again and again. Viewed historically, this was critical work—a voice of anger and subjugation elbowing its way to the front of the room, strangling the microphone in its demand to be heard. But in the case of N.W.A. that voice seems to have rapidly exhausted itself.

And not just artistically: The group soon imploded amid personal animus and financial disputes. N.W.A.'s manager, Jerry Heller, famously claimed that Suge Knight, accompanied by several pipe-and-bat-wielding henchmen, threatened to kill him if Dr. Dre wasn't released from his contract. Post-N.W.A., Eazy-E's and Ice Cube's solo careers were hit-and-miss (the latter's music grew more political and more lug-headed at the same time); AIDS killed Eazy in 1995; and the last time we heard from Yella he was directing pornos. Only Dr. Dre has stayed relevant—crucial, in fact. First he downshifted, concocting the languid, luxurious G-funk sound on 1992's *The Chronic,* where sex and menace waft over the tracks like heat distortion; then, in one of pop's rare third acts, he struck upon the shiny, hard-swinging stomps that introduced Eminem and 50 Cent to the world.

The Wu-Tang Clan probably couldn't have existed without N.W.A., who proved definitively that gangsta rappers could enjoy major success without scrubbing up. But the Clan constituted a major leap forward in terms of musical, lyrical, and, for whatever it's worth, moral sophistication. While N.W.A.'s MCs are constantly telling us what they *are* ("a crazy motherfucker," "the type of nigga that's built to last," "a real nigga," "the nigga you love to hate"), the Wu-Tang prefer to talk elliptically and abstractly about what they *do* ("stick my Wu-Tang sword right through your navel," "crash at high speeds, strawberry kiwi," "keep shit stains in my drawers so I can get fizza-funky for you") as well as what they see.

From Wu-Tang's 1992 debut single, "Protect Ya Neck," forward, the self isn't expressed so much as refracted—through kung-fu and comic-book fantasies, Five-Percenter speak, and acres of left-field metaphors. The nine-man posse rechristened their native Staten Island *Shaolin,* transfiguring, ennobling, and exerting narrative control over the bleakness and desperation they saw around them. In their retelling, gangbangers became samurai, living according to a complex, otherworldly code (no wonder director Jim Jarmusch hired RZA to score his film *Ghost Dog*—he lifted its concept from him). The result was a stunning, potent paradox—the Clan were hip-hop's first magical realists.

Wu-Tang were never De La Soul–style big tenters, but their dense, gnomic lexicon and kung-fu cosmos were, in a counterintuitive way, inclusive and inviting to both gangsta obsessives and hip-hop's dorkiest, whitest fans. Wu-Tang offer worlds to explore, mythology to pore over, ciphers to crack. *Who are these gods and earths? What is the secret significance of the number thirty-six? In what way are the Wu-Tang like Voltron?* Not for nothing are Wu-Tang the only rap group to come with a manual. Like Led Zeppelin in Carhartt hoodies, they turned the sweaty-palmed iconography of geeks, outcasts, and sci-fi mystics into something impossibly cool.

Not to mention fun: N.W.A. delighted in a sort of abject hedonism, but the Wu-Tang, who resuscitated some of the old-school, crowd-rocking values that N.W.A. had shoved aside as frivolous, suffused their music with a far more exciting sense of play. The immense character in Ice Cube's voice notwithstanding, he and MC Ren could be oppressively stentorian in delivery and unvarying in cadence; Eazy-E worked a shambling, twerpy charisma, but Ice Cube ghostwrote most of his rhymes. Whereas N.W.A.'s best songs ride relatively straightforward AABBCCDD rhyme schemes, the Wu-Tang internalized the jazzy, syncopated innovations of their East Coast compatriot Rakim, and the flow of their verse is continually, dazzlingly ruptured: Their rhymes ripple with bursts of laughter, internal rhymes, snatches of song, coughs, and onomatopoeic interjections. (Sometimes, especially in the case of the marvelously unhinged Ol' Dirty Bastard, that is *all* the rhymes seem to consist of.) The Wu-Tang rappers vary in talent, but all are capable of stealing a song, and all are fascinating just to *listen* to. The smoldering Raekwon; the drunkenly mellifluous ODB; the smoky Method Man; the creased, bristly GZA; the weeping Ghostface; the excitable Inspec-tah Deck; the narcotically laid-back Masta Killa; the rumbling U-God; the viscous RZA: The latter's ear was in fine form not just when he as-sembled samples, but when he assembled the group itself.

The MCs' gifts, of course, aren't just formal. On Wu-Tang's 1993 debut, *Enter the Wu-Tang (36 Chambers),* the song "Can It Be All So Simple" is a devastating assault on back-in-the-day nostalgia ("My pops was a fiend since sixteen," Raekwon raps, describing a distinctly un-Edenic childhood); "C.R.E.A.M." is a 360-degree inner-city survey in which our gun-toting narrators are anything but invincible; and "Tearz" stands as a grim elaboration on (refutation of?) N.W.A.'s narrowly con-ceived "reality rap": In two little morality plays that offer no easy morals, a corner boy faces the violent death of a loved one and a pussy-hound is infected with HIV. Wu-Tang were professed comic-book geeks, but it's in N.W.A.'s music that supermen act brazenly and without consequence.

Women barely appear in *36 Chambers*' lyrics—the album is a boys-only tree house. As *Wu-Tang Forever*'s scuzzy "Maria" or Ghostface's wrathful "Wildflower" would later reveal, the Clan had their share of girl trouble, but they also suggested that deep scorn for women didn't need to be a gangsta tenet. In Method Man's sublimely eerie "You're All I Need to Get By," a love object is addressed adoringly as "my nigga"—fairly transgressive gender politics for a thug. (Between "All I Need" and Ghostface's "Camay," the Wu-Tang were great at shadowy, idiosyncratic ladies' jams long before ladies' jams became a market-tested must.)

As a producer, RZA is hip-hop's great experimentalist—too enamored with unfinished edges and loose ends, too uninterested in hooks and traditional song form to ever make much of a dent in radio playlists ("C.R.E.A.M.," Wu-Tang's biggest hit, topped out at number sixty on the pop charts). For him, samples aren't meant to play in simple, endless loops: They're raw material to be dismantled and skewered, often past the point of recognition. The savings accounts of Timbaland and the Neptunes prove that there's ample room in hip-hop's mainstream for alien sounds, but there's always been something inassimilably off-kilter and atmospheric about RZA's beats, which is why his work on art-house movie soundtracks (most recently *Kill Bill* and *Afro Samurai*) makes sense, and why his popular influence is much harder to track than Dr. Dre's. (The most prominent example of RZA's legacy is the early production of Kanye West, who turned one of RZA's most haunting tricks, the sped-up, dusty vocal sample, into a brilliant commercial gimmick.)

Put roughly, RZA's beats yearn; Dr. Dre's sound marvelously *satisfied*. RZA fills even the sparest tracks with beguiling sonic riddles: voices that moan unintelligibly, minor-key melodies that never quite resolve. Most Dre beats convey an instant, magisterial gravitas—his signature device these days is an imperious, well-hammered piano chord. RZA has spent sixteen years teasing out the surprisingly expansive possibilities of a single aesthetic; Dre has not only kept pace with hip-hop's ever-shifting styles, he's done much to dictate them. Among those who agree is RZA himself: "Nobody's got a better ear in music than Dr. Dre," he recently told MTV. Still, it bears noting that RZA's music for Wu-Tang has held up far better than Dre's music for N.W.A.—his greatest innovations happened after 1991.

The Wu-Tang Clan's most lasting contribution to hip-hop might, however, be extramusical: namely, the way they reenvisioned the rap group as a business. They boast one of music's most elegant and iconic logos, which came in handy when they launched rap's first clothing line. The Wu-Wear flagship store opened in 1995 on a busy intersection in Staten Island's Tompkinsville area, and in a few years their skullcaps, sweatshirts, and jeans were in malls nationwide. This was long before Sean John and Rocawear (and Formula 50 and Pimp Juice, for that matter), so when Wu-Wear opened, the foray into "brand extension" was considered anything but global—when a sister enterprise called Wu-Nails set up shop across the street, it only reinforced the round-the-way vibe. In retrospect, the Wu-Wear storefront, now shuttered, was something like the first Starbucks or the first Wal-Mart: a trading post pitched ambitiously but modestly on the outer frontier of hip-hop's global push.

The Wu-Tang Clan's business sense manifests in another important regard—their odds-defying longevity. From the beginning, it was shrewdly stipulated in the group's contract that every member had the right to sign a solo deal with whichever label he pleased—no pipes and bats necessary. Up until very recently, the Clan's relationship has been free of the money disputes that hastened N.W.A.'s demise, and the result, to date, is five group albums and thirty-one solo albums.

This makes for a surfeit of music to navigate. If you want to explore N.W.A.'s solo afterlives, you can pick up *Eazy-Duz-It, AmeriKKKa's Most Wanted,* and *The Chronic,* download "It Was a Good Day," and ignore the rest with a pretty clean conscience. With Wu-Tang, you'll be remiss if you never hear GZA's *Liquid Swords,* Raekwon's *Only Built 4 Cuban Linx,* Ol' Dirty Bastard's *Return to the 36 Chambers,* Inspectah Deck's *Uncontrolled Substance,* and anything with the words "Ghostface

Killah" on the cover. On the ODB disc, the MC's bizarre manias dovetail with an avant-garde warping of hip-hop physics, and the best Wu-Tang projects in general are the ones that concern themselves least with the demands of the market. Ghostface in particular has been steadily and fruitfully embracing his role as a niche pleasure, delivering fantastically scatterbrained takes on current trends ("Shakey Dog" and "Maxine," true-crime nail-biters delivered with cubist perspective jumps and breathless verve) or ignoring those trends altogether ("Underwater," where he daydreams about hanging out with SpongeBob SquarePants and couture-clad mermaids).

By now N.W.A. are long gone and the Wu-Tang have retreated further and further from the mainstream—their 2007 album, *8 Diagrams,* features some of their strangest sounds yet and made an appropriately fleeting impression on the charts. But the differing visions each crew advanced as to what a gangsta could and should be are still alive and under debate today. The lines dividing camps are porous, but in one, there are those—50 Cent, the Diplomats, the Game, and Young Jeezy come to mind—who present themselves, more or less, as N.W.A.-style purists; so pure that some even hesitate to call themselves rappers, as the term suggests artifice rather than lived experience. The other— a camp that includes OutKast and Lil' Wayne—makes a Wu-Tangish case for the badass extraterrestrial.

There's no question which band had the bigger impact. N.W.A. can claim credit for harnessing rap's confrontational powers like no one before them, and for establishing hip-hop's "true" locus as the drug-ravaged, dog-eat-dog, dead-end street: To this day, any other perspective is considered a deviation from the norm. Wu-Tang's achievement hasn't been nearly as totalizing, but it's profound nonetheless. They made room for abstraction, escapism, and liberating flights of fancy within gangsta rap's no-nonsense rule book. They never lost sight of the dead-end street, but they made it a much richer place.

Devo
vs.
Kraftwerk

Tom Reynolds

Every art form has its black sheep, a what-the-hell-is-this genre that treads the line between innovation and bullshit. Pop music's idiot cousin is arguably electronica (techno, trance, trip-hop, et cetera), the repetitious hammering heard at raves and dance clubs where Hollywood ingenues pass out in the booths. But while it's tempting to dismiss as an ephemeral fad, electronica actually stretches back decades, and if we follow it far enough, the trail leads directly to two groups of a different transistor, Kraftwerk and Devo. One is an ensemble of German automatons, the other a new-wave group from Ohio—yet there is a synchronicity between the two. Besides their pioneering work with electronic gizmos, they both explore societal disconnection while creating music that's intentionally soulless. They also like robots and are out of their minds.

I attribute their insanity to seventies technology, because anyone who pursued electronica back then had to be nuts. All there was for inspiration were creepy *Switched-on Bach* LPs. There was no MIDI or digital sampling. Musicians labored with diabolical modular synthesizers, sci-fi contraptions with messy patch cords and knobs labeled VCO and LFO; only physicists could get them to work. Madmen in sound labs cranked out instruments with futuristic names like Orchestron, VCS3, Roland Jupiter-4, and ARP Odyssey. It didn't help matters when arena monsters like Yes and Emerson, Lake & Palmer got their grubby paws on them. You couldn't attend a concert without enduring interminable shrieking synth cadenzas. They made drum solos seem humble.

There were moments of ingenuity, of course. The pulsing keyboard sounds on the Who's "Won't Get Fooled Again" were generated on a Lowrey organ jerry-rigged to a crude filter bank. On the other hand, one lunatic I knew (okay, me) once plugged an electric piano into an ARP synthesizer only to create a sound akin to a grandfather clock being tossed out of an airborne Cessna. Even the staid organ had dropped acid, like the infamous Farfisa, a cheesy combo keyboard showcased on Iron Butterfly's bong anthem "In-A-Gadda-Da-Vida." It featured a "tone booster," a lever you pushed with your knee that distorted the oscillators. You don't want to know what it sounded like. Really, you don't.

It was into this atavistic techno jungle that Kraftwerk and Devo went exploring. Kraftwerk ventured first, lugging clunky analog synths, home-built electronic drums, and Teutonic attitude along with them. Ralf Hütter and Florian Schneider-Esleben are the two control freaks who founded Kraftwerk (German for *power station*) in 1970 after meeting at a Düsseldorf music conservatory. It began as an "experimental" music ensemble using electronically altered guitars, woodwinds, and organs to perform chaotic Velvet Underground–influenced instrumentals. After a few albums of arty caterwauling, Kraftwerk switched to ARP and Moog keyboards while drafting two drummers to play primitive electronic percussion seemingly assembled from pie plates and busted radios. As one of the first groups to perform electronic music in a pop context, the quartet's compositions were part sophistry, part alien, and totally mechanical. No navel-gazing ballads or Laurel Canyon vibe here. The group instead put all its efforts into being as synthetic as possible, *der Musiker als Android*. Hütter and Schneider-Esleben spent weeks twiddling the knobs on their equipment, painstakingly searching for the perfect square wave. Critics accused Kraftwerk of making machine music. Hütter and Schneider-Esleben heatedly insisted it was ... machine music. The accusation and rebuttal were the same.

Around this time, Devo was an unknown band of postcollege oddballs from Akron, Ohio. The group's name derived from Devolution, a cynical theory Devo bassist Gerald Casale conceived with early collaborator Bob Lewis, both of whom were enrolled at Kent State in 1970 when national guardsmen killed four students during antiwar demonstrations. The tragedy convinced Casale and Lewis that mankind was "devolving" to a more savage state. Fellow eccentric Mark Mothersbaugh entered the picture and Devo was born.

Essentially a guitar group with Casale on bass and Mothersbaugh wielding defective keyboards, Devo gleefully did everything wrong from the start. In an era of hirsute groups doing "Free Bird" guitar jams, Devo instead performed spasmodic non sequitur songs, sounding like refugees from a Samuel Beckett play fronting a surf band. The group mocked consumerism and conformity, dressing in matching yellow hazmat coveralls and cheap 3-D glasses. Devo's jittery music was way ahead of its time—so far that audiences predictably hated it. (Video clips of early Devo performances posted on the Internet confirm this.)

While Devo was getting fired from gigs, sometimes midsong, Kraftwerk's Germanic electronica made its debut, of all places, on the Billboard Top 100. It was 1974, an inauspicious year in pop-music history with some of the worst songs ever released. Dreck like Paul Anka's "(You're) Havin' My Baby" and Paper Lace's "The Night Chicago Died" were in regular rotation on the radio. The Grammy Awards were a chomp fest of the lowest kind, anointing Roberta Flack's dreary "Killing Me Softly with His Song" as both record *and* song of the year. It was a party that needed crashing, which Kraftwerk did with "Autobahn." A strange twenty-two-minute-long track culled down to a four-minute single, it managed to crawl to number twenty-five on the charts with a wheezy all-synthesizer music bed and lyrics that sounded like *Fun, fun, fun on the autobahn, fun, fun, fun on the autobahn.* . . . A closer listen revealed the verses were in German, translating to *We are driving on the autobahn, we are driving on the autobahn.* . . . The song stood out like a black-clad existentialist in a roomful of polyester-wearing Abba fans. *Willkommen nach Amerika,* Kraftwerk.

As for Devo, the band slogged away until it got a boost via a film short entitled *The Truth About Devolution,* essentially an extended music video they produced themselves. Cutting-edge at the time (and silly today), the movie caught the attention of David Bowie, which led to their 1977 debut album, *Q: Are We Not Men? A: We Are Devo!,* produced by Brian Eno. A few months later, *Saturday Night Live* showcased Devo performing a twisted cover of the Rolling Stones' hoary "Satisfaction" that was catchier than the original. It sneaked onto the charts and once again Seventies Singles Night had been crashed.

Kraftwerk's and Devo's careers were relatively noneventful. Neither group ever got arrested or lost members to drugs or Syd Barrett–like mental breakdowns. They didn't squabble like Oasis. They most certainly didn't ravage groupies, the least of their problems. The only drama was Kraftwerk's two original electronic drummers quitting in exasperation over Hütter and Schneider-Esleben's anal-retentive studio methods, while Devo's early collaborator Bob Lewis, after being dismissed as band manager in 1978, filed suit for intellectual property theft, claiming he cocreated the group's Devolution concept, and won.

The two groups were oceans apart both geographically and demographically. As Kraftwerk never repeated the U.S. success of "Autobahn," its fan base was almost exclusively European art fetishists; Devo's consisted of computer nerds and philosophy majors. Despite this, the two worked opposite sides of the same techno boulevard. Both employed robotlike body language onstage, except, and this is an important distinction, Devo's was meant as parody while Kraftwerk was going for verisimilitude. Kraftwerk embraced automation; Devo mocked it. Kraftwerk used synthesizers like well-oiled machines. Devo treated them like bombs waiting to go off; if they worked improperly, so much the better. Mothersbaugh has claimed he got his Moogs repaired only if they didn't work at all, requesting they be put back into their previously malfunctioning states. Suffice to say, when it came to synthesizer technique, Kraftwerk was the mannered professor poring over his data and Devo the drunk frat boy who broke into the science lab to light things on fire with the Bunsen burners.

If they sometimes resulted in botched performances, Devo's methods lent an anarchic energy to its live shows. Kraftwerk rarely experienced technical glitches. Produced like PowerPoint presentations, Kraftwerk concerts were *Groundhog Day* experiences where you swore you were reliving the same evening over and over: four stone-faced humanoids standing stiffly, punching buttons, the music entirely programmed and sequenced in advance, the lone human element Hütter's monotone vocals (and God knows if those were real). The term "live Kraftwerk" would become an oxymoron. Whereas Devo, despite its growing reliance on electronics, still used guitars and could get you to pogo.

The widest divergence between the two, however, was in their lyrics. From the semiscandalous "Mongoloid" to the Darwinian "Jocko Homo," Devo's songs were iconoclastic, perverse, and puzzling. Though anyone with the IQ of a hubcap could understand the lyrics to "Whip It," their subtext was obscured by S&M double entendre. Kraftwerk's lyrics were willfully inane, odd considering the egghead nature of Hütter and Schneider-Esleben. Songs like "The Robots" ("We are the robots . . . we are the robots . . .") and "Pocket Calculator" ("I'm the operator of my pocket calculator . . . I am adding . . . and subtracting . . .") set new heights in banality.

Devo vs. Kraftwerk

The two bands took different paths during the eighties, with Devo zigzagging from one gimmick to another while Kraftwerk marched the straight line to Androidville. Devo employed more synthesizers and machine beats into their solipsistic songs while attempting to reach audiences via the nascent MTV. "Whip It" reached number fourteen in the United States and helped Devo's third album, 1981's *Freedom of Choice,* go platinum. Kraftwerk continued pursuing their machinery obsessions until they reached the point of absurdity, i.e., the group's members wearing neckties outfitted with blinking LED lights. While "Autobahn" was a masterful taming of the Moog beast, developments in digital technology only made Kraftwerk become more mechanical, artificial, and tedious. The instruments literally played themselves, and nobody was happier about it than Hütter and Schneider-Esleben. (They even staged concerts with robotlike mannequins helming the equipment.) Unlike Devo's prankster ways, Kraftwerk was serious about its cyborg image. The song and music video "The Robots," meant as a send-up of the group's automaton reputation, was too humorless to be recognized as satire (if indeed that's what it was). It just looked like Kraftwerk being weird. As usual.

After this, it's difficult to gauge either group's career without tripping over ennui. Following the success of *Freedom of Choice,* it was all downhill for Devo. "Whip It" was seen more as a novelty song than a parody of self-empowerment anthems, and the group's Devolution concept and subversive irony were too obscure and nerdy in a marketplace filled with Go-Go's and Pat Benatar albums. Critics yawned and sales faltered. Devo broke up in 1984.

Kraftwerk soldiered on, releasing twenty-plus albums over its thirty-five-year-and-counting career. (A forty-gigabyte hard drive goes to anyone who can tell the difference between them.) To be fair, Kraftwerk largely succeeded in its machine-music methods, its pioneering work influencing everyone from rapper Afrika Bambaataa, who sampled both "Numbers" and "Trans-Europe Express" for his song "Planet Rock," and Bowie, who, in a sly homage to Schneider-Esleben, entitled an electronica instrumental from the 1977 album *"Heroes"* "V-2 Schnei-der." (Side two has Kraftwerk's doomy German conceit all over it.) As for Devo, even die-hard fans admit the band peaked artistically on their debut album, while quality-wise, its five subsequent releases ranged from inconsistent (*Freedom of Choice*) to downright terrible (*Oh No! It's Devo, Shout*).

Still, it's the absurdist Ohio band that should be counted the victor in any artistic competition. True, Devo failed just as often as it succeeded, but no artists can bat a thousand, and the more avant-garde and experimental they are, the more often they strike out. Devo took far more chances, pushed more envelopes, and tweaked more noses than Kraftwerk ever did with its software-created blooping tracks. While it's difficult to know what to make of the red "energy domes" they wore on their heads, Devo's members never phoned it in or got lazy. Dormant for decades—not counting Mothersbaugh and Casale's individual successes scoring movies, television, and commercials, likely from being forced to work within the structured framework of mass media—the original lineup has reunited in recent years for brief tours and corporate shows, the latter venue somewhat surprising considering their anticorporate stance. True, it's a little disconcerting seeing men in their late fifties dressed in hazmat suits, and they perform "Satisfaction" far slower than they did in previous years, but the Devo charm and subversive humor remain intact. Gerald Casale was asked about Kraftwerk during a 2003 interview with *Vermont Review* magazine. He chuckled and responded, "Ah, well, good Nazis. I love Kraftwerk. I remember seeing their famous robot tour." He could've been referring to Kraftwerk's entire career.

Britney Spears

vs.

Christina Aguilera

Sara Barron

For those of you who do not live your lives as
I live mine, according to the demarcation B.T.F.O.B. (Before the Fall of
Britney) and A.T.F.O.B. (After the Fall of Britney), if perchance you're
busy shaping your existence around something other than tabloid headlines—your wedding day? The birth of your first child?—lest you've
forgotten what once was, let me remind you of a day before a head was
shaved, a marriage failed, a vagina exposed: It is September 6, 2000, and
Britney Spears appears on the MTV Video Music Awards in black fe-
dora and pinstripe suit, groaning her way through the opening refrain
of the Rolling Stones' iconic "Satisfaction."

"What's this?" you think. "The Stones? By Britney? A suit? On Britney?"

But this is no average suit. This little number outfits Spears at the top of her game, and as such comes off in one deft yank of a hand to reveal a bejeweled brassiere. She looks spectacular—like the world's most agile, most expensive hooker—then segues into her own chart-topping smash, "Oops! . . . I Did It Again."

"Why, yes, you did," you think, ogling the impassioned whip-around of her meticulously crimped extensions. "You certainly did."

Spears, on the entertainment scene for three years by the summer of 2000, with two platinum albums and countless Billboard hits under her belt (". . . Baby One More Time," "Crazy," "Sometimes," "Stronger," the oft-forgot, stylistically atypical, saccharine ballad "From the Bottom of My Broken Heart"), had again hit the top, if not of this arena—critical praise in the music industry—then of this: the Best of the Blondes, a group of four including Britney, Christina Aguilera, Jessica Simpson, and Mandy Moore. All pert, blonde, adorable, all *Mickey Mouse Club* alums, all with an image crafted on the tail end of the one who'd come before, then tweaked with minor variations, e.g., after Brit's debut, Christina's: blonde and midriff baring like her predecessor, but blessed with a decent vocal range. Then Jessica's: blonde and pretty like the others, but possessing of a loudly touted virginity to juxtapose myriad spread-eagle cover shots on *Maxim, Stuff,* et cetera. Then Mandy's: blonde yet again, but with a voice so flimsy, with dance skills so inexpert, she quickly (wisely) abandons her Pop Princess ambitions to peddle her good on the indie-film, fashion, celebrity-girlfriend circuits. (Her lovely mug had to be good for something, didn't it? And in the early '00s, Mandy Moore, with publicist, manager, and agent in tow, would be damned if she couldn't figure out what.) In 2000 these four reigned supreme—a sizable faction of the commercially successful music "artists" of the day. But Simpson and Moore are mere blips—hangers-on, if you ask me—to the meat on the bones of the pop-icon personas of Brit and Christina.

Britney Spears vs. Christina Aguilera

Some people—those busied with newspapers, books, keeping their heads shoved under a rock, away from the glare of pop culture—think Brit and Christina are one and the same. This is strange to me. Naïve. A.T.F.O.B. they don't even have the same hair, for God's sake. Christina, a study in white-blonde platinum, looks nothing like Britney in her multitude of urine-colored wigs. To the keener observer, their only comparable aspect (besides a shared affection for the half shirt) is their lyrical ability.

Christina: "I'm a genie in a bottle / You've got to rub me the right way."

Britney: "Sometimes I run / Sometimes I hide / Sometimes I'm scared of you."

Christina: "Oooo / Gimme some room / Oooo / I'm comin' through."

Britney: "You drive me crazy / I'm in too deep / I'm so excited / I just can't sleep."

Lennon or McCartney they're not, churning out sentences so simplistic in their construction you'd think they wrote them themselves. They claim as much, after all, but I don't buy it. Never have. At best I suspect they toss out the occasional topic—"What if I sang a song about how much I've grown?"—then someone else puts pen to paper. But the similarities end there.

B.T.F.O.B.: In 1999 a seventeen-year-old Spears appears in her now exhaustively chronicled schoolgirl costume to launch her debut single ". . . Baby One More Time." Months later and minus the knee-high socks and pleated skirt, Aguilera does the same with "Genie in a Bottle." Christina's appeal is clear: She's cute, she belts; washboard stomach, Grammy win. Spears, on the other hand, grabs the country by the balls with greater fervor. And why? There's no two ways around the fact that Christina is the stronger singer. And yet Brit's appeal was—has always been—more complex. With a button-down shirt tied a foot above her navel, she screamed jailbait. No one could pout that effectively, eye the camera that seductively, sweat sex out of pores on so perfectly sculpted a body, then revert with equal agility to sweet-as-sugar Southern lass.

253

"I'm not that innocent," she'd bray onstage, in music videos, then back-pedal later to the nearest microphone-clad interviewer: "But seriously, y'all? I *am* that innocent!" and attribute her pigtails and shiny splays of flesh not to a blatant exploitation of her nubile physique, but rather to clever practicality. "The reason I tied up my shirt," Brit would explain, "is 'cause that's how we do it down South, y'all." This is B.T.F.O.B, re-member, when the quality of her speaking voice was addled not by quaaludes, coke, or Valium, but rather the high-pitched, honeyed good-ness that only a meteoric rise to worldwide music domination can pro-vide: ". . . and in the summer, when I'd go to dance class, that's what all of us would do: Tie up our shirts! Put up our hair!" She repeats this mantra of efficiency to Regis and Kathie Lee, to Howie Mandel, to the good people composing her one-hour special at E! She references her Louisiana roots, tosses in a "y'all" for good measure. When asked about the overtly risqué, bejeweled, nude brassiere she wore at the 2000 VMAs, she says, "I'm just a girly girl, y'all. I just wanted to look pretty and sparkly!"

Bullshit, I say. And what genius, to pin these choices on an aw-shucksishness instead of acknowledging what Brit and her handlers were *really* up to: creating an entity that appealed (gender and sexual orientation depending) to the borderline pedophile or aspiring vixen in all of us.

So complex. So enrapturing.

This is why all events A.T.F.O.B. have so powerfully transfixed the nation. (This includes you. Oh, yes it does. *Someone's* buying those tabloid mags. Or at the very least sneaking peeks in line at the grocery store.) I read an article in the *Chicago Tribune* recently that called Spears, from a paparazzi standpoint, "the top of the A-List, the most lucrative celebrity photo op there is." She's held this position for the better part of a decade and that's no easy task—staying that interesting for that long in a pop culture as fickle as our own—and it's a feat owed to her unpre-dictability. Where Britney's concerned, we have to know what happens next. If an all-knowing presence descended from on high to report that she will be, five years from now, an Oscar nominee who channeled her psychological dysfunction to become the next great actress of our time; if she—lithe once more and therefore triumphant by Hollywood standards—stole leading roles from a Winslet or Blanchett, I'd believe it. And if she died of an overdose or accidentally drowned a baby in a bathtub, I'd believe that, too.

Not so with Christina. Her career has been—will continue to be—so much more predictable. She'll give us an up-tempo dance smash ("Genie in a Bottle"), then a ballad ("I Turn to You"), then a dance smash ("Dirrty"), then a ballad ("Beautiful"). "I'm sexy! And hip!" she reminds us with the release of each new fast-paced concoction. Then—and you could set your watch by it—comes the ballad; one month following the release of its sexy, catchy predecessor, it too will plague the airwaves to remind us, "Christina *can* slut it up in chaps and a half shirt, but she doesn't *have* to. *Her* success is contingent on her vocal chops. Why, look! A ballad!"

Sure, she can sing, but how much does that count for? Think of Madonna's feeble pipes. Recall the late-eighties peak of Paula Abdul's career. Ashlee Simpson. The Pussycat Dolls. Must I remind you of the wretched and guttural vibrato sewn into the front man of Nickelback. Ugh. The list goes on and its members lack range, pitch, and/or power. A decent voice these days is more bonus than requisite, and so Christina's impressive, natural talent will illicit just a bleary-eyed yawn from me.

Just as predictable is her personal life. She blows Fred Durst, gains weight, does yoga, maybe lipo, loses weight, gets married, has a baby. Christina's classy now, all red lipstick, pressed, platinum curls, fitted couture gowns. On her most recent album, *Back to Basics,* she covers Herbie Hancock, Lena Horne. Where will *she* be in five years? Easy: a couple kids popped out, continued commercial success, a fashion line, perfume perhaps. Ho-hum. Where are the extremes, I ask you? What kind of twenty-first-century entertainment is this supposed to be? These days we demand more violent emotional swings. (I admit that as I write this, the story has broken of Owen Wilson's suicide attempt. And my first thought when I heard it, glued as I always am to the "news" reports on E!, was, "Wow. He's cooler than I thought. He's got some shit going *on.*" Here I'd had him pegged as another Hollywood frathead with little to do in his downtime besides banging blondes. Shows what I know. But Owen, by virtue of his now public, psychotic, debilitating depression, has established himself as something more than we all thought he was. And trust me: His career, if he can manage to mood-stabilize even a little, will skyrocket. He'll start competing with the Downeys and Di-Caprios for the choicest of roles. Then what? Oscar nod. You heard it here first.) Sad though it may be—junior high schoolish in its pretentious veneration of the tortured artist, offensive in its exploitation of our base, human impulse to want to watch the car crash—the unstable teeter-totter of the broken bird is always most engaging.

Remember the B.T.F.O.B. "Like a Virgin" resurrection performed in 2003 with Britney and Christina, both outfitted in dime-store bachelorette-party paraphernalia and flanking Madonna's black-clad "groom"? You'll recall Madonna kissed them both: open-mouth action with Britney first, then on to Christina. (As Madonna described it, and I'm paraphrasing here, but only slightly, "I told my daughter, 'I'm the big mommy pop star and I'm passing my spirit on to the little pop stars so they can learn lessons from me!' ") I didn't even know women still did that: feign lesbian proclivities to titillate the penis-clad masses dumb enough to buy it. But that's neither here nor there. The two young ladies were lip-locked with equal vigor for equal amounts of time. Yet there was only one star of *that* cheap-as-Pabst-Blue-Ribbon-beer attempt to get attention. The TV interviews, the tabloid stories, the newspaper headlines—all coverage about the Kiss was Britney's. The people wanted desperately to know what she'd been thinking. But the most she'd offer up was, "I'd never kissed a girl before. And it was different, I guess. But I just didn't think it would be *that* big a deal."

Christina, on the other hand, at the peak of her "I'm a dirrty girl/ Look at my cornrows" phase, would surely have talked, filled us in on the nitty-gritty, if only anyone had thought to ask. But no one did. Even Madonna, on a post-Kiss visit to *TRL,* found it necessary to remind viewers, "Don't forget about the *other* girl I kissed." In all fairness, Britney garnered at least a portion of the attention she did because in Christina's moment of glory the camera cut to Britney's recent ex, Justin Timberlake—"What'll he do?! What will he say?!"—and poor Christina got robbed of airtime. But even the decision on the part of the show's producers to sacrifice Christina's "watch *me* authenticate *my* wild-girl image" to the cause of Britney's celebrity says something about the latter's intrigue. Its power is crushing. It dominates. It has— it will—for years. Regardless of the path Brit stumbles along: Whether up the avenue toward the Comeback or down the dark alley toward eventual bankruptcy and crack addiction, we'll follow.

These days the onslaught of reality everything has steered us away from a reverential approach to creative talent and artistry. Ruled by schadenfreude we are, and so we favor compelling people, i.e., lunatics, instead of those excelling at a single artist's craft. What's a strong voice, clever lyrics, a decent script when measured against the "real" events and personalities documented on TV and in the papers? The aforementioned skills pale in their ability to hold our collective, cultural interest. I'd take a smackdown of VH1's latest reality stars over a half hour of any scripted sitcom, steal a glance at *Us Weekly* before swinging through the fiction section of my nearest Barnes and Noble. And which would you prefer: Christina singing live at an awards show or a bald, umbrella-wielding Britney lunging at the paparazzi? Christina in her latest choice couture, discussing her "God-given talent" with Ryan Seacrest, or Britney, one fake eyelash peeling off, sharing ruminations on motherhood with Matt Lauer? Christina merely performs "adventuress," while Britney—with ex-husband, estranged mother, two kids, presumed addiction, weight gain, and a wardrobe that looks pulled from the basement bin at Daffy's in tow—is busy living it.

When entertainers discuss the importance of their work, what it is that makes them worthwhile contributors to the greater good, the stock answer includes something like, "[*fill in the blank*] brings people to-gether" or "if I've made someone's day a little brighter by [*insert activity*], then I've done my job"; then there's the accompanying anecdote about us average Joes who approach the Entertainer to say how much their work has meant to us. (It's something that I, for one, might mumble shamefacedly were I standing alongside a UNICEF employee or chil-dren's-cancer specialist, but still: a vaguely valid point.) And Britney's work has meant a lot to me. It may not have soothed me through rough times, may not have challenged me with fresh, compelling insights, but she sure as shit has kept me entertained: B.T.F.O.B., a dancey tune to make a treadmill jaunt go faster; A.T.F.O.B., just one YouTube search away from the reminder that things could in fact be worse.

Have I accrued credit-card debt? Yes.

White-rapper baby daddy? No.

Psoriasis? Yes.

Bad weave? No.

Not only is she my most prized entertainment; Spears also comes complete with a healthy dose of perspective.

Michael Jackson

vs.

Prince

Touré

In the summer of 1958, in two Midwestern families, boys were born who'd grow up to be two entirely different sorts of freaky. In June, in Minneapolis, a mixed-race couple with a musician father and a singer mother welcomed their first child, Prince Rogers Nelson. In August, 437 miles away in Gary, Indiana, a musician father and a Jehovah's Witness mother welcomed the seventh of their ten children, Michael Joseph Jackson.

Within ten years Michael was a household name, the lead singer of the Jackson 5, whose first four singles hit number one: "I Want You Back," "ABC," "The Love You Save," and "I'll Be There." Michael was the cutest black boy in America with one of the best voices in the business—a voice bright, clear, and so big it was a surprise to see it come out of that little face. He was a star from Motown, the factory where Berry Gordy constructed classy negroes palatable to white record buyers, and young MJ was a clean, smiling, polite black boy whom any white family would be happy to have over for dinner. That, perhaps, is a key to why the two careers unfolded as they did: While Prince wanted stardom badly and was able to grow up before he got it, Michael had massive fame thrust upon him as a child and had to grow up in public as if his life were a reality show.

In the eighties Michael became the biggest star in the world. His first adult solo album, 1979's *Off the Wall,* is still one of the greatest albums ever made. Scintillating pop-disco rhythms bubbling and percolating, compelling you to dance, and Michael's incredible voice urging you to ecstasy. It was enthusiastic, hopeful, sensitive dance music; it was high-tech soul. His next album, *Thriller,* is the best-selling album of all time, over one hundred million sold, and it made Michael the most famous person on the planet besides Jesus. *Thriller* was bold, theatrical rock music with soul. Every song seemed to suggest it was from a movie, perhaps a sci-fi-ish musical, and Michael supplied MTV with a series of unforgettable, expensive, high-concept minimovies.

In the eighties MTV showed videos. Back then they showed pretty much nothing but videos, and most kids who cared about music watched. So instead of kids discovering new music through the radio they found it through MTV. That changed the sort of artist who'd find success, putting more emphasis on looks, fashion, flair, and showmanship rather than on songwriting and sound quality. For example, two of the best-selling artists of the seventies are the Carpenters and the Bee Gees, both of whom sang very well and wrote great songs, as opposed to, say, Madonna and Duran Duran, big stars of the early MTV era, neither of whom sang or danced well, but knew how to create a spectacle and looked sexy on a small screen. The rise of MTV led to a more cohesive national conversation about music because millions were watching as one. It was the perfect storm—it was the yuppie decade, when more people had more disposable income than ever and millions of them were obsessively watching MTV and using CDs, Walkmans, and boom boxes, which made music ultraportable, creating the potential for bigger album sales and bigger stars than ever.

There was a widespread loss of innocence in the eighties. In Atlanta twenty-nine black children were killed by a mysterious serial killer. At several child-care facilities across the country children were molested or abused, most notably at the McMartin preschool in California. After so many successful missions into outer space that launches were no longer big news and we switched from launching spaceships to sending up shuttles, a word suggesting a journey that's quick and easy, after that came the shocking *Challenger* disaster, which took the lives of six astronauts and a schoolteacher from New Hampshire and crippled the space program. And sex, which in the sixties was linked to freedom, was now linked to death. AIDS made us think any sexual encounter could be the end. Casual sex seemed like Russian roulette. For those who didn't want to be scared, Prince talked so freely and so often about nasty sex he seemed to be a welcome antidote. Where we were losing our innocence, Prince seemed to never have had any. At a glance you could tell he would fuck you like you've never been fucked before. It would last hours, it would be sinful, he'd do things you've never thought of, he'd turn you out. He was the wild son of Jimi, the younger brother of Rick James and Richard Pryor, the ultrasexual black Casanova who told you up front he had a dirty mind.

Michael held the opposite appeal. His music was often about escaping through dance or being hopeful about the world, and he came across as super-innocent, so undersexed he seemed emotionally retarded. He was eccentric, but the bizarre behavior that would later envelop him wasn't visible at his peak. The dueling personalities of the "Thriller" video looked funny, not an indicator of a dark side. On "Billie Jean" he protested a paternity claim, but no one thought him possible of paternity. He seemed asexual like Pee-wee Herman, a self-appointed force of goodness like Princess Diana. He cowrote and spearheaded "We Are the World." In the eighties you'd have felt safe leaving your kids to be babysat by Michael Jackson. As the great philosopher Paul Mooney once said, he was the only black man who could've chosen Brooke Shields, one of the most beautiful white women in America, as his date for the Grammys without getting into trouble—because America knew Michael was not going to have sex with Brooke.

Both were girlish guys, drama queens, who pulled from white and black culture to form their personas and their sound, as opposed to LL Cool J, Big Daddy Kane, and Rakim, who were ultramasculine and so black they seemed to have never met a white person. Michael and Prince's sexual and racial androgyny made them more palatable and less threatening and made it easier for them to break glass ceilings in the music industry and enjoy the wave of racial integration going on in the eighties, when Jesse Jackson ran for president twice, Oprah became a hot talk-show host without pandering to the lowest common denominator, Spike Lee directed thoughtful films about black life, and Bill Cosby starred in the number one television show in the country, telling the ups and downs of a rich black family.

Both Michael and Prince set the world on its ear in the fall of 1982. At the end of October, Prince released *1999,* his fifth album but first big seller, and at the beginning of December, Michael unleashed *Thriller.* Back then most radio stations had segregated playlists—they played either white rock or black urban music, not a mix. But *1999* and *Thriller* sounded at home on both and were so intensely requested that no station could afford not to play them. At first MTV followed the lead of segregated radio and played no black artists. But when Michael released *Thriller* he became their Jackie Robinson, the first black to break in. For a time MTV played "Thriller" every hour at the top of the hour. Soon after Prince showed up on the channel with "Little Red Corvette," a song that wasn't about a car but a girl who had a pocketful of horses, Trojans, and some of them used.

Prince seemed caricaturishly oversexed, but he couldn't have been having as much sex as he suggested because he was putting out an album a year, an unheard-of pace, and writing, producing, and playing almost every instrument. His sixth album, *Purple Rain,* and the autobiographical movie of the same name, with its incredible performance scenes, made him a household name. He recorded it with his group, the Revolution, sometimes recording the full band live rather than recording the entire thing by himself, and the result was a fuller sound—guitar-god rock with electro-funk, urban R&B, and pop—almost like a rock opera.

Michael was coming out once every four years like a president. *Thriller* was so hot there was no inkling that he had just one great album left in him, *Dangerous,* where the grooves got less rock-influenced and more funky thanks to producer Teddy Riley. Despite a few great songs like "The Way You Make Me Feel" and "Smooth Criminal," Michael's prior album *Bad* lived up to its name in the traditional meaning of the word, not the black-English meaning.

I saw Michael live in Paris in '88 when he was promoting that bad album. That was my third concert ever and it was insane. It was in a big open-air stadium and Michael came out around seven thirty P.M. wearing one of those military-inspired jackets that made him look like the dictator of a banana republic. He whipped us into a god-worship frenzy as he danced like a modern dancer with his own language of shakes and hip twists and finger points and did virtual magic tricks, disappearing from one part of the stage and reappearing far away, too quickly to have run there. And sang, because that voice is a gift from God. People all around me passed out as if in the presence of a religious superfigure as he took them through the oeuvre that showed him to be a hopeless romantic in love with love and optimistic about the world. He did his tough-guy posturing, but Mike's so soft you knew it was just that, a set-up for all those songs at the end urging you to be a good person, reminding you the children are our future, urging you to make a change in the world and to start by looking at the man in the mirror.

I've seen Prince several times, but you haven't really seen Prince till you've been lucky enough to find out where the after show is and get in. Whenever Prince finished rocking the arena in your town he'd jump in his limo and go to a much smaller place and jam there. I've seen him do two hours in L.A., one hour at Club USA in Times Square, but the most memorable of the after shows I saw was the shortest.

One night in the late nineties Prince went to S.O.B.'s, a little night-club in Manhattan, and at two A.M. he strolled out with D'Angelo and Questlove from the Roots. D played keyboards, Quest played drums, Prince played bass. It was just the three of them but the air was electric because Prince is one of the greatest musical performers of all time. Give him a guitar and a piano and he can entertain all night long with the way he commands the guitar and the emotion and color in his falsetto and the brilliance of his writing about love and sex and twisted relation-ships. Who else has had an oeuvre-long conversation about how to com-bine wild sexuality, deep spirituality, and true love in one chaotic life? And that Prince sound. He's like a genre unto himself, pulling from George Clintonish funk, James Brownish R&B, Sly Stoneish soul, Led Zeppelinish drama rock.

The threesome came out as more than three hundred people squeezed in together, screaming in anticipation of an unpredictable show. How long would it last? What would they play? They started out just vamping together, just testing out a groove to see how it felt. After a few minutes they went into "Brown Sugar," D'Angelo's first hit. D sang and all three looked at one another throughout the song, giggling to themselves like schoolboys playing a trick. But they rocked and they sounded great and the crowd was captivated. "Brown Sugar" went on for a while, they kept on vamping after the last verse, and then Quest-love got the idea to try to get Prince to play one of his old songs. This was dangerous. This was during the Symbol Man era, when Prince had changed his name to an unpronounceable symbol. He'd said he'd never again perform any of those old songs. It was like asking Dad if you could drive the 1963 Porsche 911 he had under a tarp in the garage, the car he loved and said he'd never again drive. Would Prince be insulted?

Would he storm off? Questlove just had to ask; he loved those old Prince songs so much, he had to try. He winked at D and the two of them went into "Darling Nikki," one of the verboten songs, one of Prince's best songs. Prince laughed and played along for a moment, and then I blinked and he was gone. Playing that song spooked him and he ran, ending the show after twenty unforgettable minutes.

The Symbol Man era suggested that Prince had gone off the deep end, that superstaritis had finally gotten him, and the news out of Paisley Park would only get weirder from there. But renaming himself was about breaking away from his label, Warner Bros., and escaping the constraints of the record business in general. Prince wrote *slave* on his cheek and battled the label not because he was losing his mind but because he was finding it. He felt the arrangement between labels and artists was outdated and a disservice to artists. When he finally severed his relationship with Warners he made several savvy moves. He signed a deal with EMI merely to distribute his records, giving him the lion's share of the profits rather than a fraction, and later sold CDs through the Internet when that was unheard of. Nowadays Prince remains rich and viable, charging thousands a ticket for shows in Vegas, New York, and London, and performing to packed houses whenever and wherever he wants. His output since 1992's ⚥ has been less interesting than what he made during his prime, that string of classic albums—1980's *Dirty Mind*, '81's *Controversy*, '82's *1999*, '84's *Purple Rain*, '85's *Around the World in a Day*, '86's *Parade*, '87's *Sign o' the Times*, and '88's *Lovesexy*—but Prince is still releasing some good stuff. Both *Musicology* and *3121* had a few hot joints.

Meanwhile Michael fended off bankruptcy only by selling his share in the Beatles catalog. His Neverland mansion is closed. He doesn't want to live there but he's unable to sell it. He now seems to live mostly in Europe and the Middle East, the guest of insanely rich friends. And after many years of trying, the Michael Jackson brand has been ruined. A great philosopher named Chris Rock once said we loved Michael so much we forgave him the first kid, as in the first child-molestation charge. But he's been charged with child molestation at least twice, and it's difficult not to believe that something happened while he and all those ten-year-old boys were jamming in the bed. Michael hasn't helped his cause by paying double-digit millions to make these claims go away, which reeks of guilt, and by positing on *60 Minutes* that nothing is wrong with a grown man sleeping in a bed with young children. If that were his only problem, that would be a lot. But over the years Michael has savaged his face through a series of surgical procedures that've taken him from a round-faced, brown-skinned cherub to a pale-skinned Cruella de Vil. His self-mutilation screams of self-loathing and frankly he looks frightening, as if he might be able to take his nose off or pull his scalp back and reach into his brain. He's been photographed sleeping inside a hyperbaric chamber, purchased the bones of the Elephant Man, dangled one of his small children from a balcony, and makes both of his children wear creepy veils whenever they're in public. Seriously, what sort of person loves Michael Jackson now?

The word *freak* is a deep part of black English—a verb, a noun, and an adjective. The freak is a dance. To freak is to do something extraordinarily well. Or have sex. (To get freaky-deke is to have kinky sex.) To be a freak is to be sexual. Prince and Michael are both freaks, but where Prince is a freak as in a sexual monster, Michael is a freak as in a weirdo. Wacko Jacko. How about that: Prince sauntered into the culture pretending to be out of his mind, the wild nigga, but he played the game, then challenged the system, and is now sitting pretty, while the good negro Michael, who pretended to have it all together, ended up losing his money and his mind.

Makes me want to found the United Negro Superstar Fund. Because a mind is a terrible thing to waste.

Contributors

Ross Arbes, originally from Atlanta, Georgia, served as 2007–08 president of the *Harvard Lampoon.* He graduated in 2008.

Sara Barron is a writer and comedian whose first book, *People Are Unappealing: Me Too* (Random House), will be released in 2009. She's written for *Heeb* magazine and Mr. Beller's Neighborhood and appeared on the air with NPR's *Weekend Edition* and at the HBO Comedy Arts Festival in Aspen, Colorado. She lives in Brooklyn. For more information, visit www.sarabarron.com.

Tom Breihan is an associate editor at the *Village Voice,* and he writes the Status Ain't Hood blog on the *Voice* website. He's also a contributing writer at Pitchfork, and he's written for *Spin, Blender, Urb, Seattle Weekly, Baltimore City Paper,* and *D.I.W.* He lives in Brooklyn.

Laura Cantrell is an acclaimed country singer and host of the *Radio Thrift Shop* on WFMU-FM Jersey City. Cantrell's most recent album, *Humming by the Flowered Vine,* was released by Matador Records. She has toured extensively in the United Kingdom, Ireland, and the United

Contributors

States. She lives in Jackson Heights, New York, with her husband, Jeremy Tepper, and daughter, Isabella.

Daphne Carr writes about music and edits the *Best Music Writing* series. Like everyone from her hometown of Youngstown, Ohio, she has a fondness for antiquated technologies.

Jim DeRogatis is the pop-music critic at the *Chicago Sun-Times* and the author of several books about rock and roll, including *Staring at Sound: The True Story of Oklahoma's Fabulous Flaming Lips; Let It Blurt: The Life and Times of Lester Bangs, America's Greatest Rock Critic; Milk It!: Collected Musings on the Alternative Music Explosion of the '90s;* and *Turn On Your Mind: Four Decades of Great Psychedelic Rock.* Together with Greg Kot, he cohosts *Sound Opinions,* "the world's only rock and roll talk show," which originates at Chicago Public Radio, is syndicated via American Public Media, and can be heard on the Web at www.soundopinions.org. He lives on Chicago's North Side with his wife, Carmél Carrillo.

Matt Diehl is one of the foremost writers working in the pop culture arena today—at least he thinks he is. His writing has appeared everywhere from *Rolling Stone* and the *New York Times* to *Stop Smiling* and *Esquire;* he is also currently a contributing music editor at *Interview.* Diehl has published three books: *Notorious C.O.P.* (with Derrick Parker), *My So-Called Punk: How Neo-Punk Stagedived into the Mainstream,* and *No-Fall Snowboarding* (with Danny Martin and Mark Seliger). He is currently writing the feature-length screenplay for the official Devo biopic.

Joe Donnelly is the deputy editor of the *LA Weekly.* Aside from the *Weekly,* he has written for the *Washington Post,* the *Los Angeles Times,* the *Los Angeles Times Magazine,* New York *Daily News, Detour, BlackBook,* and numerous other publications. His story "Wet" appeared along with pieces by such writers as A. L. Kennedy, T. Coraghessan Boyle, and Joy Williams in the collection *Naked: Writers Uncover the Way We Live on Earth.* Donnelly received his master's in journalism from the Graduate School of Journalism at the University of California, Berkeley.

Vivien Goldman is a Londoner who became a New Yorker. *The Book of Exodus: The Making and Meaning of Bob Marley & the Wailers' Album of the Century* is her fifth book. She's currently the adjunct professor of punk and reggae at NYU, the punk professor on BBCAmerica.com, and many other things, too, including obscure post-punk cult artist, which is a permanent gig.

Elizabeth Goodman is a recovering second-grade teacher who now lives with two basset hounds and her boyfriend in New York City. She is the former writer of *NME*'s "Letter from New York" column. Her writing has appeared in *Spin, Nylon,* the *New York Post,* and *Elle,* among other publications. She is currently editor at large at *Blender.*

Ben Greenman is an editor at *The New Yorker* and the author of several books of fiction, including *Superbad, Superworse,* and *A Circle is a Balloon and Compass Both.* He has written about pop music for *The New Yorker, The Oxford American,* and other publications. He lives in Brooklyn.

Scott Gursky is a freelance designer and illustrator (and sometimes drummer) living in Brooklyn. He's done illustrations for television networks, Web design for toy companies, and T-shirts for fashion brands, but when all is said and done, he hopes people find his posters, drawings, and comics for independent and dedicated individuals to be his most notable.

Richard Hell is a novelist and essayist and rock and roll musician.

Contributors

Sean Howe is the editor of *Give Our Regards to the Atomsmashers!* (Pantheon) and the series editor of a forthcoming series of film books. He lives in Brooklyn, New York.

Dan Kois has worked as a film executive and a literary agent. He is a founding editor of Vulture, *New York* magazine's culture and entertainment blog, and has written for the *New York Times, Slate, New York, The Oxford American, Television Without Pity,* and others. He lives in New York with his wife and daughters, and is writing a book for Continuum's 33⅓ series about the Hawaiian singer Israel Kamakawiwo'ole.

Robert Lanham is the author of the "beach towel classic" *The Emerald Beach Trilogy,* which includes the acclaimed works *Pre-Coitus, Coitus,* and *Aftermath.* More recent books include the satirical anthropological studies *The Hipster Handbook; Food Court Druids, Cherohonkees and Other Creatures Unique to the Republic;* and *The Sinner's Guide to the Evangelical Right.* Lanham has written for the *New York Times, Nylon, Playboy, Maxim,* and *Time Out,* and has been a guest on CNN and NPR to discuss his work. He's the founder and editor of FREEwilliamsburg .com. Lanham lives in Brooklyn, New York.

Dan LeRoy is the director of literary arts at Lincoln Park Performing Arts Charter School in Midland, Pennsylvania. His writing has appeared in the *New York Times, Rolling Stone, Newsweek, Vibe,* the *Village Voice, National Review Online,* and *Alternative Press.* He is certainly the only person in history who has contributed to publications founded by conservative icon William F. Buckley Jr. and Gene Simmons of Kiss. He is the author of *The Greatest Music Never Sold,* a book about famous unreleased albums that was published by Backbeat/Hal Leonard in autumn 2007, and coauthor (with Michael Lipton) of *20 Years of Mountain Stage,* a history of the National Public Radio show.

Contributors

Dennis Lim is editorial director at the Museum of the Moving Image. He writes frequently for the *New York Times* and the *Los Angeles Times* and teaches in the graduate journalism program at New York University. He edited *The Village Voice Film Guide* (2006) and is working on a book about David Lynch.

Melissa Maerz is a senior editor at *Rolling Stone.*

Sean Manning is the editor of *The Show I'll Never Forget: 50 Writers Relive Their Most Memorable Concertgoing Experience.* His writing has appeared in *New York Press, The Brooklyn Rail,* and *BlackBook.*

Michaelangelo Matos is the author of *Sign O' the Times* (Continuum, 2004) and a columnist for *Idolator, The Stranger,* and Paper Thin Walls. He lives in Seattle.

Russ Meneve is a New York City–based stand-up comedian whose television credits include *The Tonight Show with Jay Leno, Late Night with Conan O'Brien, Last Call with Carson Daly, Comedy Central Presents,* and *Last Comic Standing.*

Adam Moerder is a 2007 graduate of Harvard College, where he spent three years writing for the *Harvard Lampoon* and serving as its president during the 2006 year. Born in 1984 in Reading, Pennsylvania, Adam consumed a steady diet of nutrients and vitamins until his body fully developed into an adult. He is currently working on an "Adam Moerder vs. Ross Arbes" essay for a book of *Lampoon* presidential rivalries.

Whitney Pastorek is a writer, musician, and international star of stage and screen. After fifteen years in New York City, she recently moved to Los Angeles, where she is currently on staff at *Entertainment Weekly.* Her work has appeared in the pages of *ESPN the Magazine, Sports Illus-*

trated, Budget Travel, the *Village Voice,* and the *New York Times,* among others. A list of everything is constantly in flux at www.whittlz.com.

Tom Reynolds is a writer/TV producer and the author of *I Hate Myself and Want to Die: The 52 Most Depressing Songs You've Ever Heard* and *Touch Me, I'm Sick: The 52 Creepiest Love Songs You've Ever Heard.* He lives in Los Angeles.

Rob Sheffield is the author of *Love Is a Mix Tape: Life and Loss, One Song at a Time* and a contributing editor at *Rolling Stone.* He has been a rock critic and pop-culture journalist for fifteen years and has appeared on various MTV and VH1 shows. He lives in Brooklyn.

Michael Showalter is a member of the comedy troupes the State and Stella. His screenwriting credits include *Wet Hot American Summer* and *The Baxter,* which he also directed.

Marc Spitz's writing on rock and roll has appeared in *Spin, Uncut,* the *New York Times, Vanity Fair,* and various other publications. He is the author of the novels *How Soon Is Never* and *Too Much, Too Late* and the music biographies *We Got the Neutron Bomb: The Untold Story of L.A. Punk* (coauthored with Brendan Mullen) and *Nobody Likes You: Inside the Turbulent Life, Times and Music of Green Day.*

Journalist **Katy St. Clair** writes a pseudo-nightlife column for the *SF Weekly* called "Bouncer." Her work has also appeared in Da Capo's *Best Music Writing* series and *Utne Reader.* She lives in Oakland.

Mick Stingley is a freelance writer and self-described "low-rent rock critic" for KNAC.com, *Terrorizer* (U.K.), *Metal Edge,* and *The Hollywood Reporter.* He's also written for *Hustler, Hustler Busty Beauties, FHM,* the *New York Post,* and *Men's Fitness,* among others. He lives in New York City.

Contributors

Touré is the author of *Never Drank the Kool-Aid,* a collection of essays about hip-hop, and the host of BET's *The Black Carpet* and Treasure HD's *I'll Try Anything Once.* He's also the author of *Soul City,* a novel, and *The Portable Promised Land,* a collection of short stories. He's been a contributing editor at *Rolling Stone* for more than ten years, was CNN's first pop-culture correspondent, and was the host of MTV2's *Spoke N Heard.* His writing has appeared in *The Best American Essays 1999, The Best American Sports Writing 2001, Da Capo Best Music Writing 2004,* and *The Best American Erotica 2004.* He attended Columbia University's graduate school of creative writing and lives in Fort Greene, Brooklyn, with his wife, Rita, and their baby.

Jonah Weiner is a senior editor at *Blender.* His writing has also appeared in *Slate,* the *New York Times,* and the *Village Voice.*

Gideon Yago was a dude on MTV for seven years. He has written for *Spin, Rolling Stone, Nylon, Vice,* and NPR's *This American Life.* He currently lives in Los Angeles.

Acknowledgments

For their help and encouragement, the editor thanks Jim Fitzgerald, Anne Garrett, Carrie Thornton, Brandi Bowles, Erin LaCour, Alice Peisch, everyone at Three Rivers Press, Vanessa White Wolf, Jim Manning, and Susan Manning.

Contributor Credits